UNITED
BY PRIVILEGE

UNITED
BY PRIVILEGE

SIX STEPS FOR TURNING A PRIVILEGE INTO A SHELTER

By Phidia Maingi

XULON PRESS ELITE

Xulon Press Elite
2301 Lucien Way #415
Maitland, FL 32751
407.339.4217
www.xulonpress.com

© 2021 by Phidia K Maingi

All rights reserved solely by the author. The author guarantees all contents are original and do not infringe upon the legal rights of any other person or work. No part of this book may be reproduced in any form without the permission of the author. The views expressed in this book are not necessarily those of the publisher.

Due to the changing nature of the Internet, if there are any web addresses, links, or URLs included in this manuscript, these may have been altered and may no longer be accessible. The views and opinions shared in this book belong solely to the author and do not necessarily reflect those of the publisher. The publisher, therefore, disclaims responsibility for the views or opinions expressed within the work.

Unless otherwise indicated, Scripture quotations taken from the New King James Version (NKJV). Copyright © 1982 by Thomas Nelson, Inc. Used by permission. All rights reserved.

Scripture quotations taken from the Holy Bible, New International Version (NIV). Copyright © 1973, 1978, 1984, 2011 by Biblica, Inc.™. Used by permission. All rights reserved.

Paperback ISBN-13: 978-1-6628-2537-8
Ebook ISBN-13: 978-1-6628-2538-5

Dedication

I dedicate this book to my beloved children, Queen Hadasa and Prince Joses. Your boldness (seasoned with humility) gives me great joy as a mother. When I am tempted to forget who I am, all I do is look at you. You are the best definition of the words secure, settled, and smart!

Thank you for filling my house with so many little adorable friends of all races and colors. Now we call it, "My house of many colors." Thank you for showing them unconditional love and patiently demonstrating to them how you should be treated. Through you, their parents became a dear part of my life. You challenged me to expand my appetite for diversity.

You are the generation that will find hate a strange word!

Table of Contents

Dedication v
Preface ix

Part One: Freeing Yourself So You Can Fly 1

Prologue   Embracing Your Fall as Fuel for the Flight 3

Part Two: Know Your Monster; Fight to Win 13

A Reality Check with Privilege 15

Part Three: Finding Unity Through Privilege 41

Chapter One   Make Peace With Privilege:
                            Denial is a Friendly Enemy 43

Chapter Two   Search and Advocate for the Heroes of Love:
                            When Silence is not a Virtue 68

Chapter Three   Buy Shares in Privilege: Investing in
                            Mutual Relationships with Privilege 90

Chapter Four   Change Your Weapon:
                            Shooting the Bullet of Love 138

Chapter Five   Reverse Strategy:
                            Trade Positions in the Battle of Privilege 189

Chapter Six   Keep God in Perspective:
                            A Shortcut to Loving Imperfection 218

Acknowledgements 275
About the Author 285

Preface

In my thirty-eight years of life, I have experienced and triumphed over countless fears. I have also helped others to find their place of rest, peace, and joy by subduing their own fears. Some of my worst fears included the fear of darkness, eating in public, adding, or losing weight, pain, failing, fame, death, and while I wish that my fear of rejection was my final, the list was endless!

Those that know me quite well may hardly believe that I have ever battled a single fear. At face value, I appear to have confidence that can subdue the devil himself! I grew up with a very God-fearing, loving, bold, and ambitious father who worked tirelessly to reproduce himself in me. I always looked up to him as my hero. Being a daddy's girl greatness was ingrained in me as he made me sit in front of the TV and imagine myself being the news anchor of the day. He pushed me to be my best, expected me to be bold, which I thought I was until a messy divorce "reprogrammed my software." But still, I kept that programming change to myself to make everyone believe that I was still that same confident girl.

My mother, on the other hand, is a woman of few words who listens more and smiles a lot. You will know her faith by her actions. She never lets anything stop her from her dreams and although she rarely will say it, you will see it. Kindness, gentleness, and compassion are the hallmarks of her personality. What a sweet soul she is! I have a combination of both personalities in me which plays a major role in delivering the objective of this book.

The energy spent in keeping the secret of our struggles is often twice as much as that spent in handling the misjudgments and perceptions that follow the confession. This feels like a license to get vulnerable, so let's get going!

This book is the product of a quest to survive the raging storm of racial discrimination for my beloved children, Queen Hadasa and Prince Joses. It once was our "Keep the Dream Alive" manual. A messy divorce at a tender age, followed by an unexpected relocation from Kenya to the U.S. left our bucket of challenges overflowing. I watched my little hero and heroine (who were born leaders) gasp for breath as the storms of discrimination attempted to drown them. At six and nine years of age, the dark forces roared at them, threatening to devour their identity and possibly assassinate their once blossoming dreams.

I became an anxious mother, as I observed my dear children fighting to keep their heads above the rising waters of prejudice attempting to drown them. It was their frantic quest to make just one friend that really bothered me. The question they frequently asked, "Could you please be my friend?" which was often followed by a heartbreak and then their desperate sobs. The random notes I occasionally found written "I wish I were not different," or, "I wish I could just fit in" simply tore my heart out. The helpless cries from my son lamenting how he had no one to play with or that he was kicked for no reason with the details of the ordeal obvious on his tearful, scared, and despairing face.

If only that were all. It was the innocent conversations I stumbled upon between my two little souls inside their bedroom, a talk engulfed with fear on how they had to sit by themselves when everyone else had company during recess and lunch. And a boy who said, "I am doing you a favor by having you on my team because no one else will choose you." How about my daughter narrating with tears how her friend hugged everybody and restrained her when she just thought it was her turn? These shattered my heart into pieces. The suspicious stares from doubting faces that screamed, "You really are different," endorsed with isolation were the culmination of many experiences, both subtle and obvious, that made it so hard for these tender souls to keep their feet steady.

My kids became imposters, forced to adopt a fraudulent identity as a coping mechanism under the prevailing circumstances. The once playful outgoing children became dull and introverted. This sucked my joy and confidence, becoming the salt to the wound of my fear of rejection that was triggered by a ruthless execution of my marriage of eight years, when my husband decided to marry our adopted daughter. Yes, I was a wounded heroine with two little souls looking up to me for their survival.

And then here was Terry, a fellow parent at my children's elementary school, very oblivious of what I was dealing with. So, when she said to me, "I have seen black people, but you people are way *too* black," she must have been genuine or so I thought, although I was very hurt and somewhat confused. That statement gave me social anxiety on behalf of my kids. I wanted to shield them from ever hearing this. So many times, I contemplated returning to my homeland and surrendering myself to whatever I fled from. But this felt like a betrayal to the African American who had no other place to call home. The words of my little boy saying, "Mom, I am not afraid of death, but rejection scares me to death," triggered my adrenaline. Mission accomplished. With a mixture of apprehension and excitement, I accepted the call to be my children's "swim coach."

I folded my sleeves to rescue their identity while mine was still lost somewhere in the woods! Sometimes, *all we need is to fight others' battles to win our own*, I was just about to make this discovery.

It was 5:17 a.m. on a Wednesday morning and I had been sitting at my usual prayer and meditation spot for more than an hour fighting this call.

The days that followed, we adopted an intense discipline of spending thirty minutes every weekday to discuss our discrimination experiences, face our fears, and find solutions. It was an intense program, but we made it fun so that everyone looked forward to every session. Within six months or so, this process tremendously boosted our confidence in handling interracial relationships.

What a joy to watch these same kids assert their value with boldness, grace, and humility! The struggle is no longer to make friends but rather how to choose long-term friends. The leader in them became alive again! My daughter became the president of her elementary school in 2019. My son was selected for the Gifted and Talented seminar class in 2020 and during a feedback session his teacher said, "Joses leads with love, compassion, fairness and respect." We did it, yay!

The unfortunate killing of George Floyd, who happened to be a black man, by a white police officer, and its aftermath was an urgent call for me to share this manual as an effort to heal a divided nation. (My heart goes out to George's family, friends, and relatives.) At the time, I was writing a book on passion which is a subject of immense interest for me and therefore this call felt like an interruption whose urgency I could not resist.

We live in a world of privileges, and everyone has *one* if not multiple. White privilege is just one of them. It is difficult to do away with them because they are imbedded in the fabric of our society.

Our aim should, therefore, be creating the right relationship with these privileges, so that they do not turn into a dividing factor. Privilege is power, and power without control is destructive. We should direct our privileges, whether white, black, brown, or yellow and not vice versa. That way, privileges can become a unifying factor.

The biggest problem of America is not systemic racism in my opinion, but people who have lost control over their privileges and are drunk with the power of their own privilege. I believe that good people can survive bad systems, and this does not excuse anyone from their responsibility. And while we point fingers at white privilege, how many more privileges are being mishandled in the background?

By taking a bipartisan approach towards racism and privilege, this book uses real life stories to empower you to take charge of your privileges and, consequently, your relationships. You will learn how to create authentic mutual connections and heal the broken ones. This book demonstrates how to turn your battle into a blessing by showing you how the somewhat contentious white privilege can be transformed into a *shelter* for all races, making it a *real* value for the privileged. Isn't it real value when your privilege works to benefit everybody, then the same people stand to defend it? And then, you sit peacefully and enjoy that same privilege without feeling the pressure to protect it, wow!

PART ONE

Freeing Yourself So You Can Fly

"The greatness of a man's power is the measure of his surrender."
—William Booth

PROLOGUE

Embracing Your Fall as Fuel for the Flight

> *"Failure is an option here. If things are not failing, you are not innovating enough."*
> —*Elon Musk*

I was STILL mourning the loss of a husband and a daughter through a messy divorce when one of my friends, Tirzah, asked me a heartbreaking question. Here, heartbreaking is an understatement.

"Phidia, what role did you play in the breakup of your marriage?" I still can't believe the damage that simple question did to me. I began sweating, I was choking with anger and pride. I was bitter, offended, and defensive. Something was tearing my intestines apart or so it seemed. What was it? It took me several days to identify it and here it was. *How on earth could someone like me fail?* Wasn't I the offended one? How could she overlook the grievous act of my husband taking our adopted daughter for a wife? What role could I have played in that?

Didn't I deserve a serious apology? Not even an apology, I needed a pity party and a ceremony to curse my offenders just because I couldn't find a better way to punish them for *their* crime. How could she have been so insensitive? Or was she playing the devil's advocate? There was no one to answer my questions unfortunately. As far as I was concerned, I had *nothing* to do with this mess. I was the victim, and shocked that she did not realize how much I was entitled to be understood. I had worked so hard for thirty years to keep up a perfect image and now someone wanted to call me a failure? I had no intention of talking to her again unless she realized how offensive her question was and apologized.

I carried a heavyweight of fear from that day forward, explaining to everyone who seemed to question my cleanness in the divorce how I did not contribute to the failed marriage, even though they did not ask for the information. Unfortunately, the more I explained, the more explanation they wanted. Humans are very difficult sometimes. Until one day, I took a piece of paper and wrote in bold letters, I FAILED. My body was experiencing a storm as it fought back, but I held my peace to the end. I thought heaven and earth would be torn into pieces before I got to the letter D, but nothing, everything was business as usual. Then I realized, it's never that serious after all. I had such incredible peace from that declaration, and never again have I ever felt the need to explain my failure to anyone. I just surrendered myself to the freedom to make mistakes and live life. *Oh, what a joy!*

I come from Kenya, in the Eastern part of Africa. This country has about forty-two tribes, which constitute a population of about 54 million people. Each tribe has a unique dialect which binds its members together. I come from the Kamba tribe, which currently is among the top five in terms of population. The Kamba community is further subdivided into clans. I am a descendant of a highly respected clan known as the Kitondos. The Kitondo girls are known to be badass women; tough, fierce, no nonsense, and relentless fighters who don't believe in the existence of the word *fail*. If you marry one, you better be a strong person because she can manage you, the family, and the entire clan if the men sleep on the job. A Kitondo girl likes to see everything under control and if it is not, she takes charge. She may not actually realize that she is doing that because it is so woven in the very fabric of her being. She is allergic to stalling, she keeps things in motion. She always shows up ready for the occasion and is hardly ever intimidated.

It takes a secure spouse to handle this woman, otherwise you will have to use some manipulation to subdue her. I promise this had nothing to do with my divorce, just if you thought that your "research" is almost falling into place. Kitondo girls rarely seek battles, but when they do, they don't abandon their mission halfway. The concept of surrender does not exist in their world. You can hardly overlook a Kitondo girl because she has a huge presence. She is loyal and selfless, and her success is shared by the entire clan. On a scale of 1:10, I consider myself a 9 of this type of girl, but Lilian, who is my special Kenyan friend, and kinswoman is a perfect definition of this girl. I hope you meet her someday then you can have some appreciation for the girls of my clan. If this girl defines you, regardless of your color and gender, then welcome to Kitondo Girl Power! We have room for every bird of our feather. The only problem is that these girls will practically "kill someone" before you get them to admit that they failed. That explains the "hurricane" I experienced as I attempted to trespass the parameters of a "perfect" Kitondo girl.

Failure is a crime as far as Kitondo girls are concerned, which mirrors the woes of the entire humanity. Our society tells us in so many ways that we must not fail. But here is the upside of failure– *It is the most affordable and effective training for any aspiring teacher.* It happens to be the least competitive though because fewer people send in their applications. The fear of failure keeps a vast majority of people from attempting something new or challenging. People who fall the hardest tend to make the best teachers of the very subject they failed, though the world usually doesn't seem to give them a chance to be teachers. If they ever get the chance, though, it is painfully earned by crashing through tightly closed and highly guarded doors into a world that has already written them off. Unfortunately, not many of them possess the willpower to exercise this level of what I would call "positive violence," which is the apparent reason why we only get to see a few survivors as millions get trapped in the merciless pit of negativity and ill-fated opinions.

Some people may wonder who this Phidia person is and what moral authority she has, to advise others? After all, she failed hard! Fair enough, I did. But, as for me, I see *failure as the magic hole of endowment for every professional.* I have so much respect for those that have never failed but I also owe a double of the same regard to those that have made the best out of the pit they fell in. Heroes and heroines who spent their pit days by not fussing over the pit but establishing the foundations that would hold them high later deserve much respect because it is never easy to dig your way out of a hole.

Four years of condoning an unfaithful spouse, followed by three more years of shamelessly and consciously sharing him sexually with my adopted daughter left me feeling like a complete failure as far as self-respect and relationships were concerned. I was certain that I would never talk about relationships from a positive point of view. But who would have imagined that this would be the "certificate" I needed to master the art of relationship?

Are you ready to write the two-word sentence that scares you to death? Even at the cost of your fear, pride, and self-perception? Do you realize that your lemons are not meant for the proverbial trash can and that the world is waiting to taste your lemonade? Are you ready to admit that you have a role in the racial turmoil of this country? Or will you insist on your entitlement to an apology or vindication? Do you realize that *both* blacks and whites and every other race have a role in steering the ship of privilege?

Once you admit your failure and role in creating it, then we can proceed with the process of delivering "baby" Shelter from the pregnant "mother" White Privilege by acting responsibly and ultimately duplicate this for every other privilege. Only then, can we work together, different races and colors, but with the same objective with our eyes focused on the beauty of a shelter of protection for all races, nations, and tongues, a shelter born of this very privilege, which in the time past has been a point of contention. Then, the world of privileges can learn from us how to handle benefits, whether white, black, brown, yellow or whatever other color they may present themselves in.

The State of the Messenger

I wish I could keep this to myself, but if you are reading this book, you deserve to know at least some of my secrets. Though I am confident about so many issues, when the call to write this book came to me, I did not feel like the best candidate for it. At the time, I was a housekeeper having fun with cleaning, which just happens to be one of my passions, crazy as that may sound to some. I wondered if anyone would be interested in listening to a housekeeper, especially in our current world where class seems to be everything. While I considered myself to be a housekeeper *with* class, by default, my title condemned me from joining the "advisory board." Moreover, I had only been in this country for two years. I felt that there were other candidates who could do this better. Nevertheless, I refused to get intimidated when I realized that I wasn't meant to change everybody, but just those that destiny has allocated to me. So, I had nothing to lose by obeying the call and so I did.

The Message and The Promise

This book is full of real-life stories with countless teachable moments delivered with humor. This is not a boring book, so tighten your belt for a rollercoaster of fun. This book is not about black and white folks, though they are the main characters but instead handling privilege and relationships like a pro and making the best out of the worst. It does not suggest the *idea* of perfect relationships but rather a consistent commitment (with the right attitude) to make the best of ourselves and others through practical, honoring unconditional love for self and for others.

The concepts used are very simple, practical, tried and tested. This book is a personal life testimony and an invitation to share my best practices. I share universal relationship principles that can accelerate reconciliation for humanity and create lasting relationships, both at a personal and corporate level. The simplicity with which this book is written makes it easy for anyone, including children, to read it.

Most of us should be familiar with the word privilege, which is an essential topic in our day. Every one of us has got one or more privileges. No wonder we use the words underprivileged instead of *non-privileged*. These privileges are, in my perspective, a big dividing factor across the world. In this book white and black folks are the main characters used to represent the privileged and the underprivileged across the world respectively, who seek to specifically address the issue of racism in relation to the white privilege.

In this book, white privilege is discussed from a **UNIFYING** perspective, rather than the traditional negative viewpoint. This is a total shift of mindset, changing the focus from the somewhat futile macro approach in which the responsibility to tame the white privilege and bring reconciliation is placed on legislators, to individual responsibility. This book does not seek to undermine the responsibility of legislators in combating systemic racism. However, it does focus on *changing the people who make systemic racism relevant by giving into hate*. In short, this book advocates the view that good people can survive bad systems as they wait for systems to change. Bad people will still ruin good systems regardless. That's human nature, always selfish and inclined to evil.

This is more of a relationship book, which means that it is not limited to the predicaments of blacks and whites. The principles in this book can be applied universally to build interpersonal, interracial, and intercountry relationships.

The words in this book I hope will inspire you to embrace any fall as fuel for your flight; to realize that *the fall is not the future*. And what a privilege that someone who failed in her marriage for doing silly stuff would have the opportunity of helping someone else get it right!

Me Too Moments

To help you identify with my journey, I have rectangular segments strategically placed in every chapter, which I call a "Me Too Moment." That should help you overcome your tendency to think, *why me?* One of the strategies that the enemy of your destiny uses is to make you think that your case is isolated, and something is very wrong with you. This is the way he sucks your energy out, the very energy you need to take action for (and in) your life.

Our society does not seem to embrace challenges very much. We are taught how to conquer but never taught how to handle falling. As a result, we grow up with the picture of a perfect life until we are met with reality. *There is a safe way to fall,* believe it or not. In this book, you are allowed to struggle, to fail, and to cry as long as you don't stay in that pit of despair for too long. That pit is supposed to be just a layover as you board your next flight to success.

Please note that you are not limited to the designated "Me Too Moment" segments. Anytime you feel the need to add a "me too" in the middle of a sentence, that's exactly what you should do. The more authentic you are with yourself, the more hope of having a better relationship with yourself and others as a result. **Racism is a sign of a troubled self, escalating to the world around.** By the time you finish reading this book, it should be decorated with several "me toos" with a pen of your favorite color. That should be evidence of the countless possibilities you have to impact the world for the better.

The "me too" tables mostly encourage you to describe your experiences into one word which is aimed at helping you get even more involved as you connect with your feelings, which is crucial for any real change.

The 'Practicals' of Love

You might be familiar with the word "practicals" from scientific laboratory experiments in which the theory learned is translated into action in a real-life situation. This is the concept behind this section. Each chapter concludes with inspired action steps to help you make what you have learned count for you. This book contains great concepts but what makes it even applicable for you is the action that you take after reading. These actions include:

- Meditation
- Journaling
- Personal and interpersonal dialogues
- Exercises and affirmations
- Open discussions with an accountability partner about personal experiences, challenges, and victories.
- Interracial club fun activities
- Assignments that help you exercise interracial love and take part in creating a shelter out of privilege as we turn this benefit into a *real* value for the privileged.

Since this book is essentially my life, I can assure you that these actions have transformed my life and others and the same can happen to you and your loved ones. Through this book, you can further enjoy your life and relationships, whatever kind, spreading love, peace, joy, and abundance to others to heal humanity as you create the world you want without making racial differences or anything else an excuse. You will feel and touch the progress as you journal through your feelings, emotions, and actions.

How to Sign the Guarantee

For this book to produce maximum results for you, I recommend that you form an interracial club with about five to seven like-minded people. Let us call it, "My Coat of Many Colors Club" abbreviated as MCMC or Double MC Club. Feel free to give it a different name, as long as you keep the words "my" and "many colors" to remind you of your relationship with different races. The purpose of this club is to practice the book by having social fun as you get acquainted with and find appreciation for other cultures to strengthen interracial relationships right from the grassroots. This club should be a haven for you to be yourself without being insensitive or fear of judgement. It should be the place where you are free to identify with and express your culture without being inconsiderate of others.

Explain whatever you are doing before you do it, so it doesn't come as a shock. Have fun activities, get adventurous with culture, talk openly about your practices and beliefs, cook, and eat foods you haven't eaten before, write, pray, and/or complement one another, appreciate the beauty of each other's skin color and culture openly as you read this book together. Remember, you can read this book as many times as is needed for love to prevail.

For faster results and in consideration of people's busy schedules, I recommend that the club meets bi-weekly to give members time to read ahead in readiness for the club reading and activities. You can do virtual meetings if your club has members that cannot meet in person though in person is highly recommended where possible. Hopefully, after your book club has finished reading this book you will continue to meet and/or do things together.

It will be helpful if everyone keeps a *Double MC* journal to capture their experiences, connect with their thoughts and emotions and track their progress.

I recommend that these clubs also be formed in schools with the help of teachers so we can minimize racial bullying and create **interracial possibility** as we raise a generation that will find *hate strange and diversity fascinating*. Elementary school is the developmental stage where a lot goes so wrong and forever affects the future. By so doing we can turn around a society for generations as we work to heal our racially divided world directly from the grassroots.

I urge religious organizations and every institution that values love to champion formation of these clubs so we can close the interracial gap faster and heal ourselves.

Remember to be patient, as we are coming a long way, and the results may not be evident overnight.

PART TWO

Know Your Monster; Fight to Win

*"Experience is the best teacher, and the worst experiences teach the **best lessons**."*
—Jordan Peterson

A Reality Check with Privilege

Burying the 'Golden' Kid

Marilyn and I were in the same department after the bank we worked for transferred me from Personal to Business banking segment. We were each heading a team of business development officers. However, based on my experience and education, I was earning a better paycheck, and we both knew it – the bank's managerial grading system made it easy to guess such information. Before the move, Thomas, the head of Personal and Business banking department held a performance feedback session with me. He evidently could not hide his pleasure over what I had accomplished within nine months as one of the five sales managers within the personal banking segment which prompted this transfer.

In my prologue, I mentioned that I am a Kitondo girl of the Kamba tribe (which is somewhat highly regarded in my country). Considering the description that I gave of this girl and the social status of my tribe, that should help you in a way to appreciate my competitive self. In that regard, I was the top sales manager, which, while significant, did not imply that I lived on the golden side of life. I sort of did in my teenage and early twenties. Back in those days, I was the pride of my parents, teachers, church, and community leaders because everything seemed to be going so well for me. My peers looked up to me with admiration and I was treated as the egg-laying goose while paying for it with my freedom.

With many expectations pressing from all directions, I was pushed to some unsafe levels of perfectionism and standards to maintain. I felt I was living a fraudulent life while everyone was celebrating. I was the kid who "never" made mistakes, even one as simple as losing a pen. One mistake could mean that I cried for a day or days, depending on how grave I considered my mistake to be. Perhaps I was an extremist of some sort when it came to perfectionism, but so be it. I had a good name after all. I'm not sure if this qualified to be considered OCD, but whatever the case, I was still human and soon would discover that this kind of life was neither fun living, nor was it sustainable.

Have you ever felt like you owe life so much for the person that you have turned out to be today? That's precisely my position at the moment. I am simply indebted to life, whoever that is, for teaching me so many invaluable lessons. The good thing about life is that it has a way of teaching you in a manner that the lesson becomes unforgettable. Life has beaten me so hard that perfection is no longer an issue for me anymore. Now, all that matters is wrapped up in one word—a word that many people talk about but have no relationship with and one that holds tons of meaning to me, and that word is *consistency*. As for my younger self, you could be thinking, what a weird kid you were! I am sure this is a "Me too" moment for many others reading this book. I recently encountered one such a child, a little girl who at twelve years of age cried the entire day because she lost a piece of paper that contained the password for her school account. You may wonder why a lost piece of paper containing a password (which can easily be changed) would make her cry an entire day. She had the option of sitting her little butt down and changing the password, right? But there she was, crying for hours on end. It was on her birthday, but this little paper ruined it. I was attending what should have been a party for her, which never happened.

All of us were forced to search for the "magical" piece of paper. But why was little intelligent Lisa crying so hard and sending all of us into anxiety and panic? When I asked her what her worst fear was, tearful Lisa paused the crying and with sheer disappointment said, "I can't believe I lost the paper. I don't make such stupid mistakes! That's just me, and there's nothing I can do about it." Then, she resumed crying even harder this time. "Are you sure there is nothing you can do about it?" I cautiously asked. "Nothing! Everyone knows it!" she replied with anger and frustration as if to say, *a no-go zone!* So, I was the only stranger because everyone understood her? Sure, they did because no one seemed bothered about the crying except for me. *How kind of them! I hope life would also understand this cutie,* I said to myself.

Mind you, all the while, she has not changed her password, she just had to finish mourning her failed perfectionism and then only afterwards can she take cover from the account hackers. Poor thing! I just hope that on that fateful day these heartless fellows were on vacation. When all reasoning failed, I asked her if she could change the password for friendship's sake and she accepted! So, she was okay with doing it for me, but not for her own self that had terribly failed her standards. The good thing is that experience is a great voluntary teacher to all of us. No amount of talking can change such people. They only need to make as many grievous mistakes as possible until the fate of their real self has been sealed, and they have nothing else to hide. I watched my old self in little Lisa as if I were watching a movie, an insecure self, hidden in the words "perfectionism" and "being in control." Imagine now a "combo" of this type of Lisa-girl, and a Kitondo girl put together in one person! Now you know the kind of person Marilyn, my banking colleague, had to deal with, and this unpleasant part of my self was about to be tested through fire.

ME TOO MOMENT	Have you ever felt like you owe life for the person you have turned out to be?
	In one word, what is the main lesson life has ever taught you?

A Shoe for Two!

"I am proud to present to you the upcoming Area Sales Manager for our business banking Segment; a self-made talent, our very own Phidia Maingi, formerly a sales manager within the personal banking segment! As you all know, she has proven herself to be an inspirational, yet business-driven leader and the evidence is clear from her unchallenged performance record for three quarters in a row."

Before Thomas could finish his statement, the room was filled with passionate claps and ululations from well-wishing colleagues who had seen this coming. He took a breath as he allowed the celebration to diffuse the tension that had preceded this impromptu meeting. "Phidia is the next big thing in Business Banking leadership. She is the space to watch," he concluded as he invited me to join him and other departmental leaders in front to make my maiden speech. From the front, I could notice the excitement on the faces of the other managers except one. Marilyn, who was not only a colleague but also a friend, looked very disappointed for some reason.

When Thomas moved me, he did so with the intention to groom me to lead the other seven business banking sales managers. This was a new role being introduced in the segment whose main objective was to simplify the workload for the department head. Thomas had discussed it with me and Jared, my immediate boss. The rest of the team was also privy to the creation of this new position, and a few of the sales managers, including Marilyn and I, had expressed interest in it, but now the decision had been made, and the other hopefuls had to back off. Jared congratulated me during a joint meeting with the sales managers from both Personal and Business banking segments. A week later, this unexpected meeting was convened solely to make an official announcement of my transition.

This morning, as I watched Marilyn from the front where I was making my speech, I kept wondering to myself, what on earth could have triggered this kind of fury? Why was everyone else excited for me except Marilyn, a very close friend, one that we had shared so many details of our lives? It wouldn't be too long before I found out.

Am I safe with your privilege?

I was excited to work with the new team, but Marilyn wasn't for some reason. She distanced herself from me, developed a strange attitude and tried to incite the team against me. A month into my new role, I received an acting appointment letter. I was to "act" for six months before I was officially confirmed. Part of my responsibilities were to collate and report daily performance. This was just the beginning of hell breaking loose on me! Before it was just a cold war, but now the battle became more obvious and intense. Marilyn would delay sending her team's performance, which had a ripple effect by impacting my reporting timelines. I would ask a couple of times on the phone and with email upon which she would just yell from her office, "Phidia, I don't report to you." She would then send her team's performance directly to Thomas. The irony was that Thomas did not see any issue with her sending the reports directly to him based on his comments when I raised the issue with him. Was there a special rule for Marilyn? I just wondered, yet I didn't have the guts to face my boss about the issue. I knew that the two had a *personal* relationship, which Marilyn was very loud about. I was afraid that raising any issues could possibly turn out to be career limiting for me.

Day in and day out, Marilyn and I had issues to fight over. She made my in-house team meetings difficult. She was deliberate about making sure that she did not comply with anything I requested. Then, she would run to the head office to discuss things with Thomas any time I pressured her to comply with my requests. So often did she have something to discuss with him, that she made sure that the rest of the managers, including myself, knew that she was headed once again to meet the boss. Maybe this was a strategy of intimidation? I may never know but the content of the meetings remained a mystery, at least to me.

You, of course, know that humans by default tend to keep their noses clean regardless of what it costs others. Even though the good person inside ourselves would want to admit our liabilities, more often it never wins the battle and so the other party ends up taking the blame. It's even worse when the discussion happens in the absence of the "rival" party because it denies us a chance to understand both sides of the coin. Having said this, we can predict the outcome of these meetings that Marilyn held with Thomas.

On this other end, I was busy trying to keep it as professional as I could and to stay in charge while Marilyn was seemingly using what I would call "the law of the jungle." I thought that leadership meant fighting my battles by myself, maybe not. I had no intention to overwhelm my boss this early, until I was sure things had gotten out of hand. What I did not realize was that early as it was, the issue was already out of control. By the time I decided to talk with Thomas, it was the third month in my new role, and he had been fed with so much negative stuff about me that he had no space for anything else.

"Phidia, I am disappointed that I chose you for this role," he said after patiently listening to my challenges with Marilyn. "You have simply failed in your role, no wonder Marilyn has to do it for you," he said. "If you don't get your house in order, then we may have to get someone else to do it instead." I had no time to internalize everything I heard within those five minutes that he spoke to me. Few words they were but, they carried tons of weight. He seemed to have made up his mind on my fate. *But how soon? This is unfair!* My heart was screaming to an imaginary audience hoping someone could see my point.

Maybe I should at this point introduce you to Marilyn. She was a strong lady who could be intimidated by nothing. She believed in herself and her dreams. She had infectious energy to attract the beasts of the field and the birds of the air! She was the kind of person who loved her life, something I admired about her. But as fate would have it, each coin has two sides. She also had a sneaky side of her that enjoyed picking fights with people that she felt got into her path or challenged her in some way. She not only made their lives difficult, but she celebrated it. Before the current situation, both Marilyn and I had a mantra that said, "Give some grace," which reminded us to be kind in the face of a conflict. I'm not sure how often she applied it, but it did help a few times. Every time one of us tried to be evil, the other would say that statement and we would burst out loud with laughter and change the topic as a sign that the message was home. Surprisingly, I loved both sides of Marilyn. One side was a reminder of my father's inherited solid and ambitious personality. At the same time, the other side of her challenged the delicate part of me, which was passed on from my mother, to embrace contention and stretch my conflict-handling skills.

I am sure you have similar people in your circle who enjoy conflict. I wish I were that kind of person; perhaps my life would have been a lot easier. I love peace, but I also admit that a bit of conflict can create real and lasting peace. It's just that whenever I have to face it, it feels strange. So, when I meet people like Marilyn who search for conflict and enjoy the process, there is something to admire about them. Having a fun relationship with conflict? Who doesn't want that? Now you understand why I couldn't just remove Marilyn from my circle of friends. With reference to her personality and this situation, I knew what Marilyn was capable of. Henceforth, I fastened my seatbelt for a rough "drive."

The Dirty Game Empowered?

On that fateful day, I left my supervisor's office with a troubled soul. There were a couple of things that bothered me, but one weighed me down the most—that he did not see any issue with Marilyn sending the performance of her team directly when he had appointed a manager for that responsibility. Why did he appoint me to this role if he wasn't going to support me? I wondered silently. Did I expect too much of Thomas? Maybe it wasn't his business to stop her from sending the reports directly. But how was I going to stop her when the *boss* was on her side? Was I being used as a guinea pig? Was this a setup to prove a point and make room for someone else or was I just a failure? I should have been asking rhetorical questions. With a lost relationship with Marilyn, and little to no power, I was fighting a lost battle. I was just a ceremonial manager with a temporary title. The system seemed to scream at me, *you are on your own!* I was sitting on a time bomb that would explode in no time. I felt very confused and helpless.

When Marilyn saw that Thomas was not bothered with her reporting directly to him, she was motivated to push things a little further. The next couple of weeks, she was determined to rub it in! I remember a few days after this conversation, sitting in our weekly head office meeting feeling lost but faking to be in charge. Thomas had spent a few minutes emphasizing the importance of leading by example when Marilyn raised her hand to say something. "Some of our leaders don't seem to understand the issues of business banking, which is a shame. It has to start from the top," she finished her weighty remarks. She sure had a point and though she mentioned no names, it was rather obvious who she was referring to. She had accusations about my capability which the team and Thomas were aware of. I was hoping that my team leader would ask for facts, but he never did. He only had one message which just added salt to the injury. "People must bear their own crosses." I was lost in trying to understand his statement. *What exactly was my cross in this case?* I asked myself but found no answer.

Even though Marilyn had been prospecting for this vacancy, she did not have the academic qualifications and experience. At the time, she was pursuing her college degree which was a key requirement for this role. Much as I expected her to be disappointed, it was rather evident that she wouldn't get it based on the bank's criteria for this role.

Dirty Linen

Marilyn had another strength; she was very good at making an impression. She knew the right words to say at the right time, which was kinda cool! Being a pastor's kid or a PK, I was taught to "say everything" which was supposedly a virtue of openness and sincerity. Until this situation, it had worked for me, but now it looked like I had outgrown it! There are times when the thing that has brought you up begins to bring you down. Wisdom lies in discerning the time to discontinue business as usual and learn how to safely break the rules.

Being truthful does not always mean saying everything to everyone. There is also the aspect of who hears that truth and what they could do with it. If you suspect they have ulterior motives, then they have no business hearing that truth, especially if they could take advantage of your vulnerability. This is one of the few times when keeping your dirty linen neatly stacked in your closet is best. Nevertheless, some vulnerable people will genuinely need your "dark side" to beat their pity parties and soldier on.

It is very common for people who have suffered rejection to not say anything good about themselves. Some confuse it for humility, which is supposed to be a virtue especially from a religious point of view. We have been taught that saying something positive about ourselves amounts to tooting our horns, which is considered evil and prideful. I was once that person. But in this case, it was not rejection prompting my openness, but more about being a Pastor's Kid (PK), who was always nurtured to be open and genuine. I said everything about myself without sugarcoating it.

I am the kind of person that holds very few secrets about myself, yet I am a confidante to so many people! Strange, isn't it? So, if I did not know something, I never pretended to know nor did I keep quiet about it even if I was dealing with the boss. I discovered that it wasn't the best way to do things at work. I was naive about this wisdom of "selective disclosure." Marilyn had mastered the game very well. She knew the right things to say at the right time and that was not all. She had many cards lined up for her to take advantage of the situation. In addition to her innate public relations skills, she knew the boss at a personal level. They both came from the same tribe, and Thomas had been a long-time friend of her family, a fact that both talked fondly of. I will shed additional context about the importance of this next.

ME TOO MOMENT	Have you ever unawares helped your so-called adversary to prepare your hanging gallows?
	In one word, how did realizing it make you feel?

Position vs. Power

In Kenya, while most of us are black, we differentiate ourselves by our individual ethnic tribes. Each tribe is closely knit together by their dialect and culture. This is an essential aspect of the Kenyan community because of the similarities and connections that people from the same tribe have and, at times, can be a big deal. Of course, there is a limit to everything, but more often, those limits are just in theory, and that can be a threat to inter-tribal harmony and the workplace in this case. While I suspected that we might have broken the limits in this case, who cares! Everything was falling into place for Marilyn while it was falling apart for me. She showed the right cards at the right time and never missed an opportunity while on the other hand, I was putting in hard work and being very sincere. Politics at work, *don't ya just love it?*

It was a battle of papers, position and experience versus relationship and power. I doubt Marilyn did anything to earn the power; I suppose the so-called fate, in the name of a relationship, just gave it to her. Was she privileged? If you define privilege from the dictionary point of view which describes it as *an advantage granted or available to a particular person or group,* as opposed to the "American" point of view, then we both had an advantage. She had the relationship while I had the qualifications. The only difference was in the power of an individual's privilege based on who held the system in place. So, whose privilege would have the day?

The Wickedness of a Privilege

I am only human; therefore, I do have my stretching limits. I guess I had already burst those limits. So, I decided to face Marilyn to make it clearer to her that I did not appreciate her lack of cooperation and how it was affecting the entire team. I tried to be as cordial and professional as I could be even though I was very distraught, and justifiably so in my opinion. It wasn't the most comfortable decision to make, but it was crucial. The discussion did not go very well, and she ended it with a threat.

"Phidia, you have no idea who I am. You will never call me out for such nonsense again, I promise!" she angrily declared as she stormed out of my office. *Ah! You mean that these last thirty minutes were just nonsense*? My spirit sank as I pondered what to do next. Inside, I was screaming with anger, *Idiot, just shut up or else ...* Or else what? I felt powerless. But what came out in my effort to be professional was, "I am sorry if that came off as nonsense. My objective is to create a team spirit that works for all of us and for the better of the organization." However, I don't know how much of that she heard as she swung herself out the doors so quickly. She grabbed her handbag and left for the day.

Later the following day, I saw an email to the entire department that Marilyn was taking over the acting position as the manager in charge. It was an awkward moment because I had no prior knowledge of that structural change. Though it still caught me by surprise, I had somehow seen it coming. But this was too soon, and I could feel my intestines falling apart! I had only "acted" in this position for three months, which although it felt like an eternity, I wasn't ready to let go. I am the kind that struggles to relinquish, which is both good and bad. Bad when you must hold onto a bad relationship simply because you want to prove to yourself and others a point that possibly none, but you care about, and good when letting go is the only option to getting hold of something better.

Two days after the tables were overturned, I scheduled a meeting with my boss just to understand what exactly had transpired. We discussed a couple of issues including my strained relationship with Marilyn. He said many things to me which left me with no doubt that Marilyn had a hand in the change. As the saying goes, *while words cannot break your bones, they can shatter your identity.* One statement stuck with me for years and persistently threatened my true self-perception. This was when he said to me, "You are too timid for this position." Timid because I had refrained from engaging in a battle of words with Marilyn over a position? Or did being professional mean the same thing as timid? I had to revisit my dictionary to confirm that the meaning of this word had not changed. Unfortunately, I believed him and gave up on my dreams for the next two years.

ME TOO MOMENT	Has your pursuit for peace ever landed you into a mistaken identity?
	What were you mistaken for and how did that make you feel?

Identity Assassination

For the first time in my life, I wasn't sure of myself. I thought I knew how bold I was, maybe I had successfully deceived myself! Daring was a very outstanding personality trait of myself until that day. Sometimes, our pursuit of peace will push us to a place where we get misjudged, a place where our personal brand feels threatened. But then, if this is the cost for fighting our battles without *compromising* our love for them that offend us, then so be it! Don't be offended by people rebranding you for the worst. Avoid the temptation to fight back with hate or pick battles that add no value to your destiny. Fight, but safeguard your *integrity*. Your dream can be delayed but not denied. If pursuing it involves losing your integrity and personal values, then it's not worth it.

Be bold enough to refrain from making people's opinions about you a destination; after all, it's just a passage and it's not even qualified for a stopover. One more minute of attention to destructive words makes that a stopover, which could risk it becoming a destination, so **STOP!** These are just roadside distractions from people who have no idea who you really are and what your destiny looks like. They just assume that they know you, but the truth is that they have no idea. They don't deserve your sweat. Keep your eyes ahead and fight if you must but remember to keep character at the center of your battle.

It was quite unfortunate that at the time I wasn't mature enough to rise up to this type of approach. I couldn't handle that form of mistaken identity. It shattered my courage, and I found myself struggling to engage with colleagues and customers. The prowess I once held in making presentations and engaging with people became my history. I began living as an imposter until it became part of me. This did not just happen for a few days but for at least two years. It became the defining aspect of my performance and career growth. On the other hand, Marilyn was given an official letter as the acting Manager in Charge for business banking team within the same month. The events that followed saw me downgraded to a business development officer, which meant that I worked with the same staff that I once led. It was humiliating and my resilience took a beating.

This was the first time in my life that my image stopped being a priority. You know how important this can be for a type-A personality let alone a Kitondo girl. It's often so important that it can become a hindrance to your freedom and happiness. But not anymore! At that point, I was not worried about who thinks what about my personality. Perhaps no one even noticed it in the first place. Is it possible that sometimes we overrate our importance to other people and just assume we know what they think about our value? I added the word "surrender" into my dictionary and came to peace with the fact that it too has an aspect of beauty.

A month later, I gave my notice for resignation, one of the few times in my life when quitting felt like music to my ears. Marilyn had her own share of challenges in her new role and wasn't well equipped for the new position, unfortunately. She had little experience in leadership of about seven months, a period which had been marked with several conflicts with her team members. In her new role, she ended up receiving many complaints relating to her people management skills, which consequently impacted her performance. Six months later, she lost the job for incompetence and underperformance. This position turned into a bad omen, which anyone interested in applying had to seriously think about it before sending in their resume.

The big question remained—*how did two good friends become the worst enemies, and how did such a privilege in the hands of Marilyn accomplish so much havoc?* It was so bad that it not only left the two of us jobless, but it also ushered me to think less of one of the essential parts of my identity. How did a head-on collision with privilege crash every little evidence of my true self and send me into at least two years of imprisonment for being an identity fraudster? The answer is rather obvious. We both wanted to wear the same "shoe" at the same time, and we never allowed ourselves to see any possibility of sharing it.

When you want something so much, the brain limits itself so that it does not see anything else. With a locked mind, all Marilyn could think of was how to get rid of me to make space for herself. Fortunately, or unfortunately, the universe acts independently on golden commands, one of which is to produce a harvest of the *same* kind as the seed that has been sown! She received the fruit of her labor, which meant that at the end of the day my loss became her loss as well. How sad!

The Dichotomy of Privilege

I wonder if my predicament with Marilyn resonates with the racial situation in America today. White people seem to have "the beautiful shoe," but that is not the issue. The issue is that whites often deny having it, although there is screaming evidence. And that is not all. "The shoe" only serves him, and that makes the black person who represents the underprivileged American feel left out. And not only does he feel left out, but the very shoe is pressing hard on his neck! *The fight is not because the privilege exists but because it is one-sided*, and the system which should make it right empowers the dirty game of privilege—dirty in the sense that it is the tool used to empower one person and weaken the other. Consequently, the status quo is maintained by making the weak weaker and the strong stronger. A poison to one, yet medicine to the other. What an evil game! And, yes, I refer to the shoe of oppression that was so evident in the case of George Floyd, who had a knee (like a shoe) on his neck.

Who said that this privilege isn't big enough for all of us? Or do we have to destroy one to make the other? Can't we elevate both black (underprivileged) and white (privileged) folks simultaneously instead? There is not a single justification for this dirty game in my opinion, and this filthy game has produced an angry, bitter, and yes, hateful black folk. And while we expect blacks to be the only ones feeling the pain, both parties do (what?) as black folks double their efforts to kill the source of their pain. But must we kill privilege to make two angry losers?

The world plays by very fundamental rules which cannot be twisted no matter who you are. Although some might disagree, *at no point can you make someone miserable without experiencing some of that misery yourself.* But how much of that do we remember when the egotistical part of us takes over? The lack of inclusion and misuse of privilege by white folks has prompted retaliation from black folks. The fight that once was a battle for inclusion has now turned into a furious hate-driven fight seeking for the privilege's demise. An angry, bitter, hateful fight meant for destruction of something that can transform lives, yet none of this makes sense as the black person counts his pain and loss since the same thing causes it. How does something so beautiful (because privilege is power and power is beautiful) end up breaking so many hearts, shattering countless destinies, killing innumerable lives, not to mention the ones that die from within (like in my case where my true self died together with my dreams), creating the worst of enemies, a troubled nation, and a divided world?

A Corked Pistol in a Child's hands

Power is good only if well applied. Unfortunately, there seems to be no universal system strong enough to tame power. It's one thing to give it and another to keep it under control. How do we end up with dictatorial leadership which the very people who voted the leaders into office have little or no say over how the power is applied? Even though they are supposed to listen to the folks that voted them in, this only happens theoretically as so often leaders play by their own rules and are immune to the voice of the voters. Now, imagine a cocked pistol handed to a child with thousands seated in front of him and cheering him on to use it! You would be quickly counting the casualties and arranging for caskets.

Power is good as long as it is kept under control. Power should not use people; people should use power. White privilege is a power package on its own. Left in the wrong hands of "children" and "goons" it can destroy so many lives which, has been happening in this country for a long time. And children here mean immature people oblivious of the danger their actions pose, while goons stand for heartless humans who deliberately cause havoc for their own pleasure. We have both categories within the privilege sphere. *Maturity* is fundamental in creating a healthy relationship with this privilege and ultimately leading to a good application for the benefit of all. When you see someone "drunk" with privilege and using it to oppress the weak, please don't blame them. They do, however, need to mature or else they are actually "terrorists" at heart who derive pleasure in causing pain. Unfortunately, waiting for them to grow up and/or change their attitudes while a cocked pistol is still in their possession is sure to be a nightmare. I wish we could talk to the hands of fate to give them some time before dishing out power to them. But who is fate anyway, and where does he or she live? I wonder. The damage has already happened, and power continues to roam around untamed, all in the name of a privilege.

I hope that this book can become a catalyst for fast-tracking the growth of some of the "children," provide a change of heart to others who have been radicalized by hate and in so doing save at least one life from an early grave. And to the few (or many) privileged white heroes and heroines who have got this power contained, using it to defend and protect the oppressed, creating bridges and shelters of safety for not only black folks but all the underprivileged, I wonder how best to celebrate you! Well done! Let's take one step further by adopting the "children" and coaching them to maturity while praying and persuading the heartless "goons" to change their attitudes. Sharing this book with a friend could be the beginning of it.

The Priority of Change: Systems or People?

Privileges are here to stay, not that I enjoy writing this. The universe, in collaboration with society, creates and allocates them as it deems fit. Where I come from, being a man is a privilege. I have also discovered that in this country, being a single parent gives you some tax relief privileges. Being a beggar could also be translated into a privilege if you really want to look closely at the concept of privilege. After all, not everyone can beg and be given money! That reality simply means that we have tons and tons of privileges that humankind has to deal with.

Hats off to those that have been putting up a relentless fight against systemic racism. We need you to continue to keep up the good fight. However, with so much power vested on humanity through privilege, there is a possibility that a change of system may end up frustrated by these power-endowed humans. Again, chances are that we might end up waiting an eternity before the legislators and the government systems come through for us as far as managing privilege pertains. So, what is our fallback plan? We need to consider investing in what I call a *grassroots strategy*, which is much more within our control. That doesn't mean we scrap the old strategy; no, we should create a "combo" of the two. We have vested too much power in the government and have been left powerless. We hold too many expectations on the legislators and have abandoned our responsibility to our own detriment. It's time to take some control back for ourselves. The good thing is that we *gave* the power, and so we can withdraw it back.

Systems are made for the people, not vice versa. The truth is that the systems don't tell the people to kill underprivileged folks; it is the *drunk-with-privilege* individuals (people who have lost control over their own privilege) who do that and blame it on the system. How can we help these people to stop making systemic racism relevant?

If we can change the hate-driven individuals working in the vague system, then we may as well forget about the system, right? Because good people will *revolt* against bad systems prompting a change of the same magnitude. We are the same people that create the mess, then we run to the government to teach us a lesson! How insane is that? Our objective should shift to creating a Plan B strategy that works with the people and empowers them with *love* and *possibility* through *authentic* interracial relationships that demand *accountability*. Love enough to subdue the temptation to use the system's loopholes to act in hate. This plan is devoted to creating *mutual* relationships at a personal level, which shape other interracial interactions out there in the larger world.

Change that comes from a relationship point of view is change you can trust. While the law is good, it only bulldozes us to fake obedience for fear of pain. But, when we are driven by our own will to change, the results are more enjoyable than when the law forces us to "love" one another. How possible is it to force love in the first place? There is so much enmity that broods when the law takes its full force. Even though relationships take longer to build, not only are they the safe way to battle hate but they create a long-lasting impact.

The Gold or the Fire?

DON'T STARE AT THE FIRE TOO LONG TO MISS THE GOLD. It was a messy divorce that ushered me to a new season of rediscovering myself. From an executive banker to a passionate housekeeper and then to a speaker/author, I discovered a new world of possibilities and some magical flexibility and resilience that I never knew existed within my fabric.

It is fire that refines gold, yet we have no attachment to the fire for we know what gold looks like. We keep staring at the fire all day long not for the fire but for the expected gold to show up. For once, we must accept that there are some precious stones being produced in the fire of hate and all the nasty scenes we have recently witnessed as a reason for the privilege. All these constitute *labor pains* ahead of the new baby that I call a *shelter* of protection whom the heroes and heroines of love are about to bring forth through the troubled privilege. No wonder we are witnessing more white folks in the recent days using their privilege to shelter and advance the course of blacks and the underprivileged than I would think has ever happened in history.

There's a *golden* side to this privilege. Who doesn't know that the erupting volcano is the only means by which the earth cools its interior? Some eruption is just plain necessary. It's time to come to terms with the fact that white privilege already exists, and there is nothing much we can do about it. It will always be here with us, and if we kill this one, another one will emerge because "the world," whoever that is, has got tons of them. But what it is that we can do with this privilege is the matter on the table. We have spent decades focusing on the negative side of this privilege and this is how far we have gotten — a country weighed down with hate, bloodshed, death, confusion, depression, and a crippling economy. Remember focus has the capacity to enlarge its target. That is a principle well applied in meditation and faith. What if the object of focus is detrimental? The answer is obvious, and this feels like the case as far as focusing on the dark side of the white privilege and this country is concerned.

How much time, opportunities, and lives have we lost *fighting* privilege? What is the part of this coin that we have never seen before in all these decades? If you are born in a house with an abundance of resources because your father had the privilege of accessing or amassing them, then how is that supposed to be your fault? It just happened for you; you had nothing to do with it. I can choose to spend my energy hating you and trying to pull you down so that we can be equal a move I wish to respectfully consider as cowardice. Alternatively, I could invest the same energy (or less of it) in creating a *mutual* relationship with you so I can make use of your advantage to rise too, rising not to where you are, but to the best version of myself. Life is not meant to be a game of competition against each other but rather, against our most authentic self. The moment we lose sight of who our competitor really is and focus on each other's progress, this broods negativity, envy, anger, bitterness, hate and a list too long for this sentence.

ME TOO MOMENT	Have you ever found yourself too engrossed with your pain to see the blessing inside the pain?
	In one word, what did that cost you?

You're Not My Competitor

Maintaining a proper perspective about ourselves and others leads to having the right attitude in this battle which is a fundamental necessity for establishing a healthy relationship for the battling sides. If the relationship is in place, then I have a ladder to climb to the height of my dreams or just fly; the choice is mine. I hold high regard for the fight against injustice which has been severely frustrated by both blacks and whites as well as the system. But now more than ever before, we need a strategy that is within our scope of control to push this agenda even further. If fighting *against* privilege led us this far, then why not fight *in favor* of the privilege? We have nothing to lose by trying. Let's find a common ground and turn the battle into a blessing instead. If a white person can *create* room for the black person to share in the privilege, then the fight to destroy would become a fight to protect this privilege. But the room has to be met by an open-minded black folk who has a willingness to *bury* the suspicions and start a new with a clean slate. I say this without dismissing the unimaginable pain that privilege has caused the black folk and the underprivileged, yet I would rather focus on what can advance his life at this point.

    I don't mean to suggest that black people should take a piece of the privilege. The privilege is not all that there is. It's a rich basket full of content that can benefit millions across the racial divide. But these contents must be produced by the bearer of the privilege based on their *relationship* with it. The bearer gives the command to the privilege to produce the basket's content, and this could go two ways. If the relationship of the person and their privilege is negative, then the orders are negative and so are the results. The opposite is also true. This explains why two privileged white folks may produce two conflicting results out of the very same privilege. I have personally experienced very loving privileged white folks and very hateful ones in equal measures and I'm sure you have as well. This book gives unlimited attention to the former; the latter will probably have to wait for another edition of this book. One of the valuable components that can be produced by privilege is a *shelter of refuge for the underprivileged*, which the white person can advance without losing anything because they might not have ever realized that it existed in the first place.

I Am Not the Privilege

Let us revisit my story in the bank. Imagine if Marilyn had thought outside the box. The team was growing rapidly. We were recruiting more business development officers and sales managers. We would soon have a vacancy for another Cluster Manager. This was not the end of the world for her. If she had given herself a little more time, she could have capitalized on our friendship to learn the ropes from my mistakes and experiences before she got her promotion. She would have also finished her degree, which she was pursuing at the time, and freed up more time to deliver better results in her aspiring role. When we think in a selfish manner, as she did, we close ourselves to a world of possibilities.

We must resist the temptation to get *overly engrossed* with the privilege. We must recognize that the privilege existed way before us, that we just found it, and that we will likely leave it here. Therefore, it beats all logic to get so preoccupied with it as though we are the privilege itself. *Both you and the privilege can exist without each other, right?* This fundamental truth will help us create a separation of power so that we can make our decisions devoid of the privilege's influence. We must see things for what they are—a prerequisite to having the right relationship with them. This is the attitude that precedes the idea of seeing outside the box. Many conflicts result from wrong perceptions and closing our eyes to what exists outside our little box of selfishness. This keeps us deceived that we are gaining while, in the real sense, we are really losing.

Is there a possibility that we tend to overrate ourselves? It's sad that this happens unconsciously which means that we could shamelessly go on and on as far as our pompous self can take us. On the contrary, the people around us can see clearly as in a mirror that we are asking for more value than we indeed are worth. How terrible can our blind spots get! I was grieved to realize how many of them I had and the number of well-wishers that I brushed off my shoulders as they tried to save me from the hour of embarrassment. I cannot overemphasize the need to take feedback whether favorable or not. This explains why we always feel more deserving than any other person, which of course, is the attitude behind racism and misuse of privilege. Having this in mind, it is therefore paramount that we *detach* from ourselves as well as the privilege and take the observer's position so we can see ourselves and the privilege as a third-party would. That's the journey to humility where we get to see ourselves just as human as the other person so we can be sober in our relationship with the privilege and with each other.

As a matter of fact, privilege is not the master; *we are!* We can give commands, and it will follow. If the white folk keeps *zero entanglements* with this privilege and sees it for what it really is, instead of elevating it to a level it doesn't deserve, then he (or she) assumes control. This is true for all privileges. After all, the so-called privilege never pledges any allegiance to us when our time to depart from this world comes. It ruthlessly abandons us to find another living human to continue manipulating like a robot. So, if the white person liberates himself to this level of approach, then he calls the shots. This means that he can *make* privilege work for others, and if it works for others, then automatically it will work for him. There is no loss in giving because it comes back to the giver "pressed, shaken, and overflowing" as the scripture in Luke 6:38 puts it, which means it comes in a better version!

Any time we include others, we are setting ourselves up for abundance. The secret of gaining is giving. The universe operates under a divine command to add to those that give. White folks stand to gain more power by sharing the privilege than by withholding it. The most powerful leaders of the world are those that share their power with the people they lead. This strategy keeps them secure with the knowledge that they don't need to fear losing their control. That, in turn, means they will have fewer sleepless nights because the person who could have been the enemy of their power is now a recruit to its security forces. This ability to give comes from a place of knowing who they are. Insecure leaders rule with dictatorial tactics and gimmicks to weaken the people they lead. Likewise, white people must get to a place where they are *secure* enough with themselves, so they can act from the abundance of their security. This will not only be good for underprivileged folks, but for white people as well.

When we empower other people, we create a chain of power for ourselves and thereby strengthening ourselves. The more underprivileged people we empower through this privilege, the less we need to worry about it. The more opportunities we create for the underprivileged community, the less shame and guilt we have to deal with. And, consequently, the less the investment we must make in protecting that privilege. Obviously, this propels our economy as well and is a win-win situation. No legislator or government or system is powerful enough for this task but the *people* themselves.

A Change of Guard!

As the main victims of this racism, we understand the pain better than the holders of the system. I bet we can address the matter more passionately and effectively at the grassroot level than at any other level.

You don't realize how much possibility exists until faced with adversity. It feels as though the recent racial turmoil has gotten us to that place called "adversity" or even worse. It's time for possibility to take the show. When someone says to me, "It's not possible," I just look at them and think, *that's not true*. Anything is possible!

The fact is that we are powerful beyond measure and strong beyond what words can describe. We possess a level of influence too high for anyone's imagination. We are endowed far above our own comprehension. But we must believe in our own capacity first so we can collaborate to avert this "privilege pandemic."

Though this may sound like a longer route, the outcomes will be long lived. Relying on the legislative system only produces a short-lived change, if any, and often creates more enmity.

Since we cannot get rid of privilege, we must find a way that is more effective and *within our reach* to turn privilege from a devouring monster into a refuge, from a battle into a blessing, and from a struggle into a strength. This means that both sides must collaborate to create a benefit for ALL out of it. However, this collaboration cannot happen unless the *basics* are addressed. It is not the white person's fault that he or she is privileged. They are only accountable for the misuse of it. This abuse of privilege by whites and the anger manifesting in the blacks is a sign of something deep that needs to be addressed. Each side must deal with their foundations before any partnership can take place. This ushers us to the six steps of finding unity through privilege by collaborating to create a shelter of refuge for all races, yes, a shelter to protect, defend and advance the underprivileged while at the same time creating **REAL** value for the privileged. Please come along with me…

PART THREE

Finding Unity Through Privilege

"When you change the way you look at things, the things you look at change."
—Dr Wayne Dyer

Six Steps of Creating a Shelter Out of Privilege

CHAPTER ONE

Make Peace With Privilege: Denial is a Friendly Enemy

SOMEONE needs to publicly assume ownership of "this thing." Someone must shout, "I got it." Just like a bouquet toss in a wedding, the bearer of this bouquet must declare themselves so that the rest of us can pull out our hopes. Even though we can see you have it, hearing it from the horse's mouth makes such a huge difference. We are still fighting over it because the horse still denies it and so we are still at war with each other. When you publicly declare something, you assume responsibility. As long as *ownership* is lacking, then *misuse* of the privilege is inevitable. It's the same reason why bullets and pistols are assigned to a specific user. Think of an unallocated bullet out there. It can cause massive destruction, yet we cannot trace the havoc to anyone.

Can you imagine how desperate we would be if, with millions of lives cut short, we had no one to prosecute all because power was left unclaimed or unallocated? It's so dangerous when power is left to just roam around! I happen to come from the heart of Africa, where a disputed election is more of a norm than the exception. I guess just because we are not the only ones, that fact doesn't make it any better. But what happens when the dispute is kept going for a long time? It costs more lives and casualties as the fight escalates. The fight will continue for as long as there's no declared leader in place. One person has to assume the position of the leader in charge for the country to move forward. How much more need I say to convince white folks to declare ownership of "this thing"?

Admitting Myself in the ICU

"I have two wives. If you don't like it, you can leave." These were not the words of a stranger but the words of my husband of more than seven years and the father of my two children. How did Phil, the man who took away my virginity, the one I proudly knew as a trusted friend, end up marrying Gladwell, our very own adopted daughter? Didn't we take this girl to offer her protection after the death of her father? So, what really went wrong? Or was this supposed to be part of the "protection" deal, and I knew it not? Would it have been better if he had cheated on me with another woman other than my own daughter? I still wonder to this day. Perhaps I will find an answer in the world to come. They say that sometimes you must choose the lesser evil when the only options on the table are evil. But which would qualify for the lesser evil in this case? It was obviously a moment of insanity courtesy of the so called first love. What if I also make this confession—that at this point, we had been sharing my husband for more than three years before this long-overdue admission came! Imagine sharing a husband with your daughter. Whew! How disgusting! Maybe disgusting is an understatement.

Out of curiosity, some people will ask me, "Phidia, how old was your daughter?" All you need to know is that where I come from, adoption is not all that complicated. You can adopt anyone in need, as long as their age is "adoptable". But that's beside the point.

Then came the divorce a year later. So, which was the most difficult to deal with? The betrayal or the divorce? You perhaps would assume the divorce, but certainly not! Something massive than the divorce was eating me up and accelerating me toward my deathbed.

I was ready to take my own life when it became just too hard for me to comprehend. I tried but I missed my calculations. I found myself still alive with a monster to face and a pregnancy to take care of. I was a few days from delivering my second child and there was no way the day was going to find me alive! Did I say a monster? Yes. It wasn't the pain of betrayal, neither was it sharing a husband with my daughter for three years. It was not even the fear of an impending divorce. The fact that I couldn't *come to terms* with the betrayal was the hardest. My entire being was screaming, "no way! This can't be true!" I wanted to sleep forever so that I wouldn't have to face the reality of this betrayal.

I consider myself a stubborn girl and at least the last seven years of my life have perfectly represented this part of me that I feel so proud about. But sometimes, it has nothing to do with stubbornness, you just find yourself completely stuck in a dumpster of a social mess. This was the case for me. I wasn't just refusing to accept the situation, it just felt like accepting it would bring the entire world crumbling into my little space and I was scared to death. There was *no way* I would accept that this was happening, that the man I fondly called my husband, the one that I gave my all to, and that which I considered my greatest value as a young girl was no longer my husband but rather, *our* husband! And to add to my frustration, he was pledging more loyalty to his newly found love than me.

I was in complete denial and not just for a few days. This became my camping station, or should I say my new home address that I would not leave for three more years, long enough to earn the title "home address." There were many "trains" to transport me from this station to a new station, but the fear of facing reality kept me clinging to a false peace. A peace that never really was true peace and never would be. I was dying in the inside, and that's how I ended up attempting suicide when the imposter peace proved that it wasn't one after all.

I Choose to Accept That ...

Phew! A ray of hope came when the long-awaited confession arrived. He finally admitted that he had two wives. For more than three years, he had denied having an affair with Gladwell despite the screaming evidence staring us in the face. This was my day of liberation. I already had enough of it and if this was the price of freedom, I was ready to let go of him and everything I had invested in for more than seven years. Free at last! I had made peace with the fact that I was sharing a husband with my daughter. I forgave myself and everyone else involved and began the journey of healing to recover myself. I was sure that I had lost Phidia. Have you ever felt like a stranger to yourself? I did.

Denial is more severe than the offense itself. Being in this state of denial for more than three years had stolen my identity and my passion to live. It had left me angry, bitter, hateful, fearful, ashamed, timid, and suicidal. I was traumatized to the level that I couldn't even pronounce the name of my adopted daughter for some time, I kid you not. How bad was that? Because the longer you stay in that station called denial, the more you destroy or lose yourself, yet no one can lead you to the place of acceptance but only you. Maybe it would be fair to give the dictionary meaning of this word denial. Though it has several definitions, I deliberately settled for this - *a person's choice to deny reality to avoid a psychologically uncomfortable truth*. I love the word "choice" because that gives us back the power, the very power we thought we had lost. That word makes us a fully active part and parcel of this situation instead of what we mostly believe to be our victimhood.

It's not that we shouldn't let ourselves *go through* some denial, but we should remember that it is only a *stopover,* and not the intended destination. Sometimes you have to stop over or pass through a certain place which is part of the route in order to get to your planned address. Some destinations have no alternative route and leave you with no choice except to go through towns that you would instead not go through; otherwise, you would have to call off the journey which would mean giving up your beautiful destination. It's said that *dangerous roads lead to beautiful destinations.* If you really want to enjoy the destination, then passing through a dreadful route is not an option.

Accepting comes with responsibility, which human beings, by default, don't like—a responsibility to take accountability, arise and keep moving, which usually makes us uncomfortable. It places the ball in our hands and all eyes on us when we really wish it was on someone else. It means taking up the burden to make things right, a solemn declaration of our commitment to dust the past off ourselves and sail against scary waves. The process is not a bed of roses which explains why people would rather spend years caught up in the thicket of denial.

Strangely enough, the longer you stay in this station, the more it feels like home for you. You successfully buy into the fact that there is nothing better than where you are. That's why people in this space may need someone to remind them that passing through is not the same as camping, because the victim may never realize the difference!

Living in deception damages your identity. If you can successfully deceive yourself, then you can't handle any truth. The long-term damage of camping in denial is so significant that it takes a long time to recover while some people never recover from it at all.

Does 'Good' Denial Exist?

Denial is not just for negative outcomes. There are several occasions when we encounter situations that are too good to believe. The impact is equally the same. When I first got my first job as a bank sales executive, I was paid on commission, as is often the case. I remember when I walked to the ATM to check my bank balance and I was actually "traumatized" by what I saw. It was too good to be true. The commission system had just changed, and I was ignorant of how it worked. That was the least of my worries at the time though.

As a competitive person, whatever the best was, that's all I wanted to be and sure enough, I did put in the hard work to claim it! That this attitude led to my new paycheck (which was 20 times my retainer) was too much to handle! It looked like the bank had credited a loan to my account erroneously. I couldn't help but worry if the bank had made a mistake! What if they came after me when the money was completely spent? What if I got kidnapped or robbed and lost all that money! I thought of discussing with a colleague but then worried that they might end up tipping the wrong people and I would end up losing the money. The bottom line is that I was so overwhelmed that I couldn't handle it for some time. After a week, I gathered the courage to talk to my team leader who confirmed that I had actually earned the money. Ridiculous as it may sound, I did not withdraw any money from that account for a week even though I needed money to pay for some stuff.

Denial of positive outcomes is as dangerous as denial of negative outcomes. It is obvious that the latter causes pain but what most people don't know is that the former causes pain too, just a different kind. Remember the anxiety I had to deal with as I struggled to come to terms with the outcomes of my hard labor? How about the fact that I couldn't use the money in *my own* account to empower myself? What a waste, all courtesy of a "good" denial! Denial is denial. It doesn't get any better based on the circumstances. Hence forth, it should not become a permanent destination. The first step to dealing with your pain is accepting the current state of affairs because only then will you figure out a solution. For the privileged, denial leads to a cover up and when the cover up fails, it makes angry people. On the other end, denial for the underprivileged leads to false hope which then leads to anger when reality eventually dawns. Both sides are hurting the same way for different circumstances.

Many people confuse accepting reality with giving in. The two are as different as West is from East. The former empowers and brings joy while the latter is disempowering and leading to hopelessness. Both the privileged and the underprivileged must come to a place of acceptance. Acceptance is a positive word that opens us up to possibility by opening our inner eyes and ushering us to a place of power and life. Denial is not a good friend you should spend time with, but an ever-sinking ground covered up with white linen. It's only a matter of time before you fall and will never be recovered. This should explain the urgency with which we should flee from it. The faster we accept the reality, the sooner we can begin to see the beauty of this privilege.

ME TOO MOMENT	Have you ever found yourself in a 'home address' called Denial?
	In one word, what was the outcome?

'Yes, I Am Privileged'

I wonder how it feels to say the words above. I suggest you try it three times before you continue reading this book and note down the emotions it elicits. We all may know that (in this country) the word privilege carries a lot of stigma with it. I had to look it up in the dictionary when I started this journey just to make sure I understood it correctly. I discovered that being in this country unconsciously forced me to redefine this word in a manner that made it uncomfortable to talk about it or even pronounce it. The dictionary defines privilege as, "An *advantage*; or a condition or circumstance that puts someone in a favorable or superior position." We live in a world of privileges where some people have more privileges than others but at least each person has one. While that might sound unfair, it is the reality of our world today and there's no changing that; it's always existed. They are a part of the society, and the universe keeps manufacturing new ones every other day. Some (and perhaps most) of the privileges we had nothing to do with acquiring them. We just found ourselves having them. Unfortunately, how many of these privileges you have depends on who you are in society and are often as a result of historical injustices that humanity procured on others.

Facing this reality is one of the most significant challenges of our time, not just for the disadvantaged person but the advantaged person as well. My eight-year-old son's favorite statement when he throws tantrums remains, "Mom, this is so unfair!" He says this with so much passion and lack of understanding how someone other than himself seems to have a more favorable situation. Each time, my response is consistent, "Son, life is not fair, you have to *make* it fair for yourself!"

The word "make," sounds like work, right? You don't just *make* something happen when you bask in the sun at the beach, you actually have to get into the factory and do the dirty work. It doesn't sound fun, right? It's not, and that's the honest truth. The opposite is to sit, observe (sometimes covetously) with anger and resentment as you complain about those who have the privilege. What you may not realize is the *responsibility,* and sometimes the shame and guilt, that the advantaged have to deal with daily, especially if there is privilege misuse. The fact that they deny the existence of the privilege tells it all. They have no boldness in facing the harsh reality that they are being treated as superhumans at the cost of their fellow humans. Knowing that they are mere humans contradicts the reality on the ground and brings unbearable dissonance. This explains why it is so difficult to admit the existence of privilege.

Thank goodness that the guilt doesn't seem to lie just on the privilege itself, that would bring misery to people who played no role in its creation. This guilt, however, has a direct relationship with how we handle privilege and how it impacts others. If you were comfortable saying the words, "I am privileged" in our previous exercise in this chapter, and you were daring enough to repeat them, then that is good news. If there was discomfort of any sort then chances are that there exists a bad relationship between you and privilege, and that you need to begin the needed work to establish a healthy relationship with privilege so you can be set free from guilt and shame. Who doesn't want freedom?

A Bittersweet Pill

"As is the culture of this organization, we always reward hard work and results. This year, we are happy to bring to you the top executive portfolio manager. She is known for her passion in delivering results with a deep touch of customer service both internally and externally. She has done an outstanding job in developing a strong team behind her and we now have the pleasure to promote her to the head office to continue her good work. She will be our new Executive Centre Head for our largest customer portfolio at the Headquarters. Congratulations, Phidia, on your new appointment! We have no doubt that this is a *well-deserved* promotion and are excited to see the *transformation* you will bring on board to make this center the pride and the joy of the entire bank!"

I just finished reading the thrilling email from the head of executive banking, an email that was shared across several segments that were impacted by this communication. I was overwhelmed with the celebration, but something kept me humble—the last sentence of my boss' email. Everything else was music to my ears until I got to the last sentence and kept on re-reading it. The expectations that were clearly spelled in this sentence shook me. *Was I really going to deliver? What if they discovered that they had expected more than I could give?* I couldn't answer all the questions that kept running through my head. The glory seemed to fade away from my head as I grappled with the responsibility and accountability that came with my promotion.

People so often chase the *glory* of privilege, but then shun the *pain* that comes with receiving it. That's why we all want and wish we had this privilege but not the responsibility. This comes as one complete package, however. You cannot have one without the other. Once you have privilege, then people begin to hold you accountable which can be uncomfortable. You become answerable to so many bosses that you are not familiar with, ruthless folks whose biography you may never know. The day you extended your hands to receive the privilege, was the same day your freedom departed. This may change your perception on how *badly* you want this privilege to be yours. Hopefully, this information helps some or all of us to stop killing each other for the so-called white privilege because it's really just a bittersweet pill. For those of us that have it, it's about time that we become responsible and accept to be held accountable on how we handle it.

ME TOO MOMENT	Have you ever received a glory whose responsibility turned to haunt you?
	In one word, what was your lesson?

Secure, Settled and Smart!

A story is told of a Mr. Peter who was given a dollar by his employer, Mitch, to trade with as the boss was going to be away for five months. The business was going to remain closed during Mitch's absence but he, being the considerate boss that he was, had a fallback plan for Peter to keep him from being jobless. The only mistake that Mitch made was to tell Peter that he was going on a vacation. So, Peter had this conversation going in his mind, "You mean all the profit I will make with my hard work will benefit a man having fun at the beach all this time? That's so unfair! Who does he think he is? I won't let this happen!" According to Peter, Mitch was just a privileged, spoiled brat, and he wasn't going to let him get away with it!

But that was not all that he had to worry about. Something else was also the matter. He was anxious that the one dollar might be stolen or misplaced, and then he would get in trouble with his boss upon his return. So, Peter hid the dollar in a safe until his boss came back. I'm not sure if he had to spend his own money to buy the safe or not. That story should interest you because it shows how financial intelligence may not be common as you expect especially when we let our attitudes overwhelm our logic. Some sentiments can be very costly.

Apparently, Peter was not the only staff member, but he happened to have some sort of fame for his attitude. He was the only one whose name is mentioned in the story. That sounds like our world today where the bad guy gets more attention than the good guy. The hater has way too many views and likes compared to the lover! No wonder so many people are breaking the *wrong* records just to join the list of "fame." What really happened to the list of shame? Someone, please help me understand…

Back to our story, there were two other staff members who were also given some money to trade with. One had two dollars and the other five. I have no idea why Peter was given the smallest amount. *The universe does not overlook your attitude.* It will give you something close to what you deserve. In fact, I would think Peter was lucky to have gotten something in the first place. On the contrary, the other two who were initially given more traded their money and doubled what they were entrusted with. Mind you, this boss made no promises to any of his employees. He only told them what to do but nothing was said about what to expect. That can be very annoying especially in our today's world where we always want to know "what is in it for us." Imagine telling the whites and blacks to just love one another without telling them what they get in return! You could be risking getting a serious punch. But these two employees were different from us and Peter. Did they know that the entire amount would go to their privileged boss? Absolutely! However, that didn't seem to bother them in any way. For some reason, they were cool with it.

Mitch overstayed his vacation, but the story doesn't say how long. We are just told that he returned after a long time. The two unnamed employees were the first to meet him upon his return. They were excited to show him what they had done. They never allowed their boss' privilege to get in their way. It didn't seem to affect their relationship with their boss but not because they were ignorant or dismissive of it. No, they simply knew *their place* as far as the privilege was concerned and were not threatened by it. In fact, they had a strategy for it. They knew how to invest the money and become shareholders. If you can't change the past, you can invest in the present and the future. Little did they know that the boss had a special reward this time, not for hard work, but their great attitude. He wasn't such a bad boss after all!

This good moment, as it were, was rudely interrupted by Peter. He not only came in *last,* but he had a bad attitude and a justification for it. "Boss, I knew you to be a hard man, reaping where you did not sow and gathering where you did not scatter," he said. "Therefore, I was afraid and hid your dollar in the ground," he explained. "So, here is what belongs to you." Sounds like he was settling some scores, right? I may never know what Peter was afraid of. However, I deduced the following about this story. First, he was worried about a couple of things, including why the boss, Mitch, would be so privileged as to make money through Peter's hard labor when he was on a vacation. Second, he had such resentment for this boss that he couldn't stand his success whichever way he arrived at it. Based on my deductions, while his fear was genuine and perhaps justified, it was also a destiny-blunder which we shall soon see as the story winds. Oh, how I wish he "postponed" his attitude for another day!

Do we sometimes find ourselves fighting not because we want justice but because we have so much hatred for the privileged person that we just can't stand their blessing at all? Is there a possibility that the biggest problem we have between black and white people in this country is an attitude issue? Peter seemed to have had a preconceived image of the kind of a person his boss was. Unfortunately, it had nothing to do with Mitch's personality but everything to do with Mitch's privilege. This was clearly seen in the words he used to address his boss—the very boss who had just rewarded the two faithful, hard-working employees, by making them shareholders of his company. Peter never even gave him a chance to express who he really was.

As fate would have it, Peter's attitude would end up costing him a sumptuous reward. Not only did he lose a significant opportunity to be promoted from employee status to a partner, but he also lost his job that day. The boss had a reason for overstaying his vacation. He wasn't testing his employees for another ordinary job promotion. No! This time around, he wanted co-partners for his splendid empire. While the two *wise* staff members just expected a paycheck as usual, he instead told them, "Enter into my joy! Whatever is mine shall henceforth be yours!" Sounds like winning a lottery, doesn't it! They slept poor as servants, and they woke up rich as masters. Sometimes smart can be confused for foolish but in the end, results are what really counts!

What opportunities have you missed in this saga? Have you let your attitude towards white privilege interfere with your perceptions and *ability to receive*? Just like Peter, people with attitude tend to come in last as far as opportunities are concerned. No wonder Peter showed up last. On the contrary, people with good attitudes attract opportunities and blessings. While I respect that there is *immense* pain associated with white privilege, we have no excuse for letting our negative experiences shape our destiny because that only worsens the situation. Our circumstances should not be used as excuses to miss our moment whatsoever. Why waste your energy by carrying your own casket? And, yes, that's exactly what that is! Anger, bitterness, and resentment are components of a bad attitude, and they can rightfully be compared to a casket because they are catastrophic. If you must carry any weight, ensure it adds value to you. If it deteriorates your value, then it's simply not worth your effort.

A bad attitude leads you to a destination called Fear. Now, we can certainly understand why Peter was afraid. He was in a place full of anger, anxiety, bitterness, resentment, enmity, and revenge. Does this sound like a description of what has been manifesting with blacks and whites in this country? Perhaps. Is it justifiable? Absolutely! Does it make life better for them? I doubt it. Is it going to stop white privilege? So far it has not. This is what I would call a real blunder when we let emotions poison our blessings. Everything begins and ends with accepting the existence of this privilege. Once we accept, from whichever side of the divide we stand, then that acceptance leads us to *knowing our place*.

The moment we take our rightful position in privilege, we are ushered into a state of being *secure* and *settled* and that is the zone within which we can make *smart* decisions that elevate our lives and that of others. We need this three S's both in blacks and whites to make the collaboration possible otherwise insecurity will defile whatever efforts we put in. You might think that this example of the two wise servants is far-fetched and wonder if there exist such secure, settled, and smart people within the white privilege, and yes, they do. I also have several examples of such people in the black community but for the sake of advocacy allow me to talk about the "other" side where the power dwells.

Kathleen, who happens to be one of my close friends, is the most secure white privileged woman I've ever met. Her security is not fake because I have witnessed fraudulent security. If your security is dependent on external factors, then that is not really security in the first place. For Kathleen, it's all within. A pretty lady for whom the biased American definition of a perfect body would deny her the right to be named a beauty queen. But that does nothing to Kathleen. You have to find something else to "get" to her.

Evidently, she knows who she is whether she tells you or not. She engages with people with so much calm, humility, and boldness that it's impressive. She was the first person that boldly and compassionately said to me, "Phidia, I am privileged, and I may never understand what it feels to be you, a black single mom raising a black boy in this country." The comfort with which she admitted to the privilege shocked me, because I had never witnessed that before. She is disciplined but not obsessed with rules. I used to be the goddess of rules, until I met her and realized that too many rules were a sign of insecurity. We tend to believe that the more rules you have, the more disciplined you are. But, when you overdo rules, then the message changes. You end up being choked with rules trying to prove that you are perfect and/or in control to a world that doesn't really care about it. Kathleen plays within those boundaries very well. She is so secure and settled, you can see it written all over her just in the way she carries herself. But it doesn't stop there. She is very smart in how she applies privilege to make it better for all.

These are three important S's (secure, settled, and smart) to have more so as a privileged person. The underprivileged also need to find this place of rest, otherwise they will not be able to give, receive or engage in mutual interracial relationships. Remember that the underprivileged Peter had the capacity to give to privileged Mitch just as Mitch did. He just allowed his attitude to prevent him from making profit with the dollar. So, no one has an excuse for not pursuing the three S's.

Most people who get to the second "s" which stands for "settle" tend to stop there, which only benefits themselves. Being settled only makes you peaceful from within, and that's about it. It just changes your world, nobody else's. But if you find someone who has the three, they are such a force and a blessing to the world around them, irresistible humans with a delightful presence! Kathleen has all three. Perhaps this explains why she could entrust a black immigrant named Phidia with her daughter Toni for a play date with my children even before knowing what car I drove. All she needed was to know my values. That was it. Toni has now become a great friend to my kids. Did the words *black immigrant* make you chuckle? Then that could be a sign of insecurity. Don't those words give a perfect description of myself? Can't I say that I am black without feeling some fear of rejection? I should be able to describe my friend as white without any pressure, right? That is supposed to be a beautiful description, but hate has taught us to be afraid to mention our races. Being secure and settled includes *embracing our identities, both physical and nonphysical, and refusing to let racism kidnap us into abandoning them for whatever reason.* We must address these basics before we can make smart decisions for the advancement of all races, colors, nations, and tongues. Your actions with regards to privilege will tell us where you stand as far as attitude, secure, settled, and smart are concerned.

ME TOO MOMENT	Have you ever lost an opportunity because of a bad attitude?
	In one word, how did that feel?

Clear the Carcass!

When my daughter was in fifth grade, she ran for school council president. We had several black friends who warned us not to try running for it. They felt that it was a waste of time and would just leave her little soul crushed. Their concerns were very genuine and thoughtful but limited. I listened to them, but my decisions were based on some personal values which I stand for.

"You have nothing to lose, Hadasa," I said. "Whether you get it or not, just smile and meet every student with love." "Okay, Mum," she responded. I expected an objection but fortunately, I was met with a positive vibe. She had chosen to be gracious with or without the win, and that what she became or did not become would have nothing to do with her attitude. I doubt she really understood the weight of my request, but she seemed to be prepared.

For the remaining ten days before the election, I kept reminding her, "You must love people first before you can lead them." She became more aware of people's needs than she was before. She connected with more people with a smile. She asked as many people as she thought had a need if they were okay and if they needed any help — not just at school but also at home. Her election in a school whose majority were white kids proved to us that people care less about your skin color and more about your attitude.

Attitude is one of the most difficult things to hide. People notice attitudes. They may say nothing and that may provide some imaginary solace, but they still can see it. Even when your words don't match your attitude, people can still tell. A lousy attitude stinks. It attracts "flies," however much you try to cover it. Please don't waste time fighting the flies, they are in their rightful place. If you don't like the outcomes, all you have to do is change your input in this case your attitude, and the results will comply. How can you find peace with privilege unless your attitude is fixed?

Hangovers Versus Partying

In 2018, I finally took my kids to Disney World after years of promising to do so. Before I honored the promise, they had called me all sorts of names that equated to me being a liar. What they didn't know was how much I had to do "behind the scenes" to make their dream come true. So, when we got there, they read the signage and, with a mix of anxiety and excitement, began asking, "Mom, is this the real Disney World?" "Are we just passing by or staying?" They could barely breathe because they continuously asked questions and were peeping and peeking around. You can be sure that I did not answer the first question, but I was gracious enough to respond to the second. "This will be your home for the next five days," I said, keeping my calm like a boss. I watched my little pumpkins shrink with shame and guilt over how they had treated me in the past. It was so bad that it almost got into their way of celebrating the moment they had waited for so long. Out of the abundance of my kindness and compassion, I had to step in with a justification for how they had treated me just to help them cope.

Even though this might sound annoying, the white privilege could be the test of a lifetime for black and white folks. More than ever before, it's a test of our *attitudes* and there's no test without reward. How comfortable people are in undertaking this test can only be determined by two factors: How well the two parties have accepted the existence of privilege and what position they stand in as far as their relationship with it pertains. Passing the test is not just the final score, the *how* you pass the test is where the rubber meets the road and is equally important. If you cheated in the exam by compromising your integrity, that will annul the score. Will you be ashamed at the end of this shelter creation process? When we have ultimately resolved the dilemma between the blacks and whites, is there a possibility that you will be too ashamed to join the "birthday party" as we celebrate a new relationship milestone, because of the delivery of baby shelter? How faithful will you be in this unifying process? Will you let your integrity down in obedience to the orders of the egotistical self? Will you be confident enough to say, I have fought a good fight? Because not every fight should be celebrated unless it's a good one; one that does not compromise the soldier's character.

There is hope that this racial enmity storm will calm down; a hope that one day black and white folks will unite in a beautiful relationship together and create a shelter within the privilege. I lose nothing for this hope. We are closer than you could ever think with some heroes already making it happen at the grassroots. I see the current intensity of racial struggle in relation to the privilege as birth pangs for a beautiful creation. But what will your state of mind be when that happens? What will you say that day? Will you need someone to help you cope with the avoidable aftermath for atrocious things you said or did in the heat of the moment, like my little pumpkins had to? Hold onto your integrity regardless of the pressure to give it up. It will save you the hangovers of guilt and shame that might otherwise haunt your celebration when the party has officially commenced. But first things first. Everything rests on acceptance and positioning for you to see things as you should and consequently act things out properly.

Privileged and Gracious

When I first met Alyssa there was no sign that she would turn out to be my "destiny incubator". She did not look like it from first glance. She was the typical American girl, with flawless skin, average height and weight, beautiful waist-length hair, she drove the perfect car, lived in a well-to-do neighborhood, and she had just won a big contract courtesy of her fifth book. Right before my eyes stood the true definition of beauty, brains, and excellence. I met her to interview for her new housekeeper position. I am not the kind of person that gets easily intimidated, speaking of the transformed me. But I will admit that this encounter was a little harassing at first not because of anything she did but everything she looked. I wasn't sure what to expect.

Even though I have amazing white friends, my mind kept defaulting to the ugly narrative I mistakenly attributed to that type of a privileged woman. I was determined to keep an open mind though. I wanted to give her a chance to manifest her love without resorting to my own biased judgements. Whether or not Alyssa noticed the struggle, I may never know. I appeared confident displaying my bubbly self and usual smile. I had become a pro in faking it when I didn't have it. Being a minority in a white neighborhood called for a great attitude to build the kind of reputation I had, and this is what I dealt with every single day. It was this reputation that brought me into contact with Alyssa through generous compliments from my satisfied clients.

I was in for the shock of my life. Alyssa was one of the most loving, sweet, humble, thoughtful, God-fearing, and intelligent ladies I had ever met. It took me a while before the rude revelation came that the bookshelf next to me was an exhibit of her brains at work! *She was the author of all these books, yet so down to earth?* I couldn't marry the two ideas. She was so warm and loving that on the second meeting, I let down my guard and decided to confide in her that I was an aspiring author.

When I disclosed my upcoming book, her reaction was priceless! "Phidia, I saw it in you!" she said. "You are not just a housekeeper; I see so much more than that in you," she continued. It took so much restraint to keep my tears away as I listened to her. "You mean that a "perfect" privileged white girl believed in me?" I wondered. To me, that was a big deal at the time for some reason. I had shared my authorial aspirations with several friends who, perhaps due to my financial status, did not believe I had anything to offer to the world. Does it ever surprise you that economic poverty is often equated to mental poverty? Not when dealing with Alyssa! Here I was, face to face with the beautiful side of privilege. How could this privileged stranger think so highly of me while my own "tribe" hardly did! She seemed to soak everything I said like a dry sponge would soak in water! I could tell without a doubt that she "bought" everything I "sold" to her. She immediately initiated a plan for a coffee date to hear more about my book. Until then, she hadn't told me that she was the author of five books.

Soaring With the Privilege

Three weeks later, we met and the rest, as they say, is history. I went to our first meeting as a mere housekeeper who was trying to write her first book. I left with an endorsement from an actual author! She handed me a signed copy of her most popular book and said, "You are hereby commissioned to be an author. Phidia, write, write, write!" Then she had some advice for me, "Phidia, you have a very unique approach to this issue of privilege, I suggest that you don't consult any other approach until you are done with the book so you can deliver your authenticity," she said. Those words from a privileged girl fueled my confidence. She became my accountability partner in making sure that I stayed on course with my writing timelines. She wore several hats as my sister, champion, confidant, prayer partner, cheerleader and much more. The big question remains—how did I feel so safe with such a successful, privileged white lady barely a month into our relationship? I still wonder about that to this day. But the undeniable truth is that her beautiful *attitude* manifested itself past her privilege.

We should not miss the beauty of this privilege by focusing on the ugliness. We must come to the table with a clean slate. Nothing in the universe is one-sided. Maybe focusing on the beauty of this privilege would be the best way to appreciate it and stop spending our time and energy trying to cover or kill it. First, we must wear the right attitude to see the beauty, just like a mirror which is only a reflection of what we give. You receive what you put out in the world! This concept has been tried and tested. If you are negative and full of hate, you will most likely end up missing love and positivity when there is so much of it around you. Always look for the *smallest sign of love* in your interactions because it so often affects how the interaction unfolds.

We might have different views on how beneficial the white privilege is, but the bottom line is that it exists whether we use it or not. White folks have wasted so much valuable time in attempting to cover up their privilege, while blacks have been working overtime to kill it. It is not our fault that privilege exists, but ours that we make it a battlefield instead of translating it into a blessing. Both sides have a role to play in making a shelter out of privilege. Just remember, everything begins at finding peace with privilege, but your attitude determines how fast you get to that place of peace.

The 'Practicals' of Love

Remember, denial is not meant to be your new home address but merely a stopover for your next flight. We tend to make denial our resting place without considering the danger it poses to our lives. For our country, we have millions of lives that have been lost as a result of our collective inability to accept the existence of white privilege. Whichever side of the privilege we stand, we shouldn't allow ourselves to live in denial for one more day because the damage is fatal. Below are the steps we need to take to rescue our lives and our country before it is too late.

1. Identify: Most people live in denial for so long that it looks like reality. Actually, a good number of people don't even realize that they are living in denial. There are many signs of it, but they all lead to one thing—anger and bitterness. If you get irate on a certain issue, that could be a sign that you are living in denial. Trace your anger back to its root cause. For this stage, you may need help from your Double MC club members or a friend's help to identify what is causing your anger or the reality that you are denying.

2. Admit: You simply must realize that you are living in denial. For this stage, I recommend that you get what I call a "I accept that ..." journal. Document and say out loud what it is that you intend to accept. Expect resistance and emotional outbursts in this stage; you are allowed to cry, rant and vent your feelings. In my case, simply saying that "I accept that Phil has been cheating on me with Gladwell," almost killed me. As pertaining to privilege, we should expect admissions like, "I accept that white folks are privileged and that I cannot change that," or "I admit that historical social injustices made me privileged and that is not my fault." You must be specific and genuine with yourself as much as possible. Don't leave any grey areas. Experience all your possible pain points so you can move forward. Again, a friend can help you get through this. Let them know that they should not interrupt you until you are done. Their presence is the most important thing, not their actions, comments, or opinions. Note: Admitting something doesn't equal conceding defeat; it just gives you a new slate to begin a new chapter.

3. Moving On: Acceptance is the hardest part; if you get through step two, then you can handle this next step when you focus on finding your options. Write down as many as your mind can imagine. Some may be irrational because you may still have some anger to deal with and that anger could influence some of your options. The only way to discern irrationality is by writing down the expected outcomes at the end of every option.

In my case, there was the option of never speaking to him again but there were children involved, that would have made this decision selfish and irrational. The white person can decide— I will not let anyone take away this privilege from me; I will maximize my benefit regardless of the cost to others. On the other hand, the black folks could decide, I will do all I can to destroy this privilege so that everyone suffers. But then, what are the expected outcomes of those decisions?

Or, better still, the white person could decide, "Oh, what a privilege this is, I will make the best of it to protect and advance the underprivileged as I create more abundance for myself, while the black folk could decide, "Oh, what an opportunity! I will collaborate with the privileged to make my life and others better.

One decision has negative outcomes while the other has positive outcomes. That should make it easy to settle upon your choices.

4. Fastrack Your Options: In this step, you need to come up with specific actions toward your choice from step 3. What are you going to do to protect or collaborate? If you are in a Double MC club, this part will be way easier because you can work as a team. The list can be as long as your mind can envision and can include actions like:

- Create more interracial relationships. You can give yourself a target within a certain time frame. Pursue to have a close friend who is not of your race.
- Speak up for the other race or races that are deemed rivals by your race.
- Advocate for other races in your friends' circles
- Attend activities organized by various races.
- Plan and participate in fun interracial activities.

5. Track the Progress: How have those activities changed how you feel about yourself and other races? What have you discovered about this race that you did not know before? What stereotypes and misconceptions have you debunked? How many mutual interracial relationships have you successfully formed?

6. Share and Recommend: Based on your progress, share this newfound information with others in your race, and ask them to try these things and share with you their experiences. There is nothing more rewarding than peace. By so doing, you are creating a ripple effect of interracial love and painting the world with the beauty of love. This step is designed to make activists for interracial relationships. This is where your interracial club could be formed if it wasn't done earlier because perceptions have now been changed and walls collapsed. Remember to have fun, eat foods that you have not eaten before, be free to be yourself as you would be in your community without being insensitive to others through open communication. Exchange cultural gifts and complement each other's diversity as you read this book together. There is simply no caveat as to how many times you can read this book.

CHAPTER TWO

Search and Advocate for the Heroes of Love: When Silence is not a Virtue

A Stubborn Passion

In a new country with no relatives and two children to care for, I needed some source of regular income. I had spent eleven years of my career as a successful banker, which, surprisingly, was nothing close to being my passion! It was simply the blunder of the so-called "first love" that saw me follow my then-husband's career. When I met Phil at the university, he convinced me to change my degree course to align myself with job opportunities in the bank, which I happily did. Then, four years later, when he asked me to apply for a job in the bank, I couldn't help but fantasize about the beauty of working with my first love! That "demon of love" was big enough to get me through eight years of a soul-sucking career which was my best bet for keeping our marriage going. Then, I would still put another three more years in that field after our relationship ended.

    Eleven years of career endurance was just enough, and so "enough" that the word banker was loathsome to me. I am not sure if traumatized was too big of a word, nonetheless, hearing it left a very bitter taste in my mouth. It gave me chills, perhaps because of the traumatic experiences I associated with my ex-husband. All in all, I wanted nothing to do with that occupation or industry anymore. One thing was nagging at me: reconnecting with my childhood passion of being a public speaker and author. Despite the pressure of providing for my two children and paying bills, I was determined to say no to jobs until I found a career that suited my passion. It felt like a now or never moment!

After a few months of living in the U.S., I was offered an opportunity in one of the well-known banks. Under the prevailing circumstances, I was tempted to take it. I was just one step away from accepting the offer when the alarm sounded! It was a memory from my past just on time to trigger the adrenaline I needed to flee from a convenient but soul-sucking offer. If I couldn't find a job involving motivational speaking, then I wanted to do something else I was passionate about, whatever the name was. And here it was, cleaning homes believe it or not! Oh, how I loved cleaning! For me, it was a kind of music that required no beat to dance to! When I was a banker, whenever I visited my girlfriends, I would ask them to let the visit be a hangout for me to clean. The process of cleaning was unbelievably therapeutic and fun for me.

At the time, I was being hosted by a friend who often had to check on me because I was always cleaning. In the morning when she left, I would be cleaning. In the evening when she came home, I would still be cleaning. "What is wrong with you?" she would often ask, sometimes angrily. I tried to answer her without being disrespectful. There was nothing wrong with the house in terms of how it looked, I simply was a perfectionist when it came to cleaning; it was my (albeit weird) passion. There was no hope of stopping the cleaner in me, so why couldn't this be translated into income, I wondered?

I can't tell you how disappointed Jackie, my then host, was when I told her that I wasn't taking a bank job. "Where will this cleaning get you?" she asked with genuine frustration. "You need wisdom, Phidia,"

Jackie said with caution. In a new country, with two kids and no job, with only few dollars left between me and poverty, stuck in a hotel room, this woman accepted to open her home for us. What a risk and a daring love? She deserved an answer because she was supporting me while I got on my feet financially. How much respect do you think I owed her? A lot. And her, being the "queen of wisdom", she was keen to politely tell me how unwise my decision was. Logically, she had a point, but she was met with a stubborn passion. "This knack for cleaning will get me to my dream life," I said to myself while giving her my harmless but somewhat unyielding smile. Poor woman! She may have been dealing with the best version of my stubbornness; she deserved better. I just wish I could have made it easier for her without sacrificing my passion.

The Gift Inside Sandpaper

And so, I began marketing myself in our neighborhood as a housekeeper. But being a foreigner with a serious accent, it was hard to find business in a very white neighborhood. I needed someone from the community and better still, a white person to recommend me. I don't mean that this community was racist, there is no hidden meaning in that statement. I just believe that it is a normal part of the human nature to trust someone of their "kind" than a stranger. I see it as a safety measure and given the same situation, I would do the same thing.

Here I was, with a business to start and no trusted source of advertisement. I cold called and got my first customer, but she wasn't white, nor had she been in the community for very long. Tammy had just relocated from a different state, she was very gentle, sweet, and had quite a reserved personality. She did a great job of helping me get my first few clients through her recommendations.

But there was this white lady I had met at the community pool. Mickie had the "I dare you" kind of face. To me, she looked like a snob at first sight. She had a pile of papers she was going through while her kids were swimming, I thought to myself, "Is she working on a degree or something?" But, since I had so much to worry about, I just said "Hi" and went on with my life. When it was time to leave the pool, she said to me, "You have such adorable kids." I looked at her in bewilderment. "Oh, really?" I responded. "Absolutely, they are super sweet!" Quite frankly, I wasn't so sure if she was referring to my kids or perhaps confusing them with a neighbor's. Not that my kids are not sweet, but the "super sweet" coming from the very person I had already judged otherwise was a little overwhelming. I was just so surprised at how loving, sweet-hearted, down to earth, caring, and kind she was to me. It was a total contrast from what I had first imagined by looking at her face.

One Roof with The Privilege

After a few days of knowing Mickie, she invited me to her house where they used to have a Christian fellowship every Sunday. I was surprised to see how comfortable she was interacting with us. She made me feel that we were no different at all because of her genuine appreciation for me and my kids. Our kids became the best of friends. Mickie was surprisingly very easy to interact with. Gradually, we got so free with one another that we could discuss our cultural differences without fear. She became a cultural bridge by giving me a complete mental shift on my perceptions for the white community which acted as the license I needed to approach more white clients with extra confidence.

Our racial anxiety often stems from knowing very little, or almost nothing, about a particular race. Through a close relationship with Mickie, I learned about white culture, including the dos and don'ts that had often given me panic attacks time and time again. I could ask her the weirdest questions without fear of judgement, and she gracefully took it in stride. With our racial differences and my obvious accent, I can't tell you how many times I suffered some kind of social anxiety whenever I held a conversation with a white person. This anxiety would only serve to escalate my accent. Thanks to Mickie, I broke through this huddle, which had always felt like a sprint run up a steep hill. That's the power of having secure, loving, privileged human beings around us! They can help you across a scary raging sea simply by controlling their privilege through the power of their selfless love.

The more I learned about white folks, the more I loved them and the more I debunked the stereotypes I had once held against them. This lady brought the "magic prescription" that I needed to grow my business. How I almost missed my angel because she didn't look like one at first sight! How many have you missed in this racial discrimination saga and life generally?

ME TOO MOMENT	Have you ever misjudged someone at first sight only to realize they were the exact opposite after an interaction with them?
	In one word, how did that make you feel?

Sold by The Privilege

Mickie spoke highly of me to everyone who cared to listen among her white friends. People who would have taken me years to connect with, I was able to within days because she advocated for me to her own people; they easily believed her more than they would a stranger. I can't get over her words when she introduced me to a ladies' networking/prayer group. "Meet Phidia, my Kenyan friend, she is such a pleasant lady. She is currently doing housekeeping for me, something she does with such a passion. I'm sure you will totally love her," she said. Those few words sunk in deep, settling in my heart like an anchor. I was fully "sold by a stranger" that had barely known me for three months, yet she saw and trusted my heart. Her love broke through the boundaries of race, country, and continent; none of which, including skin color was going to deter her from using her power to toot my horn. Oh, what a beauty she is! My kids and I were safely *sheltered* by the power of a white privilege under control.

It might surprise you that when I met Mickie, I had no car. Being new in the country, I was just trying to find my footing. With no money to afford a taxi and living in a rich neighborhood with limited or no public transport, I used to walk miles to meet and serve my clients. Imagine a *real* black girl walking ten miles or more on a real hot summer day in California with a backpack of cleaning supplies! But that did not deter a white privileged Mickie who had seen me a few times walking beside traffic from connecting with me. She actually convinced her mother-in law to help me with her car for two months! She was out not only to use her privilege to empower me, but also take some discomfort on my behalf. If this is not a *secure, settled, and smart* privilege, then someone needs to help me understand what it really is!

It was through this amazing lady that I met some incredible ladies, like Ashley and Amelia. These two became my clients as well as destiny cheerleaders whose faith in me despite my circumstances at the time sparked the fire to my success. These were among the few privileged white friends who believed in my dream when I changed my profile overnight from a housekeeper into a public speaker. Though they knew the reality on the ground, my circumstances did not deter them from believing in my potential. They faithfully cheered me through my social media pages to the person I am today. Sometimes *it's not the mountain you move or the sea you part, but that one drop of love that you add into a doubting heart that awakens the giant within them to conquer their mountain.* Small actions of love could be what matters most in uniting different races by turning this privilege into a shelter for the underprivileged and a *real* value for the privileged.

Mickie and I discovered that we had several things in common, including a shared birthday and us both being strong-willed go-getters. We had more similarities than differences, and her genuine love for me and my children, I could compare it to one of a blood-sister. I should be right to say that I also found a sister inside this white privilege. How lucky was I?

The Good Traitor

Imagine if Mickie observed my pleasantness and kept saying to me, "Oh Phidia, you are such a pleasant person!" I would feel good about that comment, and that would build my confidence, something which I needed. If she decided to tell every black person she met, "I have a pleasant black woman who is very close to my family," that would possibly make black folks happy knowing that one of their own is so highly regarded and so are they. Now, such a statement doesn't "cost" much energy to say, but when she decided to tell her *own* people, it was not easy. First, she laid her life on the line because she could lose her place in her tribe, her own haven. She could be seen as the traitor who advocates for a stranger, and this could have caused her to be shunned for being different. In a society where the relationship between black and white folks has been so embattled, it's hard to comprehend what she may have had to deal with just to say those words.

Do you know how many people from my tribe changed their attitude toward me for writing this book? "How could she dare say something good about privilege," has been the matter. This tells you how close to home this reality can get. I doubt if this is a subject that can make a black girl and especially an immigrant popular anyway. I had to rely on my personal convictions and values to speak for what I believe in and still extend compassion to them that think otherwise. I figured out that prioritizing my *inner* peace by doing the right thing would make it easier to afterwards make peace with my tribe as much as possible, because the peace starts from within.

The fear of losing our position in our tribe often keeps us from interracial advocacy within our race. Have you ever noticed how it's easier to tell another race how good they are in the *absence* of your own race? How about telling your tribe how wonderful the other race is? I recently was talking to some black women who are a bit older than me about the objective of this book. I was surprised to realize how difficult it was to portray the white privilege in a positive way. It was even harder acknowledging that white privileged folks also go through pain as a result of privilege. I was afraid to look like a traitor. I realized that it was easier said than done.

Suddenly, I found myself too intimidated to stick to my bipartisan message and more inclined to portray "my tribe" as the victims. Fear of being deserted by "my people" almost tempted me to water down my message. I was guilty of betraying my calling, therefore, I quickly repented from within my heart and tried to immediately figure out how to get myself back on track. So, I began asking them questions to understand their perceptions on the impact of the privilege and the possibility of uniting the two divides. Phew! I was so relieved to pledge my allegiance to the truth I believe in despite the circumstances. I discovered the power of using questions to engage compassionately and yet still boldly in a difficult but fruitful conversation without compromising your stand. *Let us be gracious with our advocacy acknowledging that the other party might not be on the same page with us.* Being conscious not to create more hate as we try to resolve hate is key but again, compromising with evil is not an option. It is boldness with humility and compassion that does the magic. We can't force them to take our view, but we can gently through questions lead them to denounce hate and embrace unity.

But what really ails us here? Why was it so hard to advocate the positive side of privilege to my people, yet I have so much fun doing it with the privileged? The answer is simple—there is always an unconscious default inclination toward people who are *like us*. We often don't even notice that we are doing it. We possess a kind of *phobia* toward anything different from us or what we are used to. So, every time we (by default) want to be in good standing with our own, we are careful of what we say out loud. Anything that makes us look like the "devil's advocate" is avoided. That fear has always hindered us from pulling down the walls of diversity.

Consider how many black people will be transformed in their perceptions about white people simply because I decided to share the story of Mickie's impact on my life. Who wouldn't want to hear this story? Only the devil, and he is not welcome to read this book. If I choose to keep it in my heart or toot her horn anywhere else but within my tribal gates, I deny millions in my tribe a golden moment to build bridges, tear down racial walls and create relationships that favor the delivery of a shelter out of the privilege.

The Question is, Where?

Remember, it's not enough to press simply *toot a horn*—where you toot it matters the most. Go fly my flag in your compound for your tribe to see it. Don't fly it here in my compound because it will only be a feel-good moment and that's it. Your people need it most, and they see you as the only sheep worthy of being trusted while the rest of us are scary "wolves." But we know you and you know us because we have a shared experience with one another, and the two of us know each other for who or what we really are. So, we are counting on you to tell your people the truth about who we really are and what we stand for and help change their perception of us. Help us break the stigma between the two sides so they can work together. Until then, the "midwives" and the "surgeons" cannot really begin the delivery process for baby Shelter. If you keep quiet, that does not acquit you of the guilt. You are simply an accomplice to a crime and deserve to be prosecuted for it.

What does it take for me to disclose that I was mostly helped by a majority white people to grow my business? Does my nose drop off somewhere for saying this? Or do I lose a pound of my goodness for admitting to the goodness of someone else? Thus far, I have only had one black person in my client portfolio, I don't know why but perhaps because the community is majority white. Or is there an in-house racism amongst the black folks themselves? What about the white folks? That deserves a thought, too. White-blonde hair or white-black or brown hair, what is the issue? After all, white is standard for both of us. African-American or African immigrant, aren't we sharing the African? Black human or white human, aren't we all human? So, what really is the big deal? On a different note, is there a possibility that we have an overwhelming number of racists in other races that are not in the spotlight? People who feel safe to engage in racism because all eyes are on the white and black person, and if by any chance they get noticed, their bigotry could easily pass for something else just because they are not black or white? That might be worthy of our attention.

If it turns out that this in-house or internal racism exists, then the mission of advocacy is going to be a hard nut to crack for a simple reason: I am more internally threatened than I would be under normal circumstances and therefore, in the best interest of my life, I will choose to play safe. That's where most of us are playing in my opinion. I have yet to see one successful case of the so-called "confidential" love. Tell me how good I am and that you love me in front of the people that matter, yes, them that think otherwise. Let us not allow internal racism to overpower us because that is our peace and abundance at stake. I write from experience and personal conviction; it is worth it. There will always be a few people within our tribes who want to walk with us. These are people who believe in the good of the "other" side and know that there are certain people who speak our language and dance to our song from the other tribe. These believers of interracial good are the heroes we need to hold hands with as we advocate for the other side, so we don't grow weary. Two are better than one, for when one falls, the other will raise him. We must chase after these stars within our tribes because they make the advocacy business more efficient and fun. I assure you it will be well worth your time.

Priorities must be set right! Let us begin interracial advocacy right inside our tribes now with one person and pass on the baton to another then we can sit back and watch this privilege turn into a refuge and *real* value for all people and our economy too. I say *real* because currently what we deem as value is a fake one that has left the custodians of privilege troubled. *Real value is when your privilege rallies its adopted beneficiaries to its protection and all you have to do is to figure out the best way to enjoy it!* Let us remember, we will be the *first* beneficiaries of our advocacy before anyone else does.

ME TOO MOMENT	Do you remember someone you did not expect who used their benefit to help you achieve a scary dream or overcome a difficult challenge?
	In one word, describe how you felt.

Distress and the Privilege Handshake

With Covid-19 flipping the world upside down, most people worried about getting sick during the past year. As for me, I had double trouble. My lease couldn't be renewed because my landlady was relocating, and she had different plans. I couldn't find a house that matched my financial capacity. Consequently, this led to homelessness. A quarantine order was in place, with two kids and nowhere to quarantine. That was stressful enough for me to lose my hair if not my entire head. Luckily, one of my white customers knew about my situation and took me under her wing with unbelievable commitment. Gwen used all the avenues she knew of to help me find a place including posting on Next Door page, which is a neighborhood communications platform. I did not ask her to do it, but she felt obligated as the true heroine she is. Gwen acted as though someone had commissioned her to help me. At first, I kept wondering how much the "invoice" would be. If you are used to negativity, some unexpected good in your life can sweep you off your feet right into the dumpster of suspicion.

Unfortunately, none of our efforts with the house search worked out and the last day of our lease finally arrived. That's when Gwen did the most incredible thing ever! I saw a truck pull beside our parking space, which of course was crowded with our personal stuff that was ready for transport to storage. Driving the truck was Gwen's husband. He was responding to "orders" from his beautiful wife to move us into our "surprise" new home where we would stay for the interim. The next two months would be spent in Gwen's house! This was not as easy as it sounds. Imagine moving a typical African woman with two "crazy" African kids into a typical American home with two relatively quiet American teenage boys. The disparities, especially those of a cultural nature, are too irreconcilable to describe! Later, I came to discover that she had negotiated with her sons to have us move in.

If this is not a sign of a love heroine, then someone needs to tell me what else it could possibly be.

Why would someone who shares no blood relationship or ethnicity make such a big sacrifice for a stranger? We had only known each other for about six months therefore, I considered myself to have been a total stranger to her as far as sharing a house is concerned. Personally, I don't have such guts. As a matter of policy, my past experience with my adopted daughter taught me to never "try this at home," especially where a husband is involved. You never know when you invite the devil to rampage your rather peaceful home. I don't mean to suggest that all situations should be treated the same way, but once beaten twice shy. I expect this could be a genuine concern for any woman. Sadly, for Gwen, I suppose she might have had to deal with much more than just the ordinary. You know how there are some "special" characters with some "extraordinary" issues? The kind of humans who have an extra something on top of everything and so you just have to be extra something to deal with them? I could be one of those people.

Graced by The Privilege

Sharing a kitchen with the "un-Americanized" me was quite something. I certainly believed it called for extra patience. So many times, I had to ask, "And what is this for?" One time my daughter had to stop me while I was using the spatula to make eggs. She called in panic and with urgency, "Mum, you are embarrassing me." What she did not know was that I had been doing that for almost a week before she saw me! She also overlooked the fact that Gwen had seen me a couple times, but she had been gracious enough to mind her own business about my culinary faux pas.

So, what embarrassment was this little girl talking about? "You see all those eggs you have been eating?" I asked, "This is how I have been cooking them," I said. She almost jumped into the dishwasher to hide her shame, perhaps from Gwen, who was in the kitchen at the time courteously minding her own business. The poor girl was literally tormented with shame while I was just having fun! Clearly, we were in two different worlds. "Does the spatula do the job?" I asked. "Well, I guess," she stubbornly and hesitantly admitted. "But that looks awkward," she said. "Looks ... who is the looker?" I asked. At that point, she knew how this was going to end. She got very annoyed with me and walked away, throwing tantrums the best way she knew how.

Now, if you are feeling fidgety just reading this, that also could be a red flag for insecurity. Though I am not trying to justify my indecency. But back to this cutie pie, where on earth did such a pretty, little, smart girl collect all this insecurity? I support the part of being fashionable provided it doesn't enslave anyone. I am not the coolest of people neither am I the goofiest. I fall somewhere in the middle, at least as I see it. I may need to put things into perspective here, so you don't lose your breath for nothing.

I come from a culture where the rules of the game are not as complicated. We play by one rule known as "as long as it works." We major on results not the process. Yes, the end justifies the means. Now you hopefully understand why I had comfortably used the spatula enough times before I was stopped by a little girl who had been working hard to get me "Americanized." She calls it civilization; I call it stress. Please note: Not everyone in my community is "crazy," we have some very civilized people of course. I just happen to be a little different, but I promise I am not all that weird. Sure enough, I had been given orientation on my first day in the new home, but cooking spoons wasn't one of my worries for the day, not even for the week. I promise I looked for the cooking spoon, but I wasn't keen, neither did I try hard enough, and the eggs had to be cooked anyhow. I make the rules, they don't make me. I save time before saving my manners. That was the attitude Gwen had to deal with, yet she did so with indescribable grace.

How could you possibly cope with someone like me in the same house? You must have some sympathy for Gwen and her family for all they had to put up with as a reward for their selflessness. They didn't deserve this drama, especially since we were being hosted in a fully furnished guest room, which, having been her housekeeper, I can confide in you that it was the best part of the house. I am not sure how things happen in this country, but where I come from, you don't let children stay in such rooms. Occasionally, I can be a little mean, but this is not one of those moments. I spent the entire time we were there anxious and freaked out that these little "crazy rats" of mine were going to damage the furniture or something else, I simply refer to them as rats because they could easily tear anything up just for fun simply because they are happy, fun-loving kids. Even worse because they had to be quarantined in this room for the better part of the stay as good Covid-19-rules-abiding kids. I would wake up in the middle of the night from a nightmare about a torn couch! I wake up to find that the sofas were still intact. Ugh! When this drama is going on, my kids were having the most fun of their lives, which was probably the most annoying part of this arrangement.

The 'Crazy' and The Privileged-What a Combo!

For two good months, seven diverse humans were quarantined inside this 2,000-square-foot house! Gwen took all the risks possible to protect my children and I. You should know that her teenage boys adore their space. Most teenagers are allergic to little annoying voices around them and here we were. If you are blessed to be a parent, then you know how hard it is to control children, especially a typical African child who has tons of energy and is used to so much space and freedom to run around. I see white children as a bit tame or more manageable and have yet to encounter a real "crazy" one. I suppose my culture has more freedom than the American culture — not freedom of rights but freedom to roam around and express your energy as well as your emotions. You have one side of the freedom coin, but we have got the other side of it; at this point, I can't tell you which one is better.

I have reservations about visiting stores with my kids. The kind of stuff they do exposes the ugliest side of my insecurities—thankfully, I now know how to spot and act above them. But still, I have to keep looking around these kids like a hawk just to make sure no one is doing something they shouldn't. I try to get a little creative by asking them, "Do you see any other kid doing the things you are doing?" hoping to intimidate them to tone down their behavior. Luckily, my "sort of" goofy son always has an answer, "But mom, you said that we are unique and original." He knows what gets me. All the time, I'm thinking, *yes, I love the word unique, but I did not mean this kind!* Imagine, this energy had to be quarantined indoors?

What do you think this family had to deal with by taking us in! It wasn't easy, but somehow, we survived because the grace of privilege came through for us. We experienced a white privilege under the stewardship of security, maturity, and humility. Thus, we had the freedom to be our original and authentic selves. Privilege in the right hands empowered us. I don't mean to suggest that we had a walk in the park, no! But we handled our challenges with perseverance because love was kept at the center of it all. When I finally found a house, Gwen and her husband gave us our first dining table, and they even set it up for us. A white privilege walked with us all the way.

Iron Sharpens Iron!

One time, there was an organization that didn't treat me fairly. Looking at all facts, Gwen and I were convinced that it was a case of racial discrimination. Even then, I did not have to fight the battle alone. Gwen and her husband joined forces with me, and the perpetrator had no choice but to give me my rights when she was called out by one of her own. Oh, how beautiful can this privilege get! These two have done everything that qualifies them to be called my siblings. They became the family that I never had in a foreign country.

Whenever I encounter a difficult white person, Gwen is always my "go to" for the obvious reason that she understands her people better than I do. She is always willing to take on my battles. I remember one time when she tamed someone that was making my life difficult, and I said to her, "Thank you for covering my back." Her response was priceless. "I am here to protect your sanity so you can function for your kids." Awww! That sank deep within my heart; I still have those words in my journal highlighted with red ink! What a beautiful collaboration with the white privilege!

My relationship with Gwen is one of the few relationships where I feel like I get more than I give. Yet, that doesn't add a single pound of pressure on me because the giver doesn't seem to have any expectations for reciprocity. I believe that our giving is not a comparison business and that giving takes many forms. But as a matter of principle, I believe in engaging in relationships in which I give back a good portion of what I receive. However, this one challenges my principles in so many ways but at the same time, I seem to be cool with it just because Gwen doesn't appear bothered in the least. She takes pleasure in using her privilege to shelter the exposed. I am sure she is peaceful and blessed. That being the case, I promise to work on my input portion for this relationship, but that isn't a priority at the moment because I am in a relationship with a settled privilege. I have simply encountered a privilege with no demands. Lucky me!

When You See One, Look for Two

What more should I say to confirm that white privilege has its golden side? It only depends on the attitude of the person who has it and the viewer too. This chapter is dedicated to all the privileged white heroes who have acted beyond the average person, men and women of their own renown who have broken records in pursuit of interracial love. Yes, those who use their privilege not to intimidate or profit unfairly but to protect, shelter and uplift the oppressed as they connect themselves to peace and abundance. These very heroes use this privilege as a source of power to empower endangered races, and, yes, endangered by misuse of the same power by self-serving privileged individuals. I am a beneficiary of a *well-applied* privilege and *power under control*. But how could Gwen and Mickie use their privilege for good unless they first made peace with it? That's the genesis of power well applied. And putting that aside, how do you feel after reading these two real life stories about a white privilege advancing a shelter of refuge and protection to a black girl? I bet a lot of perceptions have shifted for good. That is the magic of interracial advocacy. What is your story? Are you sleeping on a gold mine that can shift this privilege battle for good?

And these are not the only heroes I have encountered. Time would not serve me to talk about some of my other privileged customers whose acts have been listed in the acknowledgements section. These heroes and heroines not only trusted a black woman to clean their homes but also spoke highly of me to their neighbors. You know how difficult it is to recommend a foreigner or a person of another race to be entrusted with your neighbor's home since it's usually the most valuable asset a person owns! Worse still, being a black foreigner in a country where blacks and whites have been racially divided since inception. But fortunately, they did trust and recommend me long enough to help me build a portfolio of clients so large that I couldn't take any more. Not only was I their trusted housekeeper but also a member of their family. I shared their meals, joy, sorrow, gifts, and their lives.

Others walked with me in sickness and in health. It was not just business, they cared for me and my children. There were many other incredible heroes (and heroines) across the racial divide. But, for the purposes of this book, I decided to give a bigger focus on the white privileged love heroes as my way of walking the talk and commitment to advocacy. The agents of light are scattered across the globe, but someone from the so called "other side" has to be interested and keen enough to notice their brightness and talk about it to their tribe, long enough to bring a change of racial perceptions. I just did, will you?

"Fame-ing" Shame?

In a country with blacks and whites embattled because of inequality, stigma is inevitable. Having some understanding of how strained the relationship of the two sides has been helps you appreciate the immeasurable courage that goes into overlooking the tension in order to act for the good of each other. Those individuals that can afford this level of maturity especially within the privilege deserve a celebration; someone should definitely make them famous! Sadly, the cowards seem to take all the fame for all the wrong reasons.

We call their cowardice out as we extend a heart of compassion to them, for they know not what they do; cowards because they believe that their privilege is their power to intimidate and disenfranchise an already downtrodden and defenseless group of people. They get attention for pressing their knees on a weakened race, suffocating a breathless people, and sucking their feeble life out. Is this really worth the fame? And who is this that makes them famous? How is so much attention given to these cowards for their ugly acts of hate, so much that it fills our screens, hearts, and lips so that we surrender ourselves to it and wash every hero and heroine (of love) into the sewer?

Well, I know that we live in an upside-down world; a world that flows against the current and one that loves evil more than good. A world that has been consistent in giving the good guy lip service while all the "likes" are given to the bad guy. But we know how deep down the pit this has brought us as a country and the world. This must stop and let the fans of love shine a bright light on what deserves attention. Hey, fans of light, let us *make* love win! Subscribe NOW!

Imperfect Heroes

I don't mean to say that these heroes are perfect because that word doesn't trend in the first place! Sometimes we really fight, but we keep love in the firing line and there are those difficult moments when we have to choose what to dwell on. We must let humans be humans and focus on the beautiful aspects of each other rather than amplify the bad sides so that we can create an echo of love and trust. That way, we will begin to subdue the existing misgivings. It's not enough to know that heroes and heroines exist. Changing society calls for activism. When we resolve to advocate, we must not let our commitment be subjected to what the other side does. We are dealing with imperfection, and we must not expect a perfect encounter. Whether they reciprocate or not, we must choose to focus on the good and do what we must do because it is good and right. It's the package of peace that comes with doing good that we aim for regardless of the situation we find ourselves in. However, we also lean on our existing *mutual* interracial relationships experience as the evidence of good on the "other side," which keeps us going in those tough times.

My beautiful children have a tendency to revenge, so they always say, "But he or she also did this or that." My answer is always the same … "Does that mean that now both of you are right because each one of you is wrong?" You should see the look on their little dazzled faces as they realize how silly their statement and actions were. Two wrongs don't make a right. Revenge is a business for the children because they relatively have little undeveloped minds, and it's the lowest level an adult can get to, although far too many people still think this way.

We must heal the tainted image that each party has about the other by highlighting the effective change agents available to each side. They won't be perfect, *but* they have a warm attitude and bear the trademark of love, that is our commonality. We must persist with "fame-ing" the good long enough to wear out evil by amplifying each other's strength right from our one-on-one relationships and then to the world.

So where are the fans of good who will not overlook kindness just because it is from an embattled party or the so-called outsider? Isn't that the epitome of security and maturity combined? May the privilege become a shelter and a real value as we search from *without* and advocate for the heroes of interracial love *within* our tribes.

ME TOO MOMENT	Who is your imperfect hero or heroine of love?
	What specific quality makes them outstanding?

The 'Practicals' of Love

> *"I alone cannot change the world, but I can cast a stone across the water to create many ripples."* — Mother Teresa

Hate often spreads like a wildfire in the summer. We must raise enough heroes of love in every home, neighborhood, city, county, state, and nation to quench this fire. We don't need to start from afar but simply with the people around us. Here below is how:

1. Search Them Out: In your Double MC club, identify three heroes (of interracial love) of different races than yours. If you can't name three, then start with one. Through the interracial relationships you are forming, you will soon have more.

2. Deliberate Complimenting: Write three compliments about them; this should include physical, cultural and personality attributes, one for each category.

3. Celebrate: Write down one outstanding thing they have done. By so doing, you are including them in the list of heroes of interracial love.

4. Create a Ripple Effect: Once you are done, make a copy and share it with the person you have identified as your interracial hero or heroine of love and share the outcome of number three with your family, colleagues, people of your race and the club members. Agree on the timeline for concluding this exercise and let the club members hold you accountable.

5. Reinforce: Discuss your experiences about advocacy in your next club meeting to motivate and learn from each other. Adopt advocacy as a continuous practice.

CHAPTER THREE

Buy Shares in Privilege: Investing in Mutual Relationships with Privilege

Let this Cup Bypass me!

"I am not at peace with the requirements of this relationship. I sense that my liberty is at stake. I feel suffocated and wish to have some freedom to say 'no' when necessary and 'yes', whenever possible, without any pressure. I believe we both need some space to ourselves for this friendship to thrive. I request that we take a break from each other so we can rethink our relationship." Delivering these words to Molly, who was not only a close friend but also my treasured and kind-hearted privileged white sister, was like attempting to take a break from the fall of gravity; it just felt impossible! I was the very person who booked the appointment with her, but the pressure was becoming unbearable. I wished I could take back my words but that wouldn't have made it any better. It was certainly an overwhelming task.

Watching the clock ticking toward the hour of distress was like waiting for a death sentence. That's how difficult it was to imagine saying these words to the very person that I loved as my own sister. I kept rehearsing in front of the mirror to make sure I didn't betray myself against that hour. I am not always as weak as I sound here though, at the same time, I also don't consider myself the strongest of all people especially where breaking relationships is concerned. Perhaps a little background could put things into perspective.

This woman was special to me. She was the person that I shared my struggles with and without fear of judgment and the girl I trusted with my secrets just as much as she did. She knew what I needed without a single word from me and so did I. My kids had found a mother figure in her. She loved them as her own. You would have thought they were her kids if it weren't for the obvious differentiator, the color of their skin.

Molly's husband, Jake, was like a father to my kids. He taught my son how to groom himself and be a "little man" as they always put it. They did indoor and outdoor sports together, memories that my son still talks about fondly to this day. I was Aunty Phidia to Molly's two daughters Tracey and Lily. I loved them dearly and looked forward to "special" days just so I could give them a little treat. They were so adorable! We bore each other's pain and celebrated our successes as one big happy family. We also shared meals together and did joint fun activities. Clearly, we looked out for each other's welfare like sisters.

There was such an amazing bond of love between the two families despite our racial diversity. So special to me was Molly that I never wanted to hurt her at all. I hope by this, I can bail myself out of the guilt I felt for not being able to say no to her requests for an entire year, especially at my own cost.

A Poisoned Love

We enjoyed each other's company, but something bothered me all the time; the fact that Molly could say no to my requests whenever it was necessary for her to, but I couldn't! I had to make sacrifices in my schedule just to be with her. She never struggled to tell me that

United By Privilege

she had different plans. She was loyal to her schedule, but I wasn't. Mind you, Molly was not to blame for my inability to assert myself, she never held a gun on my neck to make me do it; I just found myself doing it like an idiot! Though I always tried to "sanitize" the situation in my head, I knew that I was getting the short end of the deal. The oppressed "queen" in me felt betrayed and her lamenting couldn't be quenched. This was driving me insane especially because I couldn't let it out. It was that little bug up my skirt that kept disrupting the party. I wanted to confront it, but just that thought alone was scary enough to shrink every bit of my willpower!

We had just celebrated one-year anniversary of our friendship when things started to look different. As much as I wanted to keep this relationship going, I was feeling emotionally drained and anxious. New friendship year with new friendship resolutions, yay! I had just begun another friendship year with a resolve to honor myself, so I had a journal to keep me on track. Then, Molly was just on time with a request to accompany her to her daughter's music performance at her school. Lily was part of a team that was going to do a Christmas carol and as part of our friendship, we would be her number one audience. Unfortunately, I had planned to work late that day, so I excused myself from attending but I promised to take her little girl for a treat afterwards. I could tell Molly was not happy with my response because she was quiet for almost ten seconds, and then she said with emphasis, "Okay," and hung up. I felt some pressure to cancel my commitment, as I had always done before, but on second thought, I decided not to. I had taken so much pressure that I couldn't take even a little bit of it any longer. I was tired of being the sacrificial lamb for everyone else's fun. I was ready to pledge allegiance to my freedom, whatever it cost!

Sometimes you don't need another word of advice. You just need to be mad enough to make a change! I was to blame for my fate. It was my very own actions that had been "feeding the monster" that was devouring me by the day. Would there be a lasting solution or artificial peace? The choice (and the power) was mine. I was hoping to keep this relationship with no casualties at the end of the day, but first things first. After all, I had been sustaining the relationship with my heart twisting in my chest for the entire time until now. Something was and had been the matter here, and I was all set to address it in the most loving yet bold way possible!

The Math of Love

Honestly, I sort of understood why my friend Molly was disappointed with my response. For a whole year, she had hardly ever heard me say "no" to any of her requests. I could literally count the number of times that I did not honor her requests and when it happened, I gave a detailed explanation. This time around, however, I just told her that I had a commitment and gave no further details. Please understand that Molly never told me to explain myself, but there was some subtle pressure from her side (and mine too). Based on how I had *positioned* myself in this relationship, I wasn't in charge, and so I needed a "reporting line," so to speak. Her subtle pressure was met by my insecurity and fear of rejection and together, they formed a mountain of coercion. Thus, every time I felt an "irresistible" urge to explain myself, and she got used to it as "her right." So, how many times do you think I said yes that year?

Now, I had pursued Mathematics and Physics for my first degree just because I did well in both in my high school, but I didn't like either subject. I have certainly done many insane things *under pressure* but never mind. As a former mathematics student, I personally loved ratios, and this was probably the only thing I loved about math. So, take a ratio of 1:1, where one represents a day while the other stands for the highest number of requests honored per day, then this would translate to 365 yes's for the whole year. Please keep in mind that requests can take different forms not just in the context of having to do something. It could be in the form of a text or an opinion from Molly which based on the relationship I would feel some pressure to take her side to keep the friendship. Again, I don't mean to suggest that Molly was needy, but all the same, that number of yes's was a sign of trouble whatever the case, especially for people who don't spend an entire day together. No deal can be all that good! I wonder if that makes a healthy relationship anyway, but I digress.

Speaking of my two precious kids, even though I love them to bits, they get countless number of no's, especially on a bad day, mind you, we tend to have more bad days than good ones. I don't think I qualify to be considered a mean mother but that's how bad it can sometimes get for the people you *love*, especially when the requests are so frequent and "offline." If you have kids, you know what I mean. That said, what was the matter between me and Molly? What was so different about this love between us?

Speak My Language

People understand you better when you use a language familiar to them. That means that in relationships, buying shares into any relationship will involve a selfless act of learning the other party's language and speaking it! There is a disclaimer to this statement though. Wisdom has to prevail throughout this process because some language is poisonous, yet it may be the only dialect some people understand. For instance, a control freak might need another control freak to help them function. How else are they supposed to get in touch with the reality of their own venom? Alternatively, a secure person would help them shape up or ship out! I was none of that. Here I was, trying to respond in my perceived humility with a language too strange for my friend to understand. Her insecurity had just encountered mine and everything was a mess.

I chose my words carefully, "Molly, I am sorry that I *might* not be able to attend this function because I have a commitment, but I will create time over the weekend to celebrate Lily," I wanted to say, "I will not," but it ended up being, "I might not." I just couldn't verbalize those words. They had too much finality in them which I wasn't used to. I was scared of being in charge. I wanted to stay as vague as possible because the idea of being in control was contrary to my religious understanding of what a "good person," especially a woman, is supposed to do and be. The latter gave me a sense of humility and submissiveness and a cushion for my fear of rejection. In any case, who wants to be the "bad girl" after being rejected by a spouse, relatives, friends and now the world? Well, so what I did was give her a polite no which wasn't supposed to "hurt that much," at least as far as I was concerned. But alas—I must have missed something in the plan. This approach seemed to hurt her even more than a simple no would. Maybe she would have better understood a hard no than the softer version of it simply because that's her language? Sadly, I might have forever missed the chance to know the answer to this question.

It may be relevant to introduce you to another side of Molly that I never mentioned before. She is not only sweet and loving but also a strong girl who is not very generous with emotions. She is very direct. She neither minces her words, nor does she sugarcoat them. If you are the kind that looks for something to stop you before you begin, then this is your go-to girl! You only need a glance from her; a stare is too much to ask for. She doesn't keep you straining your head trying to interpret her intentions. But that said, inside this rough and tough persona lies a tender sweetness and a very loving personality. What a compassionate and caring woman she is! But woe unto you if the rough girl meets you before the loving girl does. You could easily be freaked out and miss the love if you judge this book by its cover. It should fascinate you that these are the kind of people I often attract in my life whatever that means.

Molly is the perfect definition of respect for personal space. This is something I totally admire about her; it's a quality that I borrowed from this relationship although I am still miles away from becoming a "pro" at it. I was just beginning to practice it with (and on) her when she pulled out her "red card" on me. So, why was she mad with me and for what reason was I forbidden from replicating her personality style? Was it reserved just for a few superhumans? Or perhaps my refusal was different from hers? These were the questions I asked myself until I turned blue in the face and still had no answer for at the end of the day.

A Point of No Return

I had just burst Molly's first bubble, and it didn't feel like this was the last one that would be burst. Judging by this incident, the bursting spree had just begun. Sadly, the relationship would never be the same again. In my native Swahili language, we say *Kama mbaya mbaya,* whose direct translation into English would be "If it's bad, it's bad." This is an informal statement which is only used when things are hot, and you want to convince your fearful self that the job has got to be done no matter what.

In my introduction, I mentioned that there are about forty-two tribes in my country and that I am an offspring of the Kamba tribe. This tribe takes several stereotypes, one of them being their famous "brand" name, which goes by the name *Chameleon.* This name originates from their love of the "shouting" colors, which include yellow, orange, green and red. Kamba tribe members whether male, or female can easily mix all those colors together in a single outfit. Since we all know what a chameleon represents, this doesn't seem to create a positive connotation for the image of the Kamba people. In other words, this means that you take a Kamba's word at your own peril. This stereotype exposes Kambas to a very intense scrutiny, especially when it comes to leadership in which some of the Kamba leaders have been called "political chameleons." This doesn't mean that they are the only ones who have the potential to act unstably but rather that the chameleon stereotype puts them at a higher risk for instability than any other tribe, as the society sees it. This, of course, is just one side of the story. The upside to this stereotype is the beauty that goes with these shouting (or should I say) screaming colors?

Hearing it directly from the horse's mouth sometimes is the best way to clear the air. For a long time, the Kamba people have embraced these colors as their identity. They believe that these colors represent their peace-loving, calm, warm and *passionate* nature. It is their passion that led to the famous proverb that says, *if you dip one finger into shit, then it's only sensible to dip all the other fingers.* This may sound gross, but it has a beautiful meaning. Kamba's argue that shit smells and whether you touch it with one or ten fingers, you still smell either way, which of course is true. At the end of the day, the dirtier you are, the bigger your motivation to clean your entire body than just one finger. This idiom is the Kamba way of saying that once you start an assignment, you must forget about being clean; you should get yourself as dirty as is necessary if that gets the job done and then you can clean yourself afterwards. In other words, completing the assignment is the priority hence they will go all the way whatever the cost.

Now that you have that understanding of the Kamba people, and keeping in mind that I am not only a Kamba but also a Kitondo girl, let us revisit my relationship with Molly. So, what do you think this loyal daughter of a Kamba and a faithful member of the Kitondo Girl Power was going to do? She had started a battle; would she, all of a sudden, let down her ancestors who initiated her as a warrior? Was she going to let the fear of rejection get in her way of honoring a whole tribe that ranks in the top five in terms of majority? How about dropping the legacy of a highly respected Kitondo clan? Because the Kambas, before Western civilization, held the idea of communal honor and shame; in fact, they still do that to some extent, and I consider myself part of the conservative Kambas as far as that is concerned. So, no turning back for me! My failure would be a letdown to not only my ancestors but also my offspring. One finger was dirty, which was not good enough for a serious Kamba girl. A real mess was the perfect deal. So, all my fingers went down in my attempt to rescue my independence from Molly's claws at the same time striving to straighten out the relationship.

Take the Remote Control

While the only person we are at liberty to control is ourselves, we tend to undermine that responsibility as we often look for someone else to control. People use the information they have about you as the remote control on you. That means, the less the information available to them, the less control or power they have over you. So, in the weeks that followed, I downsized the information avenues that I made available to Molly. It wasn't easy because you know how insecure people sometimes tend to talk a lot in hope that they can cover up their insecurities. But I was being very deliberate about it. I even carried a note written to myself that said *Shut up!* in red every time I had to hang out with her. Sometimes, I wrote it on the palm of my left hand and put three exclamation marks on it just to remind me of the seriousness of my desire to be quiet in case I decided to ignore the words.

Insecure people are uncomfortable with silence, and I was not an exception. It makes them feel exposed and so they often feel compelled to say something just to fill the void. So, I started practicing silence and staring at people at the same time. How creepy is that? But believe it or not, this is how Molly used to get information from me! When she stared at me and said nothing, I almost died of discomfort. So, I needed to up my game to meet her somewhere in the middle, somewhere where my head would remain intact after the bullets were fired. I even did this with my kids just for practice and boy, this was a hell of torment for me. Only a person who has been insecure (especially with the fear of rejection) can possibly understand what this situation was like. Have you ever felt like silence was going to kill you? I kid you not, this was my predicament.

On and on, I went, holding onto my breath the best I knew how. I could see that Molly was getting uncomfortable in the first month of my relative silence. I did not tell her all the unimportant details as I did before. I met whoever I wanted to meet without informing her unless it was necessary. Phew! What a sense of freedom I felt! I did not realize that this relationship had become a kind of marriage, where I sort of had to get permission just to go about my life. How the heck did we get here? I had no idea really. I just found myself wallowing in a hot mess. So, now I was beginning to live again and truly enjoy our relationship but there was a lot of tension based on her reactions to me. It looked like we had traded positions. For me, it was indescribable freedom and joy! But eventually I could tell that we were very close to seeing our friendship bubble bursting. Strangely enough, that made me excited and anxious at the same time, excited for my boldness in defending my innermost "queen" and anxious at the thought of losing this relationship.

Messed Up from the Word Go

Doubtless, I loved this woman and not just her, her entire family as well. Her two daughters were my dolls, too, as they were as beautiful as their mother inside and out. Her husband, Jake, was a very down-to-earth and people-loving person. This is what I would, for lack of better words, describe as a perfect family. And who on earth wouldn't want to be in their circle of close friends? I felt *privileged* to be part of that inner circle. Hopefully by now, I have given you an adequate description of my struggle at this point. But how did I get myself this deep into such a mess? I started this relationship on the wrong foot because I was desperate to have it. I felt that I needed Molly to rescue me from my fear of rejection and racial discrimination. She must have seen that desperation written all over my face, *I need you more than you need me.*

People are usually not oblivious of your messages; they hear what you say and see what you show. As far as I know, they need no invitation, and you have no court in which to sue them for seeing, maybe for saying things. Whether they are trespassing with their eyes or not is only a question of what is made available to them. Molly did not miss her moment. She was "faithful" to see and act accordingly. She could tell that I had submitted to a *master-slave mentality* right from the beginning of our relationship. It wasn't obvious during our face-to-face interactions however, but only because I was coughing up my lungs to sustain the invisibility. Any time she asked to meet me, there were enough times that I chose to cancel my engagements to make it work. Partly because I felt that I owed her for all she had done for me, as if "my gift" to the relationship *did not count*, and the other part just because she was from the so-called power race as I saw it. I had made jokes about it enough times, jokes that we both laughed about. That's how free we were in our conversations about race. But … was it really a joke? She must have taken it to mean everything I secretly meant!

Sometimes we give people the wrong cues and forget that they, too, have insecurities and could easily create a flood with our words. I just did in this case. Molly subconsciously (or perhaps consciously with my support) made herself an *executive* with executive privileges in this relationship and I endorsed it. She had privileges to say yes and no as she wished, and with no need for explanation (which is supposed to be a good thing) while she classified my no as taboo especially if it was not well explained in her eyes. She saw it as her right to always get a yes from me.

ME TOO MOMENT	Have you ever been in a relationship that was a threat to your freedom to be?
	In one word, how did you contribute to the situation?

Self-Inviting Troublesome 'Guests'

I consider relationships to be a game of the mind. The mind gets involved in interpreting both what is said and what is unspoken. Sometimes a lot of unwanted "guests" can find their way into a rather beautiful relationship and completely taint it. These guests do not come screaming their way in though. Often, they just *creep in* and the characters may never realize when it happens. It becomes even worse because our built-in blind spots interfere with our ability to see the influence these guests have in controlling our behavior in the relationships. Could it be that Molly was one such case? Is there a possibility that she genuinely did not realize how controlling she had become in our relationship? Perhaps all she wanted was the best for our friendship, and this was the best way she could think of to work it out?

Quite frequently, our insecurities will get in the way of our connections. They are the very unannounced and uninvited guests I just discussed. They feel entitled to our business because they are a part of us and, as such, always claim their right to steer our relationships. This could happen very unconsciously. Having this understanding at the back of your mind will help you separate the person from the behavior so you can rebel against their control with *grace* and still preserve a loving heart for them. For the kind of person Molly was, I believed that this might have been the case for her. I honestly do not think she spent time in her bedroom rehearsing how to subdue me, it just manifested itself in her endeavor to make this thing work.

I am the kind of person who keeps away from conflict, but relationships have taught me how to create it (and address it) simultaneously! It is an important part and parcel of a healthy relationship if you keep conflict within the so-called safe zone and have limits. So, being who I was then, I didn't want to hurt her, but that wasn't the only reason for my behavior. As an ex-victim of rejection, losing a friend brings up painful memories and reminds me of the past. Because I had a fear of history repeating itself, I didn't realize how much I had to do just to keep her. I avoided anything that would bring any kind of conflict in the relationship. She was one of the few genuine white friends I had, which was all the more reason I tried so hard to make it work. I felt as though my world would crumble without her. I bet you possibly understand my predicament why I felt the need to explain everything to her.

Control Strategy Reloaded

Molly and I survived for almost two months under the "new management." Unfortunately, those two months felt like ten years of tension. I was very deliberate with the information I disclosed to her, and all my dirty linen remained in the laundry basket to be washed "offline." She also started acting differently. The number of invites to her house decreased. I was sort of having fun with my life, as it somehow seemed like it was getting back to normal. But something was cooking, and I could smell it. Then came the fateful Wednesday at 11:07 a.m., when the long cooking but brief text came through.

"Phidia, I am very disturbed by how you have changed recently. I need us to talk about whatever is happening with you as a matter of urgency. Can you meet me at the Pink Center today at 5 p.m.?" The text sounded urgent. Molly had often sent me compelling summons before which obviously would freak the heck out of me so that I could honor them at whatever cost. As you already know, I was trying to get back in the cockpit and take charge, so I decided to push back just a little bit.

"Hi Molly, I'm sorry to hear that something is bothering you." (As I typed this, my fingers were sweating bullets.) "Thanks for caring, though nothing out of the ordinary is really happening to me. I doubt there's anything to talk about, but if you still feel the need to do so, then I would be available on Friday afternoon. Please let me know." I skipped a heartbeat when I clicked on the send button. Where on earth did I get the audacity to suggest a different day to meet Molly than her initial suggestion? That was too courageous and disturbing! And again, did I just lie to her about everything being business as usual? I thought about that for a moment. No, I think I told her my truth. Furthermore, this is how an ordinary relationship was supposed to look like in the first place. So what? I was just trying to work it backwards to the right place! No big deal. I cleared myself of the guilt of not being as honest as my godly father taught me.

This new me wasn't part of my fabric yet, so it still felt strange. But the fun part was the adventure and uncertainty in the entire process. I am the kind of person who doesn't like knowing everything though I ask many questions, which is a different story. I love the risky part of life because it provokes the heroine in me. That may sound goofy, but I just like it that way! I might wear different personalities depending on the occasion or the objective, but this is the original version of me. The downside is that this part of me is severely caught up in a tug of war with my compassionate personality, especially when the adventure translates to another person's discomfort. Unfortunately, at times, it just is what it is, and there is only so much I can do.

Molly wouldn't buy that, so she called me. I looked at the phone call with apprehension. I did not feel ready for this, at least not a verbal engagement because that would easily betray me. That is a tip for you if you struggle with fear of rejection. You stand a better chance of asserting yourself in a *written* conversation than you would verbally, which is a story for another day. Then the phone rang again. I wasn't going to escape this. Even though I was a little shaken, the bullet was very close to my mouth, I just had to bite it or else I would lose my head. So, I decided to pick up the call.

"I don't mean to pressure you but please create time so we can meet today." I was shocked with her choice of words and the tone of her voice. She sounded *very* different. There was no entitlement in her words anymore. For once, she was asking me to create time. She respected that I could be busy and unavailable. It was like she had just realized that she didn't have as much control over me as she once thought! What was she going to do if I refused to meet her today anyway? Spank me? The power was mine all along. Good! She deserved a chance in my schedule. We scheduled a time later that evening.

The Ugly Face of Insecurity

I have no idea what transpired between 11 a.m. and 6 p.m. on this relationship-defining Wednesday. Molly seemed to have reverted to her usual controlling nature, but also found some sort of reinforcement. It started well though. "Thank you for accepting to honor this meeting despite your busy schedule." That was the first and the last gentle statement I heard from her for the rest of the meeting, which took more than an hour.

There was obviously a screaming resistance in admitting that I had a busy schedule because she almost choked on the last part of the sentence. She was evidently furious about something connected to the schedule I suppose. Was it because I had been *too* available to deserve using those words? Did she feel like *her* schedule was the only one that was entitled to "busyness"? Or perhaps she didn't mean anything bad, after all; maybe she just expected to be the top priority in my life for friendship's sake? I wasn't exactly sure what to think.

"I have noticed that you don't tell me what you are doing lately," she continued. *Neither do you, Molly, after all, it shouldn't have been just me doing that in the first place,* my thoughts were screaming at her in retaliation! I was really having a bad attitude. *Okay, Phidia, relax!* I convinced myself. Outside, I looked calm, but within me I was experiencing a severe "tornado."

"I have no idea what you are up to," she continued. "I just see posts on social media about you and your new business. All you told me was that you were starting a business, but you no longer share any details with me about it." *Wait a minute, she was right* ...I no longer shared details of my life with her since I got myself under "new management." Her anguish was justified, but while I felt her pain how did we get into this situation in the first place? Anyway, she was describing our history and I was living in the future. How I wish she would have added the words ... "just like I do" at the end of every lamentation, then this would make it a two-way deal. This initial start was just the beginning of a long rant on her part.

"Phidia, everything just feels so ridiculous to me. This is not the Phidia I once knew. You have become so vague. Whenever I ask you about anything to do with you, your responses are neither here nor there. Other people know everything about you except me." I wanted to find out who this "other" people meant but that would just get me entangled so I bullied myself into staying focused.

"You mentioned the other day that you had a meeting with some friends in your house. I was very surprised that I did not know about it." *So, my mouth had landed me into trouble again?* I thought to myself as she went on. "Phidia, it's as if you are now very independent and running your own show. I thought I could *help* you with your business, but it seems you are not interested." She went on for almost two hours. I only interjected to ask a few questions, which meant that I only took up a relatively small portion of the entire time. Trust me, it was a long list which had several repetitive comments but for most of the allegations, I stood guilty as charged.

Danger! Danger! Danger!

I know how control looks like because I have dealt with it so many times. At one point it used to feel like a big part of my life because that is all I knew. But now that I recognize it, I hardly ever miss it. So, when she began talking, all my control sirens went off ...*here comes another one ... Danger! Danger! Danger!* My "fire" alarm could not be silenced the entire time I was with her. Obviously, she had a right to express herself but then I thought to myself ...*You mean I was supposed to tell her everything I was doing, including who I met in my own home?* Of course, I would want to as long as I did it from my own free will but not through coercion. Was I losing the freedom to just be myself? Shouldn't it be a good thing that I was becoming independent? That I am no longer just a piece of baggage you lug around? And why on earth did this sound like a bad marriage? I wish I found the answers to those questions.

As a single mother with seven years of experience, independence comes as part of the package. So, should I renounce my independence to keep this relationship, which I very much needed? But how was I going to give out my value that I had gained through so much pain, even the pain of letting go of a marriage of eight years? Can't I just have the two plates at the same time? I was completely torn. Losing her would likely result in losing other friends affiliated with her. And what was I going to tell my kids if they asked why we weren't visiting Molly anymore? There were so many strings attached. I was fearful and anxious at the thought of losing this relationship but much more afraid of losing myself after working so hard to regain my self-esteem; hopefully, I still had it. I wished I could keep both, but where was the common ground? I was officially stressed and managing a serious migraine as I tried to navigate everything. I just needed to get home immediately and find a way to sleep this situation away.

At the end of the day, I did not know what I was really dealing with. Everything felt important, urgent, and overwhelming. My precious girlfriend was drowning in deep waters of insecurity right before me, and I was not far from her situation. The only difference between the two of us was that I knew that I was drowning but she had no idea what was happening to her. It was pathetic. Everything she told me that evening was undeniable evidence of an insecure woman. And here I was trying to beat my own insecurities. So, who was the priority here? We both were in ICU; therefore, I decided to rescue myself before I could make any attempt to save her. However, this decision could not be sealed that soon, which was typical of me where friendships are concerned. What if I realized that I had made a mistake? I remembered all the authentically good times we had spent together. Was I sure I wanted to let go my closest *white* girlfriend? How about hurting her? Poor Molly, I still cared for her deeply, so I just wanted to keep a safety buffer for both of us, so to speak for myself.

From Pressure to Pleasure

I wish I had delivered my verdict then and there because the load would have been off my shoulders. Then I would only be left to handle the consequences of the verdict. That was my best bet for freedom, but I would have to postpone my liberty for one more week with the current state of affairs. Molly was not ready for the verdict, and neither was I quite frankly. There was so much compassion in my heart for Molly's plight. She was genuinely having a difficult time, but I wasn't the real cause of angst; she needed to treat herself the same way I was treating myself. Nonetheless, was she willing to stop the blame game and walk the journey with me? Probably not that day. So, I said to her, "Molly, I have carefully listened to your concerns, and this seems to be a difficult situation for both of us. I need a week to think through things and get back to you."

She must have realized that I was extremely sorry, hurt, shocked, confused, anxious and every one of their "relatives" put together. Or was she guilty of something? I may never know. So, she jumped in, "Phidia, I wish to assure you that everything I said was because *I love you* and I want our relationship to get better." Oh, wow! I wish I could believe her, don't you? At first, I did not, but thinking about it later, I realized that being the genuine person she is, she probably meant those words. But unfortunately, I did not feel adventurous enough to sail her boat of insecurity, after all, I had my own waiting!

For a control freak, *if pressure seems to break the deal, they know how to use pleasure (or dangle a carrot) instead.* She just did. If pressurizing me to inflict fear, which was always her favorite strategy, did not work this time round, then this so-called "love" was supposed to make me succumb. But did I want this kind of love? Maybe before when I had no idea what love looked like, but now, I wanted nothing of it! What about the unsolicited business support? Was it supposed to be the dangling carrot? Even that wasn't worth my freedom. As much as I needed support, this price was too expensive for me. I would rather be "business-less" and free than be a "business-full" slave. With this pep talk, I felt like I knew what I wanted but I still needed someone to push me off the cliff. It was just too scary.

ME TOO MOMENT	Have you ever been enticed to compromise your freedom for a convenient benefit?
	Summarize your experience in one word.

Phidia K Maingi

Lulu the Gold Refiner

The week that followed was one of the most difficult weeks of my life. I was caught between a rock and a hard place. Trapped inside a poisonous love, I was bearing a difficult internal conflict about how to handle my predicament. I could barely eat. I am the kind that stress affects appetite downwards, I wish it were the other way round. But never mind. How was I going to eliminate the poison without messing up the love when both were mixed in the same bottle? Maybe the only option would be to empty out the entire concoction and fill the bottle with clean love. So, did that mean ending this relationship and beginning anew? Anew with who and how? Trying to answer that question just shattered me. I could see myself losing the whole bottle with its contents. Trying to resolve this puzzle left me feeling frail.

To use an analogy, *the gold had just completed the smelting process, but we were still stuck with the impurities.* We needed someone to complete the refining process so we could enjoy a clean product, a product whose name would be Phidia the Queen. From a slave to a queen—what a transition! I was excited for this metamorphosis, not just for the end product but also the adventure. But how were we supposed to get through this refining process without either of us getting hurt in the process? There was too much to worry about, a screaming indecisiveness and a threat of being trapped in the shambles forever. We needed a *heartless* refiner to thrust the messed-up queen into the sizzling furnace. I was so scared of completing what I had started.

I was still deliberating on my next move when the phone rang. It was Lulu, my financial adviser; she had something "important" to discuss. *Wrong timing!* I yelled at the phone as though Lulu was the cause of my woes. *How on earth would this business benefit me, Lulu?* I screamed to myself. I wondered how the earth was even still rotating while I was about to lose a good girlfriend. I was so mad at Lulu as if she were supposed to hold back the sun from setting. Then, I remembered that I needed someone to vent to, which gave me some sort of motivation to pick up this call.

Mission Accomplished

"Phidia, why do you sound like you are a thousand years old?" she asked jokingly. "Lulu, something is definitely wrong with me or someone else," I opened the door to my sewage. "Why does everyone around me want to take away my freedom?" I ranted. "Phidia, I love your choice of words... it seems like it's just everyone *around* you because you are a *magnet* that attracts these types of individuals." *How insensitive can you get, Lulu?* My mind was spinning as I erupted with anger from within. I was very upset about the direction this conversation was taking this early, but Lulu is the kind of person that I respect, and of course, you should have some regard for the person you invest with anyway. So, I decided to listen until she was done.

"Phidia, you are the problem. In fact, some people are all good until they come around you, and in no time at all, you poison them!" *Ah! Poison them? Really?* She knew how to mess up my emotions, didn't she? This sounded like a personal attack on my rather clean brand. You don't say such stuff to a type A personality especially a Kitondo girl unless you are looking for the fastest way to lose your head! I wanted to trash her voice in perfect wrath. I found myself with my fingers clenched tight around the phone, sweating, and shaking with anger. The poor phone must have been paying for it dearly!

I don't know any convicting truth that doesn't hurt. These words made me so furious and uncomfortable that I just couldn't take anything more. "Lulu, I have to rush to be somewhere. I will call you later." It was a Friday, two days since I had met with Molly. I was rushing to nowhere. This pain had grounded me to the point of canceling my business for the day, but how else was I going to get Lulu off my neck? I felt a little guilty for cooking and "serving" some lies to bail myself out but *good for her.* She deserved something for her "bossyness" anyway!

Surprisingly, Lulu did not get intimidated by my request. How could she be so comfortable with rejection? That was also really frustrating for me. "Okay, girl, call me when you are ready for a change," she calmly and confidently ended the discussion like a boss. *Phew! She was off my neck finally. How bossy of her and what an annoying confidence on her part!* I thought to myself. She was too cool for the insecure me. She seemed oblivious to the fact that I was not just mad at her timing and her choice of words but also envious of her self-assurance because it was a timely reminder of my failure with Molly and that drove me even more crazy.

Why did I share this with her in the first place? I wondered regrettably. I was looking for someone to make me feel good by recognizing how unfair everyone had been to me, but did she really do that? It was as though the doctor just messed up the wound in the name of cleaning. I was seriously hurting now. I could literally touch the pain with my bare hands, all joking aside. I lay down on the carpet for hours on end. Her words terrified me the entire day. The memory of her firm yet gentle voice traumatized me to the core. I tried to bury it, but it was always there with me. Didn't I ask for motivation to deal with this mammoth? And now I was angry that my prayers were answered while the words were still in my mouth? I had just bumped into a very generous giver of that very motivation by the name of Lulu, who boisterously injected me with all the necessary pain I needed! I was on "life support" the entire weekend, until Monday morning at 5 a.m. when I decided to face the situation head on.

Self-Diagnosis

I sat with my journal at my usual prayer and meditation spot and translated my feelings into the little book. Then I began conducting a soul search for their root cause. It took me more than two hours before the magic happened. How did such a few words make me feel as though my heart was literally bleeding? Something was the matter here. At first, I thought that it was just my pride that I needed to "swallow" but then as I continued journaling, I realized it was something else. It was actually fear of rejection that was hurting so much for being spotted. It was the very thing that Lulu had described as a magnet that draws control freaks to my "hood." Hearing this truth for the first time in my life, a truth that no one had ever told me for thirty-seven years of my life was a Tsunami of some sort. No wonder there was so much unrest within me.

This stranger calling themselves "Phidia's personality" was all a fraud. Their real name was "fear of rejection" and they had been living with me since 2009, when my marriage went on the rocks. I could vividly remember when I last saw the real woman, Phidia. But how did "they" manage to disguise themselves for so long that no one had ever noticed them before? Well, they had been with me for so long that they looked at home and were a part of the family. And now, someone was trying to make them homeless? You must understand why there was so much retaliation on my part. But wait a minute ... didn't they deserve all the mercy they were trying to claim? Well, I need to give you some more details before you can make a verdict for yourself.

This very stranger was the force behind my relationship woes. Though I broke away from a bad marriage, the tactful bully never left me alone. I only changed the environment not the person. The thief of my joy was still *within* me and luckily (or not) had gotten transported with all the previous "tenants" to my new home when the marriage ended. Only one thing was missing, my ex-husband. This fear of rejection continued to claim it's right to interfere with all my subsequent relationships. It determined how I *positioned* myself in every engagement. Lulu was so right that I poisoned some of the good people around me. Yes, when I took the position of servant in the relationship, what did I expect my counterparts to do? They simply had to assume the master's seat to *balance* the equation. So, why were they to blame for it?

The Ugly Screensaver

But then, why was the slave seat my default setting as far as relationships were concerned? There was more to it and here it was. Having been a victim of rejection from a husband of eight years and my adopted daughter, that was a huge enough experience to scare the heck out of me! So, any time I found myself in a relationship, my system had discovered a "cool" way to *play it safe*. I entered every relationship on a *risk-control* mode while trying to avoid a repeat of the pain. This meant that I placed myself in a *less-threatening* position in all my relationships. I am not sure how this played out in the relationship with my kids, but I must admit that there was a time I was afraid that my kids would disown me as their mother! Those were the times that I worked very hard to please my kids and to convince them that I was a great mother as if I were not already. Imagine trying to impress a six-year-old who probably has no idea what that looks like.

How insane the fear of rejection can drive us! So yes, based on the sitting positions, the control had to be. The inferior party had to dance the music of the superior, while at the same time lamenting about their pain as though someone bullied them into it. But yes, there was some "sanctified" bullying taking place from the unseen stranger who, in this case, was my fear of rejection. They had the remote control, and I was their puppet; they always dragged me to a seat I never wanted in any relationship—a servant's seat. But who cares? Everyone had their lives together except me.

Just so you know, people always know which seat you take in a relationship, and they will fairly assume the other seat that corresponds to yours. All this happens without a single word being said to that effect. If you couple white supremacy and my fear of rejection, Molly did not need to fight for the master seat. It was readily available to her from the word go. I felt as though I needed her more than she needed me. The message was evident in my actions, if not my words. It was written in bold letters, *I have nothing to offer but please rescue me,* and she knew precisely how.

There is always the option of *equality* in any relationship, but for people who have insecurities they don't get to see that position because their insecurity is drawn to the magnet of inferiority attached to the servant seat. It takes a few minutes of watching two parties in a relationship to determine where each party is seated. Body language is loud enough and woe unto you if you dare say something. The position gets sealed and secured for you. Yes, mine was such a case; it was my permanent position, my default mode, and my ugly screen saver. This always felt like my safe place where I felt no threat of rejection. I was always on the receiving end, ready for whatever would keep the relationship going. If a broken relationship was a confirmation of what a failure I was, did I want to sign off this confirmation? Never! It was a case of whatever it takes to sustain the relationship.

ME TOO MOMENT	Have you ever been in a relationship where you felt as though you needed the other party more than they needed you?
	In one word, why do you think you felt so?

The Game of Status Quo

If the controller realizes that you are trying to check out from your normal position, they will have a strategy to keep you in the same place to maintain the status quo. Even though you volunteered for the servant position, making an exit is a totally different story. Such change affects the other party in that they also have to change seats in the relationship and therefore, you must expect resistance. They will use manipulation through pressure or pleasure. Many people ask me, "Phidia, how did you stay in a bad marriage for three more years? Why on earth would you share a husband with your adopted daughter? How stupid could you have been?" These questions offend my fans big time, but not me because I now expect it. Looking from outside at the mess, I can see how insane that was, yet it was so hard to see it then because of the manipulation involved.

My ex-husband Phil was so discreet in playing this game. The moment he savagely said to me, "I love Gladwell, and if you dare bring that subject again, I will do something much worse," I was all set to give him the space to enjoy his new bride. I had been waiting for this admission for three years. So, did I have any intention to play the party pooper? Not at all. He deserved some space for being honest at least. But that did not seem like what he wanted. He sure wanted to keep both of us, a deal I did not feel brave enough to engage in whatsoever. I was still the pastor's daughter, and that arrangement did not sound familiar to me. Even if I were to get a little more open-minded, but certainly not with my adopted daughter. *Fine, I would never bring up this subject again,* I was fully decided. After all, I wanted nothing to do with him starting from that moment, so never mind! I was angry enough to move on.

I went ahead and rented a new house for me and my daughter. At the time, my son was not yet born. I had just moved some of my stuff when my kid brother, Sam, called me panicking about collecting a suicide note. It was 8 p.m. and I had one more trip to make. So, yes, I was undoubtedly done with him, but this call drove me insane. But why? I was not supposed to care whatever he did with his "damn" life, right? However, the compassionate personality inherited from my sweet mother decided to betray me. This was back in the day when compassion controlled me and dragged me wherever it wanted, (I have been a puppet to many things really). But now, I give the orders! I determine what my compassion attends to and what it does not. Even good things, if not controlled, can become toxic but that is a topic for another day. So, as for compassion, this was someone's life at risk. I could not focus on my agenda. Not with the tearing thought that my daughter's father was dead, in a place I had no idea where, and that I was supposedly the cause of his death.

I am not the strongest of the human beings, and this incidence was evidence of that. But whatever it was, Phil was on course to achieving his objective. This freaked me out, and I abandoned my evening plans to rescue a life. A whole night of frantically searching for him in a forest where I was supposed to "collect his dead body" as per the suicide note was sufficiently traumatizing that, when I finally found him, I sobbed uncontrollably with mixed feelings. I was not sure whether to be happy that the father of my daughter was still alive or sad that the drama was not yet over. But one thing was for sure, I was willing to stay in the marriage *if* that would keep him alive. I laid aside my bitterness, kissed him amid the sobs, and we cried together. *After all, he didn't mean to hurt me,* I told myself, holding on to his tears for the evidence. The stage was well managed, I was dealing with a "professional manipulator." He knew my soft spot, and I did not disappoint. My compassion was locked in place, and I gave him my promise to stay, exactly as he wanted to see it play. The strategy worked, at least long enough to blindfold me for three more years.

Do you think I should have asked him why he was still alive before shedding my precious tears? Maybe that sounds mean, but perhaps it would have helped me back to my senses. But seriously, he had written a suicide note, so why was he still around fourteen hours later? It was clear that I was being played, how could I not see that? So, when I finally decided to leave him after the three years, he still tried manipulation (it worked for him previously in the suicide case, why not try it again?). First, he tried pleasure. "Think about our kids," he said. He knew that was a soft spot for me and I guess it would be for any mother. I cried when I thought about our kids and him too because I still cared for him. You know how a person's first love can be silly. But then I remembered what this stupid love had taken me through and so I decided to cry forward and not backward. So, I said, "No problem, I will think about them while we live in separate houses." I was on top of the game this time. Not that I did not have compassion for his choices, I did, but this time around, I was the one giving orders to the compassion on what it should attend to and not vice versa.

Breaking manipulation calls for a separation of *emotions* and *logic* and this was always my pitfall, but this time I made it safely, yay! So, he moved to strategy number two because a *manipulator won't let go that easy*. They are stubborn, they need some "violent" stubbornness. Violent in the sense of acting against your wildest emotions. He knew that being a pastor's daughter, I guarded my image and reputation carefully, so he decided to mess it up. Perhaps that pressure would get me back to his trap. "She is a drunkard and a promiscuous woman," he said to everyone who cared and even to those that didn't care to listen. That hit me real hard, prompting me to think that I was better off making peace with him for my name's sake. But the go-getter in me screamed *nooo way!* So, again, I mourned my way forward NOT backwards. Hurdle number two crossed.

But he wasn't done just yet. When the defaming strategy did not work, he turned to two of my closest friends and accused them of grievous things. That they had destroyed his marriage by influencing my decisions. They bore the cross for my change, while they themselves were equally shocked about the person I had just turned out to be. I looked at them compassionately and boldly said, "I am sorry you are going through this for me, but you have to be strong because this has no point of return." They looked at me as if to ask, *are you for real?* I am the kind that takes too long to make up my mind on relationships, but once the decision is made, I execute with speed at whatever cost. It doesn't take screaming, but actions will be clear, consistent, and loud. That can be a strength and a weakness at the same time.

So, this was the case with my marriage. I was done and no manipulation, whether pressure or pleasure, would change anything. I knew what I had signed up for and this was not it. Regardless of who wanted to kill themselves for their inability to cope with my freedom, I was all set. If they did, I would cry beside their grave and amid the sobs declare, *no turning back!* And the thing is, they won't kill themselves; manipulators never will. They are too selfish with their comfort to do anything that hurts them because they don't know how to love themselves and others, so don't fool yourself in the name of pleasing them because they won't reciprocate. Don't dance their song; create your own rhythm of freedom at whatever cost and dance to it with your own beat. But remember to be compassionate with them, understanding that they have a *love deficit*.

The Swearing in Ceremony

My predicament with my ex serves to confirm that it is not enough just to realize that you took a wrong position in the relationship. This is just the beginning of a long journey. You could still get stuck forever somewhere along the way if no radical measures are put in place. It was about time to take one such step to break this nagging yoke in my relationship with Molly. I had cleared two hurdles, but the last one was breaking my spine. If I may quote the scripture in Ecclesiastes 7:8a, it says that "The end of a thing is better than its beginning," but I also believe that "better" comes with a huge cost. I wish I could cheat the system!

I was ready to pay the cost of my freedom. You cannot justify your insecurity and break out at the same time. So, I led myself to admitting my insecurity, owned up my contribution in feeding it, and immediately proceeded to renounce it. Three stages at one go! This anger was working for me. All fear was gone, and I was ready to fall into the furnace of refinement.

"For all that I poisoned, I hereby solemnly declare that I have the necessary resources and the required commitment to detox you. But, if you are attached to the poison, then, I am also committed to walking away from both of you gracefully (or violently) whatever the case may be." I had just appointed myself as my own freedom fighter and therein lay my maiden speech as evidence. Woe unto any control freak that crossed my path!

Free at Last!

"Molly, I have carefully considered your concerns and as promised, I wish to talk to you about it. How does tomorrow 5 p.m. work for you?" The text was sent, and I could not recall it. Molly was quick to respond affirmatively. The deal was sealed. I breathed a sigh of relief as though a burden had just fallen off my shoulders. I experienced a heroic instance. Is that how it felt to be the one calling the shots? Then I understood why Molly would put up such a fight to retain this seat. It was worth every penny!

What before felt like my moment of execution turned into my hour of power, a champion's moment! I felt as though the clock was not ticking fast enough, I kid you not! I couldn't wait for the meeting that a few minutes ago had twisted my intestines in a knot! This would be a chance to redefine myself correctly and accord me the honor I was due. One part of me was excited but the other part was agonizing how to shield Molly from an impending heartache. I wasn't sure how things would turn out, but the adventure was worth having just for the sake of it. I was still the very girl who is always fascinated with adventure. Then came the moment ... I walked into our usual restaurant, the "Pink Center" as we fondly referred to it. I was feeling bold and graceful. Molly was already waiting; this was as important to her as it was to me. We were trying so hard to enjoy our evening coffee as we talked about everything else but there was a tangible amount of tension in the air. This was the first meeting I had ever initiated for more than a year into our relationship. It could only be the first and the best, I told myself. It could also be the only meeting.

Did the victim turn into a villain? Time would tell. I could see on Molly's face that she had many questions. She must have wondered what I was up to as we went on with our scattered conversation. Then, I decided to drop the bomb. That is how with five sentences that opened this chapter, I rescued my freedom.

The fight for your freedom may be painful to other people only because they are *trespassing,* but you must fight to the end then once you have it you can look at the casualties of your liberty and say, "I am sorry if I hurt you in the battle for my independence." That is the kindest you could ever get. Molly was deeply hurt, she stared at me with a mix of fury and surprise. She wasn't going to have any of that! "No friendship without accountability and that's what you are running away from, Phidia," she forcefully retorted.

Well, Molly was very right for the first part of the statement, but then I had a couple of questions lingering in my head. When does this accountability cross the line into meddling or enslaving, whichever communicates the criticality of the situation? And if this was friendship as per her words, then why not let the saw cut both sides? Where was the defining line for this accountability if it at all existed? Did that mean that all the other friendships that I had were supposed to directly report to Molly? Everything sounded a little complicated. *Was I guilty of defending my space?* You don't challenge a Type A personality with accountability. She knew the words that would nail me down, but I also knew the *difference* this time.

It was very unfortunate that I didn't save the relationship, but I recovered my independence and joy. It was worth everything to me! Sometimes, it is what it is. You can only do so much. At least I had many lessons to take home with me. I take responsibility for losing a somewhat beautiful friendship by allowing the wrong foundation. This explains why I write with so much passion as pertains this subject. Perhaps it might be the rescue boat for someone who is just about to sail the wrong direction.

ME TOO MOMENT	Is there an uninvited part of you that feels like an annoying screensaver because it keeps interfering with your relationships, one that you need to claim your freedom from?
	In one word, describe it.

The Giving and Receiving Posture

You have something valuable to give to the basket, do not let yourself be intimidated that you have nothing to offer. The black person has something to offer the white person and the vice versa is true. Neither of the two parties should feel that they are giving or receiving more value because each one gives according to the *measure of their stock*. You can only give what you have, and the thing is, I can't take your place neither can you take mine. What you give is unique to the relationship and by no means can I duplicate you. That should be a sufficient reason for us to have some respect for one another.

In my native Swahili language, we say *Kinyozi hajinyoi,* which means that the barber needs someone else to shave him. So, this barber is only a "pro" when shaving others but not himself. At some point, we all need to be helped regardless of what privilege we have.

Be *bold* enough to give what you have without shame and *humble* enough to receive what others offer without feeling the pressure to *match* them in any way. Don't let the nature of your gift to the relationship intimidate or bother you.

Boldness with *humility* is a beautiful blend for a lasting relationship. Many people tend to practice one and not the other. The misperception is that both cannot exist at the same time in the same vessel. We have either seen many bold, arrogant people whose boldness is the excuse for walking on people's heads or timid, humble people who cannot face a fly! Others still confuse the two. There are those who believe that being arrogant is a demonstration of boldness while others believe that being timid is a sign of humility. Whatever the case, anything less than the real thing is a threat to any relationship more so in a relationship where the parties have a history of struggling for supremacy! Without a clear understanding of boldness and humility, we cannot practice the *right* way of giving and receiving, which is a critical part of becoming an *equal* shareholder in the white privilege and all other privileges.

The Fearful Giver

Ah! You mean there's a wrong way to give or receive? Absolutely! We have only heard of the *cheerful* giver, how about the *fearful* one? It's not enough to give or receive. The attitude accompanying the two is very important. This includes the emotions felt during the giving process and the experience afterwards. How do you feel when you receive something? Do you feel like you must pay it back? Do you feel like you must keep saying "Thank you" every time you see the person who gifted you? Are you struggling with some sort of pressure to start every text with a "Thank you for blah blah blah?" as if one gracious "Thank you" did not suffice? Is there a temptation to always talk about the gift whenever you meet or interact with the giver lest they forget you are still grateful?

And it's not just about tangible gifts, it's also about the non-tangible ones. How many times do you say you are sorry when you are wrong? What do you say when that person compliments you? Can you just say *Thank you* without feeling the pressure to also compliment them? I mean, while it is good or nice to compliment other people, if you feel pressure to do so whenever they give you a compliment, then that is a red flag. While we expect that repeating the words "thank you" should portray how grateful we are, the message might be different. The first "thank you" is supposed to bear the literal meaning, the second one is simply for emphasis. The third one and all that follow thereafter mean that *I do not deserve it, so please take it back*. Do I sound crazy to say that I lost one of my clients for being "over grateful"? That my gratitude became a toxin that made her uncomfortable and she was forced to distance herself? Am glad she was open enough to talk about it, and that helped my future interactions with other people. Always beware of the ugly and bold Mr. Insecurity within your castle the next time you are tempted to over thank someone!

I was once that person. I struggled to receive compliments, I always looked for a way to give back a compliment to the giver. I went through the phase of wanting to keep my *privileged white* friends so badly to the point that I did not know when it became dangerous to have them in my life. I struggled with all kinds of emotions possible for a person suffering with the fear of rejection. The word "privileged white" is emphasized because there was something about that type of people that placed them at a more superior position in my head. That was a huge hindrance to ever having a mutual relationship with any of them.

When receiving and giving becomes a burden, then something must be done. There is a place called "too much," I once made an emergency landing there because my identity craft malfunctioned. It got to the point where after giving, I would be left feeling that my gift was just not good enough. I even wondered if the receiver appreciated it even when their words proved that they did.

There was some kind of fear within me attached to my giving and receiving. I doubt if I was the only weird person but that didn't make it any better. Though I did a great job hiding my struggle, I was nervous throughout the process of giving and receiving. I did not enjoy the giving or the receiving. While you expect the receiving part to automatically be fun, that wasn't the case for me. When Jackie, my special friend, lent me one of her cars, it was both sweet and bitter. Sweet that I finally had a car and bitter that I didn't know what to give back that would measure up to her gift. That is the awkwardness of insecurity. It poisons your gift whether outgoing or incoming and makes it hard to enjoy the process and the gift. It can drive you insane worrying about something that doesn't and possibly will never exist or minding a business that belongs to someone else. It leads you to the deepest pit of sorrow, wondering how the housefly at the porch will find his or her meal for the day! I don't know a robber of joy as brutal as insecurity.

Too Much!

Has insecurity ever pushed you to the temptation of wanting to diagnose yourself of a personality disorder not because it's fun, but because you just don't understand what the heck is wrong with you? My heart goes out to those struggling with such disorders. You are heroes and heroines who deserve a celebration for not giving up! Even more complicated because most of these insecurities *camouflage* as our personalities and so we sometimes find ourselves recruited into their "defense forces" whenever someone tries to point them out. Now, if receiving was this complicated, perhaps giving was supposed to bring me joy, but once again, I was making it harder for myself! So it was that whenever I cleaned a house for a privileged white person, I wondered if the house was clean enough for their standards. Even after they said how amazing the house looked, I still left thinking that maybe they did not mean what they said. I bet you don't like what you are reading; me too. But hold your horses, I am not done yet. Was it possible to overcome this level of anxiety or was I just doomed? How do you think I felt when Kathy, one of my first white customers, terminated my contract within two months because she doubted that I had mopped behind the trash can?

I promise you that I did the mopping. So, what was this all about? Then two hours after she expressed her dissatisfaction, I got another text from her. Did I read the text correctly? I went over it again. *Sorry, we won't need your services anymore. Our previous housekeeper is ready to come back.* It was on Halloween weekend, and I was supposed to take my kids for the school's yearly celebration. They were dressed up waiting for me downstairs. Suddenly, I felt so sick, I had to keep the kids waiting for thirty more minutes. My legs were weak as though I had been on a prolonged fast, followed by a rumbling stomach. I felt like the entire world had terminated a cleaning contract with me. Does this sound like a medical case to you? Maybe it's just the bare minimum for a person struggling with fear of rejection!

Had I been rejected again and this time around, by a privileged white person? That was such a big deal for me at the time because of the lies I had given control over me. She just did everything I needed to justify the tearing apart of my little world. I mourned the entire weekend, paralyzed with fear that I would never convince another white customer that I was good for business. One minute she was my fan and in less than two hours, she had changed her mind. And she wasn't going alone, she would check out all the other friends she had checked in with. I cried myself to sleep that Saturday night wishing I could reverse time. Then on Sunday night, yet another rejection.

Millie, a referral from Kathy, had also realized that my service would not work for her. At this point, there were no more tears left. But what exactly brought me this far into the pit? I was ready to answer that question before another week of advertising my business found me in ruins, otherwise my two kids and I would be homeless.

Sometimes you think that your hands are full until something else shows up screaming for greater attention as if the world is ending. Then, you realize you still had some space to hold more and that "full" only exists theoretically! It should amaze you how powerful and resourceful humans can become in the face of adversity.

Rejection Redefined

As the weekend ended, I realized that it was my *definition* for the word rejection that was hurting me this bad, so I decided to introduce another meaning of the same word in my head's dictionary. You know the way one word can have several meanings? I suppose the Lords of Grammar forgot to include one of the most important meanings of this word. I was armed to correct the oversight and here I went. *Rejection is a bold attempt by which the perpetrator honorably and graciously acknowledges their inability to handle the gift within their target.* Boom! My perspective changed and I began to see rejection as a filter that keeps out of my life the people who don't deserve me and a *faithful* guard to the gates of my destiny. Based on my context I was going to stick with this meaning *forever*. Then, I had something else to add to close every loophole and silence every accusation. That *the people meant for your destiny will always give you another chance even when you goof*. Since Kathy did not, I was ready to close that chapter.

Have you heard of anyone being allergic to honor? I have never. This definition ushered me into another realm. All of me was screaming with excitement, *Bring it on! Bring it on! Bring it on!* The magic worked just perfectly. Bam! The tables had been turned. I realized the honor that Kathy had shown me through this text and how much of that honor she deserved in return. She did not publicize it to neighbors; she personally told me. She could have chosen to endure me or just give me the silent treatment, which would have been more difficult and disrespectful for both of us. So, why not give her what she was worth? Didn't she deserve a taste of the very grace she had shown me? She certainly did. Again, she did not feel graced to give me another chance, so she did not belong to my destiny. In the same spirit of honor, I needed to honorably let her go, and I was ready for this.

So, I wrote … "Kathy, what an honor it was to serve you though for a short time. In case you need my services in the future, please do not hesitate to get in touch with me. Thank you." Wow! Did I sound like a queen in charge of her own palace? I hope I did. No longer harassed by my fear of the so-called "white rejection," *woo-hoo!* I was so calm that I even doubted my intentions. This was truly a defining moment for me. I don't mean that the struggle ended there, but this became my power source where I would always fall back to gain soundness of mind and reposition myself as a queen whenever I felt threatened. What freedom, what a joy! But sure enough, that insecurity was worth gallons of poison and if I survived, anyone can.

When you have been a victim of rejection, this interracial collaboration journey will not be the easiest but watching yourself grow out of timidity into boldly articulating your value and expectations with humility and compassion will be the sweetest thing ever! We define how we want to be treated. If people treat you differently than how you expect, just show them your expected standards by adhering to them yourself and everyone will follow suit or jump ship. Don't say much. Just fold up your sleeves and show the way.

ME TOO MOMENT	All of us in one way or the other have experienced rejection. If you were to redefine rejection from a positive perspective, what would it be?
	In one word, what vibe does the new meaning give you?

Living as the King or Queen

People don't respect words as much as they do actions. The people we love most can be the most difficult to deal because of familiarity. They may not take you as seriously as you want them to. After a messy divorce, I struggled to keep my sanity because my family was all over my space. Whichever "room" I walked in for solitude and serenity they were right there. I believe they meant well, but they were driving me nuts. I had to learn to act with my mouth shut.

Do you even realize how much we misuse our mouths? The purpose of the mouth should only be to set the record straight, and that's about it. The rest should be spoken with your actions. If you keep telling people what you want, unfortunately, they will begin to take you as a mediocre. It only turns into a soothing lullaby after some time until the day you act what you want. Kings and queens create a precedence by not repeating themselves. That way, their first word takes the day, and no one waits for a second word.

When you go into the marketplace, you are out to invest value and reap the same if not more. Your money and time are at stake. You don't go out just to play games. No! A treasure for a treasure is the rule of the game. It is not a game of emotions, but a game of the mind. Imagine standing there and feeling sorry for the poor traders whose products you do not need. Then, out of sympathy, you decide to spend all the money you have buying unnecessary stuff to help promote their business. Well, they will be smiling all the way to their bank accounts as you mourn your loss all the way to poverty, courtesy of your emotions.

We are just about to step into the marketplace of privilege. We are embarking on a serious assignment with the privilege to birth a shelter and *real* value for all people from every race, color, nation, and tongue. We might have to disrupt the way the privilege operates currently to get the baby out. It will remain white privilege, nothing to worry about there as that's unlikely to change. We have no intention to lose the privilege nor the shelter. We must remember that privileges are going to be here for as long as humanity exists, and worse still new ones keep emerging. Not that I am a big fan of them, I just realize that my ability to prevent their existence is limited. The hard reality is that the futile attempts to kill them would only make for more angry brothers from the fighting races.

But we are about to set a pace for the world to handle these privileges honorably and gracefully, whether the privileges be white, black, brown, or yellow! By keeping all our emotions at bay, we can get value by investing into worthwhile relationships with those who are privileged as part of getting shares in this advantage. Likewise, the privileged too must see the peace and abundance they are missing for not partnering with the underprivileged. But the basics have to be dealt with on both sides for this to happen. Any symptom of insecurity must not be ignored. It must be traced to its roots and addressed by both the privileged and the underprivileged for us to engage in equal interracial relationships which would make us partners in the white privilege and others.

Returning to the haven of your race is not an option; you must stay out there and proactively establish as many *mutual* interracial relationships as you possibly can. If it doesn't work with one, don't give up. Move on to the next person and keep at it until you find one who is willing to partner with *equal* shareholding. Don't accept being a *minor* shareholder just because you feel desperate especially if you are the less privileged. If you do, this will put the life of Mother Privilege and Baby Shelter at stake. This principle applies to all relationships, including romantic relationships.

You have waited and persevered this long; you can wait a little longer especially with every sign of labor pain all around you. The baby you have been expecting for years is here. That's why there is so much turmoil with privilege. Don't take anything less than the original. Step out like a queen or king, engage with the privileged without fear or intimidation because you are a worthwhile partner. If you are privileged, don't let guilt, shame or whatever insecurity keep you from collaborating with the underprivileged. You have no stake in the existence of this privilege and you know what you know. That's the cost of buying shares in this privilege and finding unity so that all people, regardless of their race or ethnicity, can stand to profit.

You Ain't a Rescue Kid

I was a member of a women's fellowship a while back where we decided to contribute our help for a cancer victim. I was the only black woman, and the rest were white. When I gave my contribution, they struggled to take it. I insisted that they take it because I had *something* to offer. They looked a little surprised, but they accepted. I came to realize it perhaps wasn't their fault. They had interacted with another black lady who was always asking for help, so she spoiled it for all of us. I understand she might have been needy but sometimes, it's just *neediness in the mind*. When I gave this money, I was sharing a room with my kids because I couldn't afford to rent two rooms or an apartment. Worse still, that one room was on a subsidized rent because the normal rent rates were too high for me to afford. That should have qualified me as needy. But I believed that I had the capacity to help this cancer victim. Fifty dollars wasn't going to move me to a new house anyway!

Don't go into any relationship, whether interracial or whatever kind, as though you are being rescued. You have got something to offer to the relationship too. In case you discover that the other party sees you as inferior and is not open to receiving from you, please do yourself and that other party justice. Take the bold and humble move of walking away. And this does not only apply to people who are not open to receiving your gift; even the ones that keep receiving and never give back to you. If you give someone three likes and get none from them, please STOP! Unless they qualify to be a busy "celebrity" who has no time to create a relationship with you and you are happy to keep it one way. If all they needed was a warm-up these three likes should do the magic, otherwise they are sending you a message that they devalue you and staying is detrimental to your identity.

Walking away to honor yourself is not revenge, what matters is the *motive* in which case your objective is to honor yourself while revenge is aimed at hurting the unkind party. But don't just walk away, do so with grace and marinate it with a heart of compassion. As you take your bags to walk away, make sure to leave some love and empathy. Try to understand what they are struggling with but don't become *emotionally entangled,* just walk away! Do you realize that even a control freak deserves some compassion? Their behavior is evidence that they are struggling with some insecurities too even though most of them have a serious blind spot about this fact.

The person holding you captive is also captive to their own insecurities. They are actually not your real hosts. They are simply a physical manifestation of the invisible master of insecurity unto whom they are enslaved. If they succeed to control you, they are not to blame but *your insecurity responding to theirs* is. We must claim our freedom first from the invisible then the visible will comply.

Remember, you are not the only one facing a struggle, so please do not walk away heartlessly, wishing the controller a hell full of fire and brimstone. Be gentle but don't postpone the move; the sooner the better for both of you. Be sure to do two things, maybe three — acknowledge that their shoes are difficult to wear, explore the possibility of a hug depending on your risk assessment and immediately after that, jump ship. That is an important part of the process of buying shares into any inter-racial relationship and ultimately into the contentious privilege, and this is true for all relationships.

Don't keep a relationship that has zero shares under your name. If you do, then your efforts will not count, and at the end of the day, you will feel cheated. This will only widen the gap we are trying to close. You are likely to gain that relationship back just by walking away than you would by enduring. Genuine friends want you because you are secure, you understand yourself and you know what you deserve. So, don't shy off from your radical decision. Furthermore, you will have to lose one fake friend to create space for a more genuine one. I do not mean to downplay the pain of losing a friend but if it costs your net worth then it's better not having it at all.

If you must lose a friend, it had better be at the beginning by setting the record straight rather than later after you have invested your time, emotions, and resources like my case with Molly. Don't wait to pull out your cards in the middle of the journey. Place them at the table at the word go. Let the boundaries be clear from the beginning. This is critical for any relationship, even more so when two embattled races need to work together to build an empire out of ruins. Each person in the relationship must keep their safe space and safeguard their sanity. That doesn't make them any meaner but rather worthwhile partners in building a shelter out of privilege.

Secure and Open

Each party in this endeavor must feel secure enough with privilege if anything meaningful will develop. Being secure makes open and genuine racial discussions possible. Have you noticed how everyone in a mixed-race group stays away from discussions that pertain to racism? Why is there so much tension when that topic comes up with everyone giving it the silent treatment? Why is there so much effort to keep this matter off limits? Could it be that the parties are insecure, and that silence about the topic happens to be the only strategy they can think of to apply to safeguard their respective courts? How then can we become shareholders in the privilege and create the shelter unless we talk about privilege?

So, is there a possibility that we can talk about privilege without talking about racism? I doubt. And not just talk about it but do it with so much grace so that our eyes open to a world of new possibilities. Earlier in the book we read that we are NOT the privilege itself. Detaching ourselves from the privilege helps us to be open to whichever direction the discussion of privilege and racism goes. As long as we see ourselves as the privilege, we are bound to take it personal which really hurts and hinders our progress as far as this issue pertains.

Secure people are open. They talk about emotive issues without snapping. Most times we flare up because of some sort of insecurity. Are you tired of seeing the word "insecurity" in this book? Perhaps we should change the title of this book to "Haunting insecurity," but never mind. This should serve as a witness of how much of this "monster" I have wrestled and triumphed, no wonder I can write freely about it, and that is a statement of hope for anyone feeling overwhelmed with their struggle. When an insecure person faces a conflict, this is the kind of conversation which goes on in their mind—*How could she do that to me? Does she know who I am? I will prove to her that I am better than this!* See all the insecurity contained in that mental chat, which then leaves the victim upset and wanting to prove a point. You have no business proving what you already are or have because it is self-evident. Who you are is your basic minimum, and it runs through your fabric, so what exactly is there to prove? It seems like if we solve the issue of insecurity, we solve the issue of anger, too. People who are insecure will manifest it by being controlling or playing the servant role. There are only two seats for such people. There is no such a thing as an in-between seat.

Let us swing into action. Don't just sit there and complain that no one is giving you shares, because no one will. If this is valuable to you, then value must be deposited. Arise, and get the work done. We need these interracial relationships in every nation, state, county, city, and neighborhood. Even the privileged white police officer will not need a systemic change (although it's still critical) to stop racial killings because he has enough of these black brothers back at home and they hold him accountable. I say this without dismissing the fact that we also have very responsible, secure privileged white police officers who have their privilege under control and treat the underprivileged with dignity. I am a witness to this.

If you are still reading this, I admire your boldness and humility! This is not the kind of stuff for everybody but the chosen few. The best part of this choosing business is that you are the contestant and the judge at the same time. If you miss out on being on the list, then you only have yourself to blame. The criterion is simple: tactfully marrying the two somewhat estranged partners— boldness and humility under the roof of compassion. If you have this in place, then you are qualified to become an equal partner in the interracial relationship and in the privilege too. Congratulations for *earning* your shares in the privilege! You are ready for the next milestone. Yay!

The 'Practicals' of Love

Martin Luther King, Jr. said, "Freedom is never voluntarily given by the oppressor; it must be demanded by the oppressed," and for our case, I would add, "and demanded with boldness, compassion, and humility."

Remember you are dealing with a hurting host. The person holding you hostage is under commands from a ruthless commander known as insecurity. They don't have fun with this control business but still that doesn't justify their behavior. Separate emotions and logic and free yourself, then you can consider freeing them if that doesn't put your painfully earned liberty at stake. Be gentle with them as long as it doesn't delay or cost your freedom.

But the order must be followed, your freedom begins with subduing your insecurity before facing the visible control freak. No amount of reasoning can persuade your fear to let you go. You just have to rebel "violently." Recognizing that you are captive to your insecurity is the beginning of recovering your self-love, which is the same love you share with others. The joy of your freedom is worth every investment. It's the fuel that keeps you going until the process is complete and that liberty from your insecurity is your *ticket* to engaging in mutual relationships within the marketplace of privilege. Below I discuss this process step by step. The journey to freedom is never a smooth road. Having an accountability partner is often helpful. I hope your Double MC club will come in handy for you in this.

1. Relationships Checkpoint - Identify a relationship that is critical to you but gives you anxiety. For the main purpose of this book, an interracial relationship would be more ideal, but you are not limited to just that type. It can be a marriage relationship, sibling, parent, friend, neighbor, employer, or whatever kind of relationship is bothersome on some level. Check for red flags like the inability to say no, a temptation to overdo things like praise, appreciation, or apology, fear of giving or receiving, pressure to respond to calls or texts promptly even when you are busy, and the issue is not urgent. These are just but a few things to notice. You can add whatever is specific to your situation to the list.

2. Face the bug - Write down exactly what you are anxious about and make sure to use the person's name and see how that makes you feel. Anxiety results from fear and so being specific in my case meant writing the following sentences: I fear that Molly will not find me pleasant, which might lead her to reject me. I fear losing Molly for not meeting her standards. Here it's a freestyle sentence as long as you can articulate the object of your fear. The objective is to be as genuine with yourself as possible in identifying the fear.

3. Redefine the object of fear with a positive connotation - In my case of the fear of rejection, I gave a new meaning to the object of fear. I redefined rejection to mean "honor" and the fear was no more! Notice how changing the perception of the object affects the fear; things are as we see them.

4. Envision the end and fight - Imagine the joy, freedom, and honor of reclaiming your self-love and think about the peace you are missing out on. Here, the choice of words is as important as it is in step three. Use words that will trigger the fighter in you. I recommend the following actions for maximum value in this stage:

- Get a self-love journal.
- Write down your expected end including the feelings and emotions. For example, I will feel honored, I will cry tears of joy, I can't wait to feel the peace and freedom, or people will respect me like a queen or king.

- Take charge. This is where you break down the actionable part of the fight by taking responsibility for taking the servant seat and working backwards to your freedom. Identify the loopholes you created and begin closing them. In my case, it was cutting down on information sharing and saying "no," *even if it was just for the sake of it* in order to familiarize myself with my "new normal." If the person doesn't get the message or tries to clamp you down, speak up. You can ask for a break from the relationship depending on your assessment of the situation. Remember to show compassion and humility in your boldness. This is a place of making or breaking and you must want your freedom very much to get through this stage. You are also free to make use of a "heartless" loving friend like Lulu to thrust you through your action-taking furnace of refinement.

CHAPTER FOUR

Change Your Weapon: Shooting the Bullet of Love

Radicalized at Home

If you are a stubborn parent, what do you expect your kids to be? I bet "stubborn squared," for the love of math. My eleven-year-old daughter is my best friend, but she sure gives me a run for my money. She is "Phidia reloaded." I so often have to find the right words to convince her that there is a better way of doing things, because she often appears surer of herself than sureness itself! Being a typical African parent, now living in America, it often "vandalized" my nerves to even imagine that I needed to engage in this "convincing" business at all. This is because in a typical African home, the parent is supposed to know everything, and no one should dare challenge him or her. So, what the heck was this "negotiation" process with my child supposed to be? All I grew up with was "shape up" or "ship out." So, being the loyalist I am, I kept wondering, *shouldn't I duplicate the same parenting strategy?* If so, how was this type of parenting plan going to work under an American system where, in my opinion, the child seems to have more rights than the parent?

Poor me! It was baptism by fire to come to terms with everything. No one took the time to explain to me what was going on. I would be there, demanding obedience and citing how well I obeyed my own parents as a means of intimidation, really—anything, anyhow or anyway, just provided "it worked" for me. Then, my little girl savagely interrupting, "Mom, that was *your* generation. Welcome to America, we are the alpha generation," and her little brother cheering, "Yeah, mom," —as if to say, *Woman, you are on your own.* This boy has always held a level of reasoning above his age since he was little. It didn't surprise me when he was selected for the Gifted and Talented Program. So, I would be left thinking, "Do I want to engage with him?" Engaging him meant choosing my words, and I was rarely in the mood, so I would just swallow it. I so often ended up abandoned because my annoying little pumpkins had already moved on after their "signature" statements. I did all the screaming and yelling possible, sometimes both at the same time! These days, nothing much is left.

"I can't believe how rude you are! I won't let you talk to me like that again," I would swear to my daughter, choking with frustration. The anger itself was enough to kill me without any reinforcement. I was angry not because of the original trespass, but because my ego as a parent was being trashed. I really took it personal. My mind would race while trying to devise a quick-fix strategy to subdue these little heads and vindicate myself with urgency. Then, I would remember that I was in America and not in Africa, a land where spanking was not part of the quick-fix deal, until I realized that this was going to kill me *and* our relationship too. The more I yelled, the more reasons she gave me to yell. So, I came up with a perfect strategy — reverse psychology.

Calling Out the Potential

Instead of calling out her rudeness and disobedience in the heat of the moment, I decided that I would call out her *potential* kindness and obedience. Any time she acted defiantly I had a signature response too for her. "Baby girl, I love your kind boldness. I know you are a good kid and I trust your intentions." Was she kind? Not quite. Did I trust her intentions? Not sure. So, was I lying to her? No, I was speaking the future to a worrisome present. At first, it felt strange because the entitled part of me believed that she deserved some wrath, but with time and practice, I got the hang of it. I had to swallow gallons of pride though, and I thought I would die of poison. It was like swimming against a current all the time but thankfully I purposefully and intentionally survived.

The results of my pain were priceless. At first, she asked, "What do you mean by kind boldness, Mom," to which I said, "Just break the two apart and take them word for word." She still didn't seem to understand, neither did I bother to explain it to her. She needed to think it out herself. Then, one day she said with guilt, "I know I am bold but not very kind to you." Even with this halting admission, I still said nothing. I just looked at her, smiled and kept at it.

During the days that followed, I started noticing that she was being more open to correction and guidance and our relationship eventually changed for the better! She now makes one of my most pleasurable companies, even though we still fight a lot, as you would expect for two strong-willed girls and inborn leaders, for that matter. But we fight with love for good, because she wants to manifest that "good" and "kind" that her mother sees in her. I still use this strategy when dealing with her to this day. I call out her potential, instead of her current nasty reality even though sometimes I have to change the strategy, especially if I notice she is taking advantage of it. Does it mean that I had radicalized my own daughter by focusing on her challenges? Though I cannot assume full responsibility over her behavior, I believe I acted as an *aide* to it. If it's already bad, then why make it worse with your own words?

It is not enough to be the sober party in these interracial relationships. The fact that you don't execute hate is good but not good enough. Is there a possibility that your attitude towards the hater has contributed to more hate radicals than you can possibly comprehend? Not that I seek to excuse them for their hatred, but are they solely responsible? Are there some kind, loving humans who are now radicalized haters because of your *words and actions?* I acknowledge that my analogy is not a one-size fits all for every relationship. Different situations call for different strategies. For example, I have a different approach for my eight-year-old son. For him, I just call "the spade" on him and he will be quick to correct himself without a lot of convincing, maybe just some few tantrums. He just has a different type of personality than his sister. I am always keen not to "kill" any of my kid's personality because it is designed to serve *their* life purpose. All the time my parenting goal has been to make the best out of them without necessarily changing who they really are.

Unfortunately, we don't always have an eternity to learn people. Sometimes, it's just a spontaneous interaction, and you must be quick to figure out within those two minutes what approach to take to expose the love in that person however nasty the situation may be. On some occasions, I look at someone discriminating against me and my heart is boiling just to revenge or shame their intent. Instead, I gently say to them, *I appreciate your love and support.* Imagine how that makes them feel? You should see the executive treatment I will get the next time I come to that same office! I bet if I engaged them in a hateful fight, it would end worse for both of us. Not that I am against a fight, sometimes it's inevitable, but if love can do it then no need for an angry hateful fight against the same hate. Love and kindness should always be given the first chance (and maybe the second and the third) in resolving our differences.

People *know* when they are acting in hate. Let me say that again. People know when they are acting in hate. You probably don't need to tell them. I don't mean to downplay the role of candid feedback in defeating hate, however. But enough times, the perpetrator is very aware and actively and deliberately seeking an angry fight of hate. You can choose to engage them in a fight and *fulfil their objective* or use a gentle way to *point them* to the loving part of their heart because *everyone* has that spot, even a serial killer! So, let's swallow our pride and entitlement and call that "hidden love" from each other into existence and go about filling the world with love instead. This strategy is applicable for all relationships whether, personal or interracial, you just have to be strategic on how to apply it and be keen to know when a change of strategy is required.

Love and Hate Co-existence

I look at the heart as *dichotomous*—one side that loves and another that hates. We need both emotions within the same heart because there is a season and a target for each. If the heart doesn't stock some hate, what shall we do when evil shows up at our doorstep? We need to hate evil, right? So, yes, we need hate inside the very same heart that carries love, the secret lies in the ability to direct it the right way to a *deserving* target. This qualifies hate to be categorized as a "necessary evil," an evil that you can't do without!

When you see someone acting with hate to another, it just means that they have lost the steering wheel of their heart. They have been *kidnapped* by their own emotions. They need help to rehabilitate themselves. Both love and hate are powerful emotions, and they can seize the wheel any time if you sleep on the job. But I would consider hate the most defiant and notorious of the two especially when it comes to relating with humans. This evil world doesn't make it any easier for "him" or "her." Hate tends to have more misleading chances than love does by pursuing the wrong target out of his or her vindictive nature and having a "sensible" justification for it. No wonder we struggle controlling ourselves from hating a "deserving" interracial party.

No single human, however evil they may be, qualifies for hatred in my opinion. We must separate evil from the person so we can accord love to the person and reserve our hate for their evil act. There is a place and a partner for each of the two emotions. There is no need to "cheat" on each other. Where humans are concerned, love should be set free to adopt anyone, anywhere, anytime while hate needs to be fully tamed because it's impact can be very grave. A life could be lost, and the damage may never be reversed. Furthermore, I don't think there's anything like loving the wrong person especially in the context of interracial love. *Real love* is supposed to be safe, just make sure you don't confuse it for anything else. I should not be calling it *real* love in the first place because love is real and should be sufficient without any adjective, right?

Love is a full package, even when it comes to romantic relationships. It's the same love that should lead you out of bad relationships because love is caring, wise and bold (contrary to the traditional narrative that portrays love as weak and stupid). But so often, we just rebel against its voice and then we have the guts to blame it for the consequences. If whatever you call love doesn't protect you, then I suggest that you must give it another name. That should give us a license to love one another *freely* without fear.

Based on my previous assertion that the heart is dichotomous by nature, that means that at any given point in time, you are either giving love or giving hate. There is no in-between, nor is there a possibility of giving nothing. Have you heard someone say, "I don't hate her, neither do I love her?" Do you really believe them? I used to, but now I don't. This, in my opinion, is self-deception. I discovered that you must be giving something, however little it is. When that statement is used, it's either disingenuous or the quantity (of hate or love) being given is just so negligible that the giver has to be very *attentive* to their heart to know what they are giving.

The moment we encounter someone, whether in person or through their information, something registers in our mind as like or dislike. That "little something" is a component of love or hate. Our minds automatically pick a side and swiftly advise the heart to do the same. The more we interact with the person or their information, the more we feed that little something into a mountain of love or a flood of hate. But even before we made the mountain or the sea, we started by giving a little bit of it. That's the nature of the heart. Bottom line, the heart is always giving out something and we must be plugged in to *discern* and *direct* it.

Sword for Sword?

Let's revisit the story of my daughter being elected as the president of her elementary school at age ten. She ran for the position of council president against three other candidates of different ethnicities. Based on the location of the school, her ethnic group was not the majority. When she got the position, it was clear that she had been elected mostly by students of a different ethnicity from hers. This was a great moment of victory against racial division. During her graduation, her speech came at a time when the country was in turmoil owing to the killing of George Floyd. I noted that social media was being used to spread a lot of racism and hate. So, I thought to myself, maybe I could use this opportunity to counter the hatred by writing something positive about our racial differences. This prompted me to do a post to celebrate the little kids who had triumphed over the stigma of diversity to elect this beautiful little black schoolgirl as council president.

Unfortunately, someone interpreted my social media post to mean that I was trying to implicate the school as having no diversity. When I looked at the comments, which were a little harsh and judgmental, I had the option to add fuel to the fire by "telling the person off." That was the easiest option. It was evident, based on several reader's feedback that this person had deliberately changed my post to mean what *they* wanted. They seemed to have been fighting their own battle, which I had no knowledge about. I decided to ask one of my friends what the best response would be. "Just fire her?" she said. "What do you mean, Esther? Can I fire her without catching some fire myself, or is there a safe way to fire someone? Fire is fire, right?" I asked with some humor just to counter her boiling anger.

Some people can really get angry on your behalf, and you are left confused about whether to thank them or not. "Just tell her to keep her baggage out of your page because this post is clearly about love, period!" I thought I was breathing fire, but she was vomiting brimstones! Her response was factual, but it wasn't going to be the best for this particular situation. It was clear that her advice was from the abundance of anger and resentment for this follower. So, I prayed, "God please, just like Esther I am really annoyed, but what should I say to this person to achieve the same love that drove me to write this post?"

I believe He answered me by changing my attitude. At that point, I felt so *compassionate* for the shoes this lady was wearing, that I *chose to understand* what she might have been going through. I began to acknowledge how difficult it was to be her. That immediately changed my perspective toward her. I stopped seeing her as someone attacking me or driven purely by evil motives. I realized how much love she needed and decided to give it to her the best way I could. That changed my response drastically, as I wore a loving heart and wrote, "I am sorry this is how you felt. The main purpose of this page is to spread love and unite people. I hope your eyes can see that love and unity expressed throughout the entire post." Then I concluded my response with some love/heart emojis. Was it comfortable doing that? No, but I did it anyway and the *peace* in return was invaluable. My text deflated her wrath, she was guilty of receiving my *unexpected* love and so she went ahead to explain herself. I successfully disarmed her with love while she expected a sword.

Keeping the 'L' side Up!

See how close I got to trading my peace by creating some more hate? There was only a *thin* line separating the love from the hate. Based on the timing and her choice of words, I had all the motivation in the world to cross that "damn" line. I only needed to close my eyes, click the send button, and wake up on the other side of love called hate. They both exist in the same coin, just on different sides. If you flip that coin reading love, the other side reads hate. Never forget, it is the same heart that loves that hates too. You must constantly be *deliberate* in keeping the love (L) side of the coin up when handling humans. There's always a temptation to shoot the human and their act with the *same* bullet, which should never be the case. Each deserve a different kind of bullet. That helps us appreciate when people do insane things just how close the two divides are. Not that I am an ambassador of evil, I just choose to understand where it comes from.

But how can we stay on the L side as far as loving our interracial counterparts is concerned? Acting in the heat of the moment exposes the ugliest part of our dichotomous hearts. *Taking time* before you respond gives a chance for your mental filter to separate hostile emotions from logic. It also provides you ample time to ask someone else for their opinion. When you ask, you're disseminating the weight of the pressure to another person, which then consequently deflates you so that you can see everything for what it is and not just what it looks like on the surface.

Have you ever responded in anger and afterwards you want to bury yourself from the disgrace contained in your words? What looked and felt like victory in the heat of the moment turns out to be a disgusting package of shame. You must understand what I mean if you have ever acted in anger. I bet we all have. Things are not always what they appear to be because emotions can be very deceptive and sort of evil. Evil in the sense that they get you possessed until they plunge you into the furnace, and then standing afar off from the flames, they cry out, *fire! You are on your own; quick, escape!* If this does not constitute evil, then I am sorry for the oversight; please help me redefine this word!

We must act in defiance to these ruthless and selfish emotions as part of our efforts to defeat hate. Always stop for a moment and ask yourself, why did they write or say this to me? Your emotions will be quick to answer, "Because they hate you?" But, please don't believe them; it's all a lie. The correct answer is this: *they have a troubled self, and you just happen to have been in their hood,* so you got a feel of their world and pain. With that in mind, you have some compassion and are safe to ask the next question —What should be my reply? Once you get a response, it doesn't stop there. Move a step higher to answer the question — *why this response and what outcomes do I expect?* By the time you finish answering these four questions, the bullet of hate will have undoubtedly been overtaken by the bullet of love. It's always better to check yourself before reacting. Any time someone is hateful, their *default* weapon is hatred. Unfortunately, it usually presents itself without effort and it is always in huge supply! Never make responding to hateful comments an *emergency*. You are allowed to take your sweet time so you can say the right thing. You must be deliberate in *delaying* the process of attacking so you have time to find the weapon of love inside the crowded arsenal. It is the only weapon that doesn't leave you with a feeling of guilt when the battle is over. Such patience in reacting is worth every dime of our time!

ME TOO MOMENT	Have you ever responded to hatred with hatred, or anger with anger?
	In one word, how did you feel afterwards?

Hate ... A High-Maintenance Product

The weapon of love is rarely used, so often it lies rusty in the arsenal yet that doesn't affect its effectiveness. The peace that comes with it is worth the investment. However, we must also be deliberate in using it so *frequently* that it becomes our default weapon.

As a family, we have this mantra that goes like this ... *Both love and hate are costly, but hate is way too expensive*. Even though hate is readily available and always "on sale," it is a premium product when it comes to maintenance. It costs lives and deprives the hater the most important thing they have in life, peace! No hater is peaceful regardless of how hard they try to look the part. Hate is one of the defiant products that violate the law of demand and supply. The ultimate price of hate is way too high yet there's always an overflow of buyers and an overwhelming supply at no initial cost! Hate never runs out because our selfish sinful nature is a brooding environment for it. This explains why we must be intentional in rejecting it because it is highly stocked, which means that it's all our eyes can see when we walk into the arsenal. The temptation is always right before our own eyes.

When the deal looks good, think twice. Why don't we realize the high cost of maintenance that comes with hate? Whose fault is that really? The seller? Not at all. The disclaimer is always right below the purchase price, and it reads, "Please consult our maintenance team before committing yourself to our special products." Sadly though, only a few buyers see this disclaimer let alone read it because hate comes as an angel of light, claiming to be a friend who "fights for us". We think we are vindicating ourselves by hating, but the truth is that we are destroying ourselves. Hate roams all over the place causing havoc, creating casualties, and leaving the burden of healing to you. Though hate comes deceptively promising corner of paradise, they sure give a hell. So don't be enticed with the words "on-sale" or "for free" to forget the ultimate price you will pay. Remember, attention to details is important. Read the entire package please before you buy!

On the other hand, love is always at a high initial cost, which keeps it in low demand. The heart has a huge supply of it, though (there is surprisingly always so much love within our hearts), but many people seem to ignore love because they aren't willing to pay the purchase price. Love will never be on sale, there is always a price to pay. She will never try to market herself because she knows her worth. The seller doesn't ask for anything you don't have though. He doesn't take money, with love, only barter trade is accepted as a transacting currency. You *exchange* your selfish nature to purchase love. That makes it affordable and costly at the same time. This is because everyone has their selfish nature available to them, but letting it go is often like cutting a piece out of you.

We are so familiar with our selfish nature, that we can't envision a life without it. This could be a major reason why we have few buyers in this queue. The purchase price is a bit of a deal breaker. What we don't recognize is the free maintenance that comes with the love package. And that's not all! The love package is an *investment*. It *grows your value* each day, *manages your risks including protecting you from loss* and ultimately *spikes up your net worth*. This parcel has magic in it; it defies the math of addition and invokes high-end multiplication. This is what some people call favor — when the sacrifice of giving unmerited love triggers *a series of amazing, supernatural occurrences* within the space of the giver. I have become a beneficiary of this thing called favor enough times that I am fully convinced of what selfless love can accomplish for the giver; I will discuss this concept in further detail later in this chapter.

The Caravan of Unmerited Love

There is nothing special about loving someone that loves you. That is just the bare minimum for the average human being. But, when you lay down your selfish ambition to extend love to the so-called "unlovable" type (unlovable because they offer you zero motivation to be loved), you are setting yourself up for divine favor and exceeding kindness. You are stepping out of the ordinary to the extraordinary. I love to describe this act as the *VIP gate pass* from the natural to the supernatural, where miracles are the oxygen of the day. For what greater miracle is there but the experience of indescribable peace and joy in this life! It invokes exceeding goodness and abundance not just for you, but also the people around you and for generations to come.

Those that trade with hate attract misery not only to themselves but also those connected to them. So is love. The benefits of this package are felt by everyone around you. If you can't do it for the target, you can do it for yourself and your loved ones. I can't think of any better way to get you on board into the caravan of unmerited love.

Our beloved nation, and the broken world at large, needs unconditional love more than ever before. You might have heard of the statement borrowed from scripture that *love covers a multitude of sins*; that's what unmerited love is all about. Who of us has not committed an offense? Who among us has never found themselves in need of some cover for a mess they have personally manufactured? Then, why not do to others what we would like to see done to us? This is the business of sowing and staying back as we wait for the day of reaping to come our way. I think it is about time that we take advantage of the affordability (and the value of love) to extend this privilege into a shelter. We have, for the longest time, been fighting with hate against one another and against the privilege. That's why there is so much havoc and bad blood between black and white folks. I am quite sure the rest of the races feel the weight of it too.

Only fools use the same strategy that failed them and expect different results. We are not! It's time to load our cartridges with bullets of love as opposed to bullets of hate. I am not asking us to change the pistol; we still need the real you, but this time load yourself up with love. There is no need for rules where love is involved because love is *perfect* and makes everything right! Love cannot even be limited to the words in this book. It is both *adventurous* and *safe* at the same time. Just do it your way and let us recruit tens and thousands even millions of all races, colors, nations, and tongues into the caravan of unmerited love. We need to learn how to fight the effective, fierce fight of love! *There has never been and never will there be a weapon so powerful as love.* Let's find our commonality. If we focus on the differences, it will grow into a monster that devours us all. We are balancing on a seesaw. The weight of one keeps the other up in this socio-economic seesaw. We are not independent of one another; we are a family, yes, the human family.

The Labor of Love

Imagine anger being met with outrage! That amounts to an explosion that none of us wants to witness, much less be a part of. *Love can turn a terrorist into a peacemaker, a sinner into a saint, and a devil into an angel.* We must be stronger than our emotions. We must take charge and defy our selfish nature to produce something greater than ourselves, something beyond the obvious, simply because we have the power to do so! If we are going to *create* a shelter, then both black and white people must *labor* together with love and endurance. I call it labor because a lot of deliberate *restraint* and *self-sacrifice* are involved.

Creation doesn't happen passively. It is an active, intensive process in which something non-existent is brought into existence. It takes two to create, at least for a typical creation. But the two must labor in love to bring the creature into existence. When I was little,

I used to think making babies was an easy engagement. Then, I got married, and there were those two years of un-rewarded hard work! It was only two years, but it felt like an eternity! My heart goes out to those that have tried longer than I did; they stand as heroes regardless of the outcome. Those two years gave me a totally different perspective of the reality of conception as opposed to the ideal imagination of the naive girl I was back in the day. When our baby was finally conceived, I had such high value for the gift than I would ordinarily have if I never experienced the labor of love. I guess that will be our predicament when baby Shelter is born.

Heal Them With Kindness

The philosophy of killing them with kindness is outdated in my opinion. The motive of this type of kindness is worrisome. The scripture in Romans 12:20 says, "Therefore If your enemy is hungry, feed him; If he is thirsty, give him a drink; For in so doing you will heap coals of fire on his head." I hope that no one from the so-called "outsiders" deserves the title enemy just because they don't look like us. We are all sons and daughters of the same nation; if not nation, then we share the same earth and human species. But in case you just insist on having enemies, I have no option but to respect your wish. But, before I let you have your way, I would like to submit something to help you decide whether you still want to make anyone your enemy.

If anyone makes it to a list of your enemies, as per this scripture, you are supposed to *feed* them and *refresh* them. Sadly, there is no option number two. For those who like to keep a long list of enemies, this is not funny at all. Who wants to feed and quench the thirst of just one unlikeable person let alone a hundred? So, my appeal to you is simple, keep the "damn" list as short as possible (if at all you must have one) by looking at each person that annoys you as you would do for a difficult family member. This is where you don't have to actually like the person, but you can still figure out a way to love them without giving yourself any other options whatsoever. You can't choose family after all; it just happens, and you are stuck with them for better or for worse. Every day you (should) just focus on how to make it work. Obviously, this goes against all short-term logic. The cost of defeating hate has to beat all rationalization or else we have to prepare for the worst. This means that you don't look for any justification to love, like Nike, you *just do it*! Furthermore, some of the people we consider as enemies are simply *voluntary coaches for our destiny!* So, how does that qualify them to be enemies?

While I agree the black person is hurting and must put up a fight, the basis of this fight must be founded on love for this fight to yield results. The best way to vindicate yourself with someone who hurts you is by giving them love. The sting of love is so powerful that it leaves the offender feeling as though a heap of hot coals was placed upon their heads, yet the hot coals was NOT your goal in the first place. *Healing* the offender's wound and *refreshing* their heart was the objective of your love (because people who hurt you are already hurting). And the so-called "hot coals" are not meant to kill the person but to make them feel the heat, realize that they are standing in a dangerous position so they can make a move, *a shifting of their hateful standing to the place of love!* Wow!

So, if you were looking for a way to vindicate yourself, how much more vengeful can it get? *Isn't getting the hater to stop hating the best payback?* Else are we also haters hiding under the blanket of "love"? This is not just a religious teaching. It is practical across the divide. You have heard the saying, "Kill them with kindness," but here I mean to say, *heal them with kindness;* because they just don't hate for fun, their hearts are wounded, or they are struggling with something no wonder your kindness should be aimed at healing and not killing. Do you know that not all kindness is kind? There is some kindness which comes from a place of pride, hate, or revenge. This may shock you, but it is the truth.

The attitude behind the kindness matters a lot and makes a whole lot of difference in how we feel after giving out kindness. Love must accompany your kindness if it will bring any positive change. I don't mean to suggest that this will be easy, not at all! It is a battle for the humble and brave. So, the blacks should replace the bullet of hatred, anger and bitterness against the privilege with a bullet of love, and the white person must meet this fight of love with empathy, understanding, and compassion. *Empathy must meet empathy, compassion must encounter compassion, and love must shake hands with love* for privilege to produce the shelter. Two cannot walk together unless they agree. This is part of the agreement process where the good that is given is the good that is reciprocated. Let your *loving*-kindness heal this broken world whichever side you give it from.

Being in the Zone of Partnership

Dismissing someone's pain puts them further on edge and widens the gap even more, thus reducing the possibility of creating anything good together. The white person must acknowledge the black person's pain and vice versa because the two divides are hurting. It is not only the black person that hurts as we might have always imagined. You cannot create trouble and escape it. We live in a world of sowing and reaping, which many people refer to as karma. *The trouble you give is the trouble you get*. We can see the pain of the white folk in how he angrily and dismissively responds to the cry of the black folk. There's anger and resentment which has crippled the two sides. So, both blacks and whites need the healing and the peace that comes with this shelter. But then, the creation process is preceded by coming together and this togetherness calls us to a place of *equality*.

Perceptions about each other must be set properly. Both sides need to pull their share of the weight. In my short life, I have seen white people who can stand a black person as long as he is operating at a lower socioeconomic status in comparison. There were several relationships that worked for me provided I drove an old car and remained a housekeeper. What happened when I bought a new car and decided to reintroduce myself as a public speaker on my social media page? It was just that easy. The good thing is that you can call yourself anything and (almost) nobody will dare ask for an explanation. I just did — housekeeper and speaker — don't they rhyme? *Eazy peazy*, I was so excited.

But perhaps I trespassed the perimeters that the privileged had confined and defined me by their perceptions of me! Some clients just said, "Oh, you have a new car?" And that's the last time I saw the tip! Not that I was entitled to it, mind you, but I still thought they would finish what they had started. Or was *this* (not tipping) their way of finishing? Never mind. I was grateful that they kept me on their payroll. Others never wanted my services any longer and there seemed to be no sufficient reason for it. I couldn't figure out any other reason but my new car and title. By the way, the car wasn't that expensive; the only annoying word was maybe the "new."

Could they have felt threatened in some way? Perhaps they felt I was getting too close? *But too close to what or where?* They had their space, and I had my own, right? For most of them, I had to fill in the gaps for myself except for one Tirzah. She evidently seemed disappointed when she said, "You must be doing well now, huh?" "Yes, Tirzah, I have come a long way and you know it. I thank God and you for walking this journey with me," I answered innocently. She just looked at me and said nothing. The next cleaning wouldn't happen because she suddenly realized that she had time to clean her house. I sure wanted to believe that her decision had nothing to do with the car and the title. Let's hope that I was just overthinking it. The good thing was that these types of clients were not even a quarter of my entire client base. This brings me to the conclusion that we have *more* well-wishers in white privilege than we think, and we need to give them the attention they so richly deserve.

Still there were those who had no idea how my new life was supposed to bother them. They just minded their business, and that number was bigger. But then there were some heroes who were so very excited for my progress. They obviously had no insecurity whatsoever. Some of them even increased my paycheck as if to say, *not yet get yourself an even better car!* Others checked my posts daily and cheered me on up to the person I am today. Some could not wait to hold this book in their hands! They believed that the title motivational speaker was too low for me! Hats off to Alyssa who believed every single word of this book even before she saw it. Her faith kept me on the keyboard and held me accountable to my deadlines until this was done.

For the purposes of this book, let's now focus on the first and last type of clients. It may surprise you that these were two groups, both privileged white people manifesting themselves differently based on their perception of this black immigrant woman.

Each had a right to their perceptions of me, but the power to determine the eventual outcome was vested on me. I had to make a choice who to give my attention amongst the two groups. Spend the time wondering why group A had changed so much or give my undivided attention to building an empire within the shelter which group B erected for me. Though a white person may be willing to advance the shelter, the black person must first notice group B, which is composed of well-wishing privileged whites and focus on making the best out of their support. This cannot happen unless you are willing to break out of the pre-existing suspicion, anger, and pride to receive the shelter. If we see ourselves as equal partners, then our motivation to keep love at the firing lane will be higher than ever before. Who wants to hurt their *partner* even when they are on the wrong?

Angry and Abandoned

How can we get to the place of love unless we address the issue of anger? With our past racial experiences, we have a lot of pain and misgivings too. The only way to deal with suspicion is to give a try because you will never know until then. We must be bold to give love a chance for it is a worthwhile risk. How draining it is to stay in a place of misgiving. It is a zone filled with indecision, and you know how uncomfortable that can be. Suspicion makes angry victims —angry at themselves (and others) for their very inability to act. Anger does nothing but sip energy out of you, the very energy required to take positive steps in your life. Angry people are stagnant because anger robs them of their willpower and ability to make progress. Anger leads you to a place called *abandonment* — abandoned by friends and now your blessings because people are the bearers of your blessings. Who wants to be in the presence of an angry person? No one really. That's how you become abandoned.

As long as I was angry with my ex-husband and my adopted daughter, I was grounded. I couldn't get the job promotion I wanted for more than five years. I was sick, and the doctors couldn't diagnose me. I looked way older than my actual age, so much so, that I still marvel at the pictures I took back then. It was the first time in my career to be put on a performance improvement plan for three consecutive quarters because I was way below the bank's performance expectations. I almost lost my job were it not for my gracious boss who negotiated a grace period for me based on my previous track record. I had such a bad attitude towards men which kept interfering with my relationships. I was so emotionally drained and absent that I had to relearn how to hug my own children again! Not only was I stagnant but I was also progressing toward an early grave. I *thought* I was punishing them because that is what "they deserved." But that was like drinking poison myself and hoping that it would kill my adversary. It doesn't work that way.

The day I let them go, I was like a satisfied calf let loose on green pastures. I experienced unspeakable joy and my body and mind felt lighter. I gained back clarity and focus on my mission. My dream and passion for life was restored, and that same year, I got the job I had sought for more than five years, and my income doubled. A year later, I got another promotion! Doubling your paycheck within a year in a third-world country? It may not be a big deal to you, but where I come from, it takes magic to make that sort of thing happen. Previously, my income had barely experienced any growth in five years, but then, miracles began to happen! This couldn't be a coincidence and if it was, then this coincidence had a strong relationship with the release of my anger and inability to forgive. I wished that I could reverse time so that the forgiveness happened five years before. Since then, I have *always* operated under open heavens because I set myself up at the place of *favor* with my forgiveness. Isn't this forgiveness business so worth it?

I have witnessed many angry black folks, especially the women, perhaps because they tend to manifest their anger more than the men. You may be familiar with the phrase "angry black woman," which in and of itself is a very controversial statement. I believe a black woman (and precisely every black person in this country) has every valid reason in the world to be angry and bitter. I don't even know how she has managed to stay sane until now with all of the atrocities that have been committed upon her. However, there is a caveat to that anger especially when you want to determine the nature of outcomes for your life and your loved ones.

The actual weight of anger is usually too heavy for its bearer. It feeds on your happiness, which is your energy to live peacefully, pursue your dreams and enjoy life. It is an actual *repellent* to your blessings. It's a repulsive force that drives away the very people carrying your portion of blessings. People can somehow see the anger even when you pretend that you are just fine.

Have you ever lost an opportunity just because you were *too angry to receive it?* I agree that systemic racism is to blame for the stagnation of the black community in so many ways, but what can we do as we wait for the government (and other) systems (and people) to change? Isn't anger and unforgiveness partly to blame for the socio-economic status of the black person in this country? Has the black folk in a way been giving reinforcement to the enemies of his or her destiny?

ME TOO MOMENT	Anger is a part and parcel of our emotions and sometimes it can be very disastrous. Have you ever messed up a great opportunity because of anger?
	In one word, how did that feel?

Why Are They So Angry?

When my daughter was in the fifth grade, she served in the Safety Patrol. Normally, when your child qualifies to render services in this capacity, you, as the parent, can serve with your child. So, there I was, every Wednesday morning at the school drop-off location, helping her clear traffic and receiving all the little angels from their parents' cars as they made their way to school. I always wore a bold smile. I talked to everyone I could that crossed my path and wished them a great day ahead. It was so rewarding to give positive words and hope to these little kids, especially on bad days as they battled between being in school or at home with their parents.

I eventually noticed something strange happening. All the black parents wore a serious look on their face, and I mean all that came across my face except one that was previously known to me. For one year, serving every Wednesday, I cannot recall any one of them that smiled at me or stopped by me. This generalization doesn't feel right at all, but it is not an exaggeration either. These are my *own* people and tribe, anyway, so why would I want to taint them? They appeared to be at war with someone or something that I couldn't quite understand at first. They also *seemed* to deliberately avoid any contact with me.

Based on the school's location, most parents were white. So, there were only a handful of black parents, and *every* time I saw one, I would be so excited … as in finally, *here comes one of my own!* I would try to make eye contact to wave at them, pick their kids and make their morning as beautiful as I possibly could in a few minutes, especially thinking what being a minority they could have been facing. Unfortunately, they seemed to make every possible effort not to look at me or stop anywhere close by, just in case I decided to walk by their car. I do not remember one of them who showed interest or said anything to me. If our eyes met by pure fluke, they would quickly look away. On top of that, they looked angry, and especially if I was smiling which I possibly did the entire time. Maybe I was just being too sensitive, but this really bothered me each day.

Most of the white people acted differently. The majority seemed genuinely interested in me. A good number were very pleased to see me; they smiled and greeted me back. Some of them went even further to engage me and compliment me on how well they thought I did the job and how much I had made their day. This kept bothering me until I shared it with one of my black girlfriends just to see if she could help me understand what was going on. I had only been in the country for a year, and I had spent that first year in a very white neighborhood. I certainly had not experienced enough black folks, which made it hard for me to understand what was really happening.

At least it looked like it was "a thing" for these black people. I wasn't willing to make any assumptions though. I needed one of my own to help me understand, and Nikki was that person.

Born and brought up in this country, Nikki has experienced enough for me to believe that her diagnosis was probably right. "Phidia, it has nothing to do with you," she said. "You just remind them of their struggles. They hate their skin because of the battles they have had to fight just for being black in America," she said. I couldn't be more surprised than I was. "But why do they look so angry, especially when I am smiling?" I asked. "Because they are always in a fight-mode and your smile makes them feel guilty for not wearing one. It reminds them of what they should be doing or what they want to do deep in their hearts, which brings about an internal conflict over who they want to be and who circumstances have forced them to be. They want to be kind and gentle, but racism has taught them how to live like imposters in their own defense," Nikki concluded.

Is Love Safe Enough?

I asked because I was curious and troubled, but I wasn't really ready for the answer, and it was too late to make that decision. I had the facts now, hopefully. I was literally in tears; my heart was so messed up with compassion and sorrow. I could not hide it. Nikki must have been moved by my state when she said, "I *will* pray for you." In my head, I wondered why these prayers would be offered in the future when the need was here and then! Or was this prayer an "app" that she needed to access Wi-Fi to download? I guess I was asking too much of her. She jumped into her car and drove off for a meeting. I mourned those words the entire day. I was immensely grieved by the fact that I did not see hope of changing the fate of the blacks.

I am not the kind of person that likes to leave matters hanging, especially difficult ones that affect people's lives. I consider myself a solution provider, and now here I was, faced with a complex challenge whose solution felt impossible. This was a test of my personality. I wasn't bleeding for the adults as much as I did for the little black kids who had to learn how to be fraudsters against their own personalities just to survive racism. I wanted black folks to safely let go of their anger and let joy permeate the source of their beings. I wanted to see them live a fulfilling life just like any other American should, but I did not have a solution to the threats facing them. So, before I proceed, my question to you is, *are you that threat by any chance*? Have you in any way forced the black person and the underprivileged to commit an identity fraud just for their safety and survival? And is there any hope for the black person? It took me months to settle upon an answer.

Love! Love! Love! My research was complete with one word. And, if anger was a weapon for black folks, then it was too heavy and way expensive. I wanted a weapon that the innocent little black kids could afford and bear the weight. If you still doubt that love is sufficient to protect a black kid in such a cruel, and sort of anti-black society then I have the facts.

Horror and Love on a Date

In my short and long life, I have been held hostage twice by brutal gunmen. It should have been three times, but the third one did not feel very personalized. I was just in the company of some friends when the orders came and all I did was lie down with my wallet in the air. In a few minutes, I was a free girl but wallet-less. Not really enough drama to deserve a count, so let's work with the two that did.

For the two, I had a more personal encounter with these goons. I just hope that two is enough for a lifetime and that there won't be any need for them to come back. Nevertheless, the most traumatizing was the first one which will be our focus in this chapter, while the second will be discussed in a different chapter in this book. The bank had organized an evening town hall not far from my office. If I was to choose an AKA for myself, then it would be "hiker," if love wasn't among the choices. Hiking is my life, and so I changed into my semi-casual wear, grabbed my comfy shoes, and began the ten-minute walk to the event. At the time, I was five months pregnant with my daughter, but it wasn't very noticeable at all.

The event venue was just a minute away but there was a railroad overpass I had to transverse before getting to my destination. I believe it was about thirty feet high, though math and I have always had an estranged relationship after circumstances bullied us into one. All I know is that the distance between the overpass and the railroad was scary because I had, every now and then, looked down as I often crossed this bridge. This was a common route for me where I would hike after work as I "bought" time for my then-husband to pick me. Down from the railroad was a thick forest. There were a few people behind and ahead of me. It was about 7 p.m. and already dark. The streetlights were on, and a few traffic police officers busy at a traffic roundabout behind me, so I did not feel like there was anything to worry about.

As I stepped into the beginning of the overpass, someone grabbed me from behind and sent me flying down the cliff. Fortunately, some shrubs on the steep terrain acted as angels to reduce the speed of gravity. I was rolling and screaming but, I don't think that was all. God knows what else I did. Luckily, there was no train passing at this moment. Safely, I managed to land to then face the real nightmare. Another bully boy was now waiting for me. Or was it the same goon that had just jumped ahead of me? What idiot would be worrying about those details when death was staring them right in their face amid terrible darkness?

My little bag was still hanging on my shoulder across my chest. He grabbed my throat with one hand and placed a cold metal "something" on my forehead and then he ordered me to drop my bag and sit down. Luckily, he was logical and gracious enough to give a "break" to my head and throat as I pulled off the bag. I could barely see him as a distant railroad light beamed just brightly enough for me to see a dark figure. "Don't you dare scream, you are safer with me than anyone else," he said. He must have been teasing me or something; by then I was sweating bullets and gasping for breath. His voice was hoarse and terrifying that even the word safe didn't feel safe at all! And while at it, this "dude" was far too articulate for a Kenyan thug which still bothers me to this date! Most of them don't have such English fluency, at least as far as I know. From a personal experience, the majority use Swahili, which is an easier-to-learn native language for Kenyans. So, *was he just a learned thug or something else worth my interest?* This is a mystery I may never be able to unravel in my short lifetime. But never mind how I noticed such details while at the moment I was "prematurely standing at the gates of eternity." Sometimes you have to figure out how to do "self-care" by living in the moment and creating some comic memories out of the worst. What else can you do anyway? My worst fear wasn't death, but the thought of a sexual assault sent me into a frenzy. I was shaking uncontrollably with panic. I wanted to relax, so I could focus better but how?

Then, he placed another somewhat friendlier order, "Bring all your cards." Then, "Passwords?" as if it was his right to ask for these things. I stammered my way through and finally "bought" the freedom for my head and throat. Now I wonder why the first order to drop the bag was necessary if I would still have to reach for the same bag to give him the cards with my head under "supervision!" "They had better be correct, or I will burst your little head," he warned. "They are, boss," I answered amid shivers. But whose boss, was he? I was looking for any word that could satisfy his bloated ego. If he wanted to be called babe, I was going to do it just to escape what I feared most. Then, he blindfolded me for a couple of minutes and ordered me not to move. I could hear him talking to another person at a distance in a language that I did not understand. That felt like a million years, waiting for his "unsolicited" surprise. I would never wish my worst enemy such a moment.

Several minutes later, he was back with yet another question, as though he hadn't asked enough. "I have the money; do you have something else to offer?" I could tell he was smoking some marijuana. I immediately had a panic attack and for a few minutes, I opened my mouth, but no words came out. Do you remember having these types of nightmares? Where someone was pursuing you, and you tried to scream yet nothing came out? Well, I used to think that this was only reserved for dreams but no, here I was, face to face with it in real life. I was sobbing, shaking, and sweating — the three unwanted S's, all at one go!

He grabbed my throat forcefully and dragging words through his firm deep voice he said, "Poor thing, do you have something else to offer?" He mumbled something else I did not understand but I was ready to answer him, so never mind. I was filled with a mix of rage and fright but then I thought, I'll never know *how* the once bouncing baby boy ended up a terrorist. Maybe he deserved some *compassion!* What a loss if I died after being kind to this undeserving bully! Death is death anyway and kindness has never been too expensive for me, so I simply said, "Sir, you are stronger than me. I am so grateful to still be talking to you, for what is my life to you? What am I that you should spare me? I have nothing else to offer except my life, but I also have another life within me. I am five months pregnant. You really sound like a nice person, which I believe you are. For the sake of the life I am carrying, please show mercy and spare me." I doubt if I was as orderly as I wanted to sound, but I got the message out.

Then, in a bossy cruel tone again dragging his words, he said, "Idiot, you still have something else to offer but I will get it next time. You are lucky that I am in a *good mood.*" He pulled away the face cover and ordered me to run away without looking back. My feet had wheels even though I couldn't see my way. I forgot I was pregnant, believe it or not. I was traumatized and depressed for several months. I couldn't stand the city. I went to the countryside for weeks before I could find meaning to life again. Enough of that drama.

Love is manifested with kindness. Sometimes kindness and some little but hard humor may be the only weapon at your disposal. It would be fascinating to see how the two gracefully join hands to rescue you in your time of need. How did this bad boy get a *good mood* out of nowhere, which was a prerequisite to my freedom that fateful night? I will never know. But this is my deduction: If kindness could locate the soft spot of this heartless goon, then it should be *sufficient* to protect little black kids and everyone else. It's time to recognize anger for the *poison* it really is as opposed to the "weapon of protection" it claims to be and embrace the real weapon of love. Then we can spare our faces and hearts of the massive, unproductive weight of the so-called "defensive anger" just because there exists a less costly and more effective weapon.

ME TOO MOMENT	Do you recall a kind act to an undeserving person that saved your day?
	In one word, how did that feel?

When Love Does the Fight

One time I was looking for a house and I had to fill out an application to get the house. Abby, the community manager who was handling the process, seemed to have something against me, however. She did not seem motivated to work on my application for almost a year after I did the first interview. This was, of course, contrary to the three-month timeline that she had initially cited during my interview. I kept hoping that something would come up every month until it finally was a year and then some. By then, my lease had expired, and I had to look for a solution in the interim. Each time I called her, she had something else to ask for. One time, she made it quite clear to me that she had "bigger projects to deal with."

It so happened that I knew one of the applicants for the same housing and she was from a different race than mine. She submitted her application after I had done mine, but she was granted a house long before me. This made me angry and disgruntled. I was ready to knock this Abby lady down. Whenever I called her, she would find something else to ask for, or say my signature had expired, and that I needed to sign the paperwork again. Either she just did not like me, or she could have been discriminating against me. Being a white lady, it is unfortunate that the subject of discrimination was something that had to go through my head and of course, I wish that was not the case. Even though I shared how I felt with her, my conversations with her were very harsh. I was always on edge, and close to erupting with anger.

This back and forth was entangled with the events that led to George Floyd's death, and so I was taking great pains to keep my cool. My fight for what I deserved was driven by judgement, anger, and hatred against this woman. For more than a year, this hateful fight bore no results, until one day I decided to change the game plan. I revisited my arsenal and once again, found the *rusty yet typically effective weapon of love.* I lay down my entitlement attitude and began attacking her with love. I took charge of my harsh feelings and began to try to understand her perspective on several issues. I stopped telling her how much I needed the house, though I desperately still needed it. At the time, I was graciously being hosted by a friend as I waited for Abby's verdict.

With two children in the picture, in a borrowed housing setting, there was every temptation to let my emotions loose. But I decided to *lay down* my need to break the racial barrier first. I "created" interest in her as a person. I engaged her with questions about her experiences with applicants and showed genuine concern for her. Every time she asked for something else, I submitted it without asking a question although I really wanted to erupt. Then, as I dropped off the documents she needed, I would find some kindness to engage her with questions like: How has it been working in this office? You must be overwhelmed sometimes, huh? Do you find yourself dealing with difficult applicants? Really annoying questions for me to ask, huh?

It didn't take long before I realized that, as I sought to understand her, I began feeling better. I felt more in control of my emotions, which had previously defiled our conversations. This time, I was in a pursuit of *creating a relationship* which would serve to break the ethnicity barriers we both had created. If she had a bad experience with someone like me before, then I wanted to clean that mess as best as I could and create a new perception. I stopped being *selfish* and *short sighted*. I began to think about other people (like me) who will pass through the same office and the kind of experience I wanted them to have. I wanted to give her a different story to tell about the people of my ethnicity. They are known to be driven by anger and I could see she had been long anticipating it. *Not this time!* Things had to be different, and I was willing to walk the road of patience this situation called for if that would transform her perspective about black women.

I love my family. They have worked so hard to teach me patience, which, until they did that, had never been a part of me. A typical type A personality has no time to waste in the name of patience. Even worse when she is from the Kitondo clan of the Kamba people. Based on the elaborate description of the Kitondo girl that I gave in the prologue, you wouldn't be surprised as much to learn that this girl has a strained relationship with patience. She is always on the go and stalling is not a word for her. Time is of essence and according to her, some patience is just an enemy to that very time. So, since I disclosed that on a scale of 1 to 10, I am a 9 of that girl, I must be deliberate about patience all the time to make it work.

But thank God and life because they have a way of strategically positioning teachers our way. My family has been that teacher as far as patience is concerned. Not that they announce with a microphone that *...now we are starting a patience class*, of course not! They just act and you realize, *oh, that was supposed to be a patience lesson!* And they have a way of making the lesson so "relevant" that I have no option of exiting before the lesson is over. Some of you may know what I mean, huh? You don't realize what a gift these people are until you land in the hands of someone the likes of Abby. By then, I was armed with enough patience to handle her.

Please note that I do not mean to support the lack of professionalism. Nevertheless, when confronted with it in the name of racism, then we must keep our guns loaded with enough bullets of bold, yet humble love to accomplish the job properly. There were different options to dealing with Abby, of course. One of my white girlfriends was ready to get me an attorney for free to deal with this situation. It was a good idea, but also very predictable. I felt that it wouldn't change the person's perception towards black women. Anyone can go to court anyway, but not everyone can *lay down* their need to bring about true healing. I was looking for a less obvious option that would create a lasting change for her, myself, and others. And of course, by now, you know that this approach works. The house came two months after my changed attitude, but I couldn't take it because I had just received another better option. The fight of love not only opened the door I had been knocking but also spoiled me with *options* and established a beautiful interracial relationship at the same time.

You must know what you want and *invest* in producing it. All sorts of strategies are at your disposal, it just depends on what your end goal is. If my goal was to get the house, then a legal process would probably have done it for me. But I was determined to create a *perception-changing* relationship and an experience that would impact many people positively. It's never a small effort; many little changes can produce a big change. Just be loyal when answering your call when it comes and do the little change your space can accommodate This generation may not recognize it, but in the years to come, a story of a love hero or heroine will be shared from one hopeful soul to another amid nowhere, as they attempt to extinguish the fire of hate.

ME TOO MOMENT	Have you ever prolonged your wait for something important just because you fought for it with a judgmental attitude toward the participants?
	In one word, how did realizing your role in the delay make you feel?

The Hurting 'Grass'

In my community, we have a Swahili saying that goes, *wapiganapo fahari wawili, ziumiazo ni nyasi,* which translates to, *when two bulls fight, only the grass underneath hurts.* This implies that while we think that the fight of hate affects us alone and we are strong enough to handle it, there are other helpless victims that bear the consequences heavily. Our nation's children carry a heavy load of the impact of our collective inability to deal with racism and direct privilege. They are on the receiving end. They feel powerless and hopeless. They keep wondering to themselves why we never pull together while they want to play together. They are afraid to live in freedom and break through diversity because we created an impossibility for them.

One time, as we were watching a worship service on YouTube by one of the major black churches, my daughter asked me, "Mum, why are there no white people in this church?" What troubled me was not the absence of white people, but the fact that she was having this conversation in her head and it was the very same conversation that was going on in my head. I just had been hoping that my child would never notice and worry about such things. I wanted her to realize that we were all *one* people. She already had several white friends which she seemed to acquire without struggle or noticing their differences. I wanted her to continue approaching diversity with such openness.

But here, at this church, society was giving her a different message and leaving me to clean up their mess. "Daughter, there are a good number of white folks here, I don't think you have taken the time to notice." I had just jumped in with a coverup explanation. *I had better back up my words and defeat the devil before he claims her.* I spent the next five minutes or so trying to spot one white person. *Phew!* I finally landed on one and made my case. But did it have to be that hard? Are we so subdued by hate that it is so very evident even in a place of worship? I thought God is love and that His friends or followers should be in the front lines to carry on His agenda of unmerited love? Haven't you heard that it is written in John 13:35, "By this all will know that you are My disciples, if you love one another?" But that said, perhaps the topic of Sunday being the most segregated day of the week in America is best dealt with in a different forum.

Unconditional Love Vs. Accountability

Hate for hate does not produce love and blood for blood doesn't yield life. You may ask all sorts of questions to get to the root cause of why such and such a thing happened or find a "justification" for love. But at the end of the day, the answer is found in love. Even the pursuit of equality and social justice should be driven by love for one another.

Yes, we have been hurt very badly and a lot of water *is* under the bridge. An irreparable mess has already been created, and many lives have been lost, but that doesn't justify making it worse. Holding onto anger and unforgiveness doesn't solve the problem of hate. You may be justified in your anger and/or vindictive approach but the outcome simply will not produce love or anything better. That should be a sobering statement whenever we are tempted to use hate for a weapon of defense. Sometimes you must *look like* a fool to bring *victory* home. I don't mind being a "victorious fool," especially in the subject of love, do you?

Mind you, unconditional love does not replace accountability. It seeks to demand accountability with compassion. There is always a temptation to withhold love when demanding accountability. It is as though the brain struggles to handle the two because they wear different hats, yet they share the same mother. You must be deliberate about marrying the two. This kind of love aims to understand the other person's point of view and what drives them to their actions. When we *understand,* then we can extend compassion and overcome judgment without compromising our mission for accountability. That then places us in the right position to persuade our target to change.

Understanding them doesn't translate into supporting their actions; it just offers us the necessary platform for engagement. When people feel understood, they get vulnerable and that makes it easier for us to get the crucial information we need to build a long-term relationship. It helps us see the person independent of their actions to connect with them better. That is the very connection that transforms them from a "rival" into us becoming part of their support system. We allow ourselves to get "recruited" into their defense force to fight against a common enemy — hate. That is a beautiful way to make accountability fun. People find it easy to give accountability where there is love.

Hate does not shoot for fun but to kill. We must keep in mind that we are not fighting to destroy; we are fighting to build. We are not shooting to kill but to heal. That's a different kind of fight! Understanding the nature of this fight will affect how we do it. A shoot to kill should be reserved for an enemy. We are not enemies. We belong together; we share the same human species, sons of one nation, but one was favored right from the very beginning, and we were never part of that favoritism deal. That was the sin of our fathers, and we simply cannot perpetuate it. It is time for the children to heal this relationship otherwise there will be peace for none.

The Parents' Mess

The story behind white privilege relates closely to a famous narrative of a certain Jewish family. This is a true story. Isaac and Rebecca were blessed with two sons, Jacob, and Esau. Their mother loved Jacob more than Esau. That's how she managed to sneak Jacob, who was younger than Esau, to get the birthright which was a privilege reserved for the firstborn son as per the Jewish culture. Their father Isaac was too old to realize that the birthright went to the wrong son. The fight that ensued after this was so intense that Rebecca advised her beloved son to flee for his life. She created the mess but now it was too overwhelming for her. Jacob and Esau were caught up in a very hateful fight. Esau was determined to kill his little brother because of the privilege.

We don't see the parents anywhere once the brothers began fighting. The only thing is that Rebecca is on record asking her son Jacob to flee for his life. Once she had accomplished her own selfish ambition, she had moved on and left her kids to deal with the volcano that erupted. Of course, Isaac was sorry for the "oversight," but that was about it. Rebecca, their mother, and mastermind of the drama did not seem to worry so much except that the little privileged guy was almost losing his life. The writer of the story says that Esau hated his brother and vowed to kill him because hate leads you to *kill*. When Jacob realized that he was on his own and that his life was at risk, he fled and took asylum in another country. I am so grateful that he decided to *flee* rather than to fight back with hate because one or both would have gone down. We would be talking about a grave or graves. And not just graves because this man Jacob became the father of the Jewish people, which means his death would have cleared out an entire nation of people. That's how grave hate can be! Think of how many generations have been doomed with hopelessness, destinies, dreams, and lives cut short because of the hateful fight between the blacks and the whites in this country.

Taking asylum gave him a moment to wise up and reach into his weaponry to get the right weapon, the weapon of love. For *twenty* years, Jacob looked for the right weapon! Finally, he had found enough love in his heart to face his brother who had, at one time, tried to finish him because of *privilege*. You may wonder why Jacob felt entitled to this birthright. Well, matters were a little bit complicated by the fact that these kids had made a childish deal when they were growing up. Though they were above eighteen at the time of the deal, the nature of the deal did not sound "adult" in my opinion, but I had better let you decide for yourself.

There was a time when Esau was almost starved to *death* and the only thing available to save him was a cup of lentil soup that was in Jacob's hands. That day, Jacob agreed to help but with one condition—that Esau would forsake his birthright for Jacob. That couldn't have been a casual "pinky promise" right? The deal was sealed and most likely, Jacob told his mama because he was a mama's boy. That deal didn't make much business sense, but Jacob took it seriously. I guess he was justified because an agreement is an agreement after all he saved Esau from dying otherwise the birthright would have no meaning to him. For that reason, he had every right to fight back and slay his brother for playing him. I am glad he decided to flee instead. That for sure made him look like a serious coward though.

Fleeing the Fight of Hate

Love deserves another chance and sometimes chances and wisdom must guide you in this to know when your identity is at risk in the name of love. That wisdom was never my portion in the situation of my marriage, perhaps I gave too many chances. And even when the chances are exhausted, hate is never an option, you can still "love from a safe distance." So, twenty years went by, and now Jacob was ready to fight with love, therefore he made a trip with gifts and *words* of peace for his brother. Show me a person too strong for love, not even the worst of the goons can resist it! It melts the stoniest of the hearts and turns the toughest of the lords into adorable little boys. Not even the highest tower of hatred can withstand love; when love steps in, towers tumble down in obeisance. The anger of Esau was met with the love of Jacob, and it couldn't withstand the force of love. The walls collapsed and the two who were now humbled by love forgot their *entitlement*. They passionately embraced and kissed one another as they wept; sober minds unleashed manly sobbing. Wow! The relationship was ultimately mended, and the long fight was over.

But it had been a whooping twenty years before Jacob felt ready to handle the anger and hate of his brother. By this point, he was now a husband and a father. That's how long finding love can take sometimes. I just hope it doesn't take us that long because it has already been long! If you must stay away to avoid casualties, please do so, but don't do *nothing*, search through the arsenal and find the magic weapon. We must trust the *sufficiency* of love because love is complete; it requires no reinforcements.

It is worth noting that the privileged Jacob was fleeing from an *angry, oppressed* Esau. He wasn't fleeing because he didn't have the power but because he didn't want to kill his own brother. This man was a warrior after all. He wasn't a coward as you might imagine. He had his *power under control*. Have you ever noticed that the very skilled soldiers don't shoot aimlessly? They must have a good reason for firing, right? That was Jacob. It was not *his* fault that his mother favored him, *however*, it was his fault how he handled that privilege. He took a weaker position not because he couldn't fight but because he loved his brother. Though they had a strained relationship, he kept in mind that he was fighting with his brother and the fight had to be *different*. He was only going to fight to build not to destroy, to heal and not to kill; otherwise, the fight wasn't worth his investment.

Handling an Angry Underprivileged Esau

Esau seems to have been suffering from what I call "spontaneous-ity." I guess he has an overwhelming number of subscribers in today's society. You know how sometimes hunger can tempt you to do silly things that you regret when your stomach is full. I had a friend who overate all the time, but she wouldn't know just how full she was until the plate was empty. Then, she would start crying foul as if she were eating at gunpoint! Food can be such a temptation at times. Jacob knew that this guy might change his mind once his stomach was full, but he also had a "smart" mother whom he kept in the loop for backup. His mother never dropped the ball when the time for action came. She dressed Jacob in a hairy garment that was sufficient to confuse their blind father that the person he was giving the birthright to was Esau who was indeed a hairy man.

Sure enough, Esau came back to his senses, but it was too late. The privilege had gone to his younger brother. I call birthright a privilege because none of the kids chose what number they would be born yet the birthright was culturally meant for the first born. It just happened that one was born first and the other afterwards, hence none of them had anything to do with who was given the birthright. Does that sound familiar with the fate of blacks and whites in this country? Certainly. The current generation was never a part of this privilege allocation; it has just been caught up in the mess and forced to pay for the sins of the founders of this nation. Blacks didn't choose what color to be born neither did the whites and all other races. I do not mean that the white person is the firstborn, please do not get me wrong. However, as far as the circumstances surrounding the founding of this nation are concerned, there existed some advantages that gave white people advantages over blacks and all other races.

Whichever way we want to look at things, whites have the birthright whether fairly or unfairly. Esau struggled to come to terms with that fact just like black people have had to in this country. Not accepting this reality initially led him to a place of anger, hatred, and contemplation of murder. He had actually murdered the little privileged guy in his head; the only part left was to manifest it in the physical realm.

Now, whether it was a fair negotiation to exchange a lifetime inheritance for a bowl of lentil soup to a starving man may not be the issue. The matter is that we had a willing seller and a willing buyer, and both were adults at the time of this deal. Therefore, that means that Jacob, in his own capacity, had every *right* to fight for this privilege and rub it onto Esau. Someone that saved your life can say anything anyway, right? But Jacob acted with a lot of wisdom when the hateful fight ensued. This is how heroes do it! It takes a lot of boldness for a warrior to flee an unnecessary fight. If you are the same person to take your brother to the hospital, then what need is there to wound him? You rather maintain a safe distance if your hands try acting up! And why compromise your peace for a lifetime dealing with the guilt of your brother's scar or grave? Isn't it easier to deal with the relative peace of being deemed a coward when you know you are a hero?

Judged and Jolly

Many times, the fight of love will call you to a place where people misinterpret your actions and brand you with names. You remember the story of Marilyn, my co-worker in the beginning of part two of this book? My boss Jared had called me timid just because I did not indulge in a hateful fight with Marilyn. When you choose your battles, you also choose your weapon and that can cause serious misjudgments from people.

How comfortable with misjudgments are you? I hail from a large family and I'm so proud of it. It was amazing growing up together, making noise, playing, and fighting. There was so much life in our home, I miss it. With nine siblings and two parents, we deserve to be respected as were practically a soccer team in the making! This beautiful family wasn't perfect at all, and I wouldn't wish it was, because I would have missed the adventures if it had been. We have had our fair share of rough patches. I stopped being my father's favorite after I got divorced. Someone else took that seat and as we speak, I don't yet know who. But that's fair because the seat was meant to be shared in the first place, isn't it? (Imagine for a moment the beauty of a *shared privilege*!) But that's not the point here. You understand sibling fights and how that goes, huh? It's never that serious anyway, as long as it doesn't get to where Jacob and Esau got.

My society is very warm, but if you are a female divorcee that warmth may never be extended because you are considered a bad omen. The society will tell you in so many ways that you are useless if you lose your marriage. The man, of course, is privileged; he is the king and free to conquer another territory. But for the woman, some treat you as a threat while others treat you as an outcast. The former seems to be common across the cultures especially by married women regardless of how hard you work to prove your sanctity. I never do well with this "proving business" anyway, so much for that.

The man has his identity secure even when he divorces, but not you as the woman. You will be told in whispers or in the open that you are a *nobody* and what a *disgrace* you are. Those that are brave will tell you openly while the rest will act it out, so you can fill in the gaps for yourself. You can't miss their message — *you don't belong*. I had to create my own space and definition in society otherwise I would be doomed.

"So, you mean you won't get remarried?" That is an important question for my dad, which he cautiously asks whenever a chance shows up. I keep my answer the same all the time. "Dad, I haven't thought about it yet," his disappointment is almost audible. *Seven years down the line and you haven't thought about it yet*? I can still hear the question in his unusual silence. Then, I realize I needed to "massage" the situation. "Maybe I will someday dad," That's how I end the discussion. Sadly, I never sound convincing enough as I hope to and the repeat of this question in the "next episode" tells it all in greater detail. I understand the concerns of the old man because of the value that my society attaches to marriage, especially for the woman, even more so when you are a pastor's kid. I know it's not easy for him dealing with the judgements of having a daughter who is a divorcee. It is next to impossible that I will ever do anything in this world to cleanse myself of *that* taboo.

Wearing my father's shoes is not to be undermined at all. He has his own pressures to deal with, yet I never seem to make things better for him. How come it doesn't bother me with all the noise around me? Well, it was a big deal for me the first few years as I still struggled with rejection and the fear of it, but not anymore. I have defined who I am and where I stand in my society now. My identity is safe and secure and that has affected how I relate to my family and society at large. I handle every misjudgment with grace because the issue of my identity is now resolved within me and nothing someone says or does will affect my peace. Before then, I was ruthless with them that did not have a favorable perception toward me. Oh, how powerful understanding your identity can be!

Privileged Jacob had his identity settled. When he began the journey to meet his brother, he had two wives and two mistresses who had given him eleven sons. (Please don't judge him for having mistresses; that idea came from his two wives.) It was supposed to help raise more children, which was a major part of the Jewish culture. Sons depicted a man's strength and so with eleven sons, Jacob had *strength* to boast about. But that did not stand in his way to healing the relationship with his brother. He sent three groups of messengers ahead to meet Esau. He gave each of them a gift for his brother with the words, *this is a gift from your servant, Jacob.* And as if that was not enough, when he met him in person, Jacob himself *bowed* seven times. In the Jewish culture, this is a sign of respect. What? A privileged, rich, and strong Jacob *chose* to take the position of a servant? And he didn't even seem to struggle with bowing because he did it seven times? Don't we expect him to be full of himself, rub it in as pertaining to his privilege, brag about his wealth, show off his might with eleven sons and/or anything else that was possible to intimidate and oppress his underprivileged brother? Why would a *privileged* person come this low? What exactly did Jacob know that we don't seem to? I can't ask enough of these questions.

In chapter three, I brought a different perspective of how *evil* the servant position can be. Not in this case when it was done by the privileged to avert an impending death and heal a broken relationship. The issue here is *who* takes the seat and what their *objective* is. The effects are just not the same when the underprivileged takes that position. By default, the state of the underprivileged places them in the servant position so it's nothing extraordinary. It takes a secure privileged person to take this position to save a life and bring peace. This is the only time when taking the servant's seat can be a priceless act and the highest sign of selflessness and humility. How beautiful it is when love and maturity kiss one another under the roof of security. Titles and riches lose their value at the sight of the peace and joy that prevails.

The Family Matrix: Once a Brother Always One

I believe the hateful fight between blacks and whites is because of a failed identity. When you know who you are, you don't feel any pressure to prove a point. You will be comfortable with your brother perceiving you as a coward just because you fled a fight of hate. I use the word *brother* because *anyone whose pain affects you in a way is supposed to be viewed as a family member.* After all, when they cry, you also cry however much you wish not to. We share one economic basket both privileged and underprivileged and that is enough to make us brothers if sharing the same human species doesn't. The reality is that you may never get over the guilt of oppressing your weaker brother. You may pretend to be okay, but you truly aren't. When a strong and privileged brother runs away do not assume that they are cowards, they just *know* their position because they do not have identity issues. They are at peace with themselves to the extent that nothing you say would change them. Just like Rebecca and Isaac in the story above, the founders of this nation introduced us to a battle, and they moved on. But we the sons must know who we are to end this fight of hate. I don't mean that we should stop fighting for equality. You can't stop members of a family from fighting but you can *direct* the fight with love.

I treasure my family. They have taught me how to love imperfection, of which I am part of. They have qualified me to write about the possibility of unmerited love. I owe them for this blessing. After going through a messy divorce, I had a lot of battles to fight. My beloved siblings did not seem to make it any better. They were very oblivious to what I was going through. I had so much hate, bitterness, and anger to deal with and my only safety was to avoid them for a good two years. I knew that if they were caught by the hate within me, they wouldn't survive. I wasn't in a fight with them but because they kept crossing my path the wrong way, there was a strong likelihood that a stray bullet would find them. Thankfully, fleeing away from them helped in reminding me that they were my siblings no matter what.

If your brother decides to supply your adversary with the wood to burn you that does not make them an enemy ... yet. They just don't understand themselves, and that leads them to taking the wrong position in the fight. Giving them a grace period by *fleeing* them and taking time to reload your love bullets can be the best gift to yourself and to them. We are one family, the human family. I have yet to see angels around. You have no excuse for not creating and keeping successful interracial relationships. You have the power not only to build new ones but also to heal broken ones with unmerited love. We can set a world record where *the strong bow themselves to the weak and the privileged to the angry underprivileged* as a bold attempt by a secure people to avert wrath and stop the war from escalating further to save and advance lives. That sounds like absolute power, doesn't it? But this attitude comes from being secure with ourselves and having compassion to understand the pain of the underprivileged, just like Jacob, rather than dismissing it. I bet that sets the platform for the underprivileged to understand the pain of the privileged too because it does exist. That is where the journey to accountability begins for both sides.

Fighting an already oppressed person is cowardice. Jacob knew that solid people have no need to show off their strength; only the weak do because their power is debatable. He knew the secret to more power was using his strength to empower the frail and uplift the oppressed. That is the epitome of security and maturity. But how can the blacks and the whites in this country find this level of identity stability?

ME TOO MOMENT	Has anyone ever used their privilege to intimidate you and get their way?
	In one word, how did that feel?

Loving You Through Me

Seeking to understand your identity so you can be secure could be the highest level of love you could ever give yourself because it determines all other decisions you make. If you can't love yourself, then you can't love nobody. I know traditional religious teachings prioritize loving others and turn a blind eye or even worse demonize self-love. I grew up feeling guilty about loving myself because that was deemed selfish. But the scripture is very clear on how significant loving oneself is in being able to love others. No wonder it encourages us in Mark 12:31 to love our neighbor *as we* love ourselves. Notice that it doesn't say *friend* but *neighbor* because we cannot choose our neighbors, they are like family, they just happen to be. But that is not the point here, the issue is that the *maximum love you can give anyone cannot exceed the one you have for yourself.* You are the benchmark as far as love for others pertains.

People who struggle to love themselves also struggle to love others. When people say, "I love him or her more than myself," I don't believe them. Maybe they are confusing love for something else. How can you be giving something you don't have in the first place? Loving others is like looking yourself in a mirror; you only get what you give. And if you wonder why you can't love a particular person as you wish, the solution is simple. Turn the mirror on yourself, find means to love yourself more, and the same love will reflect on that person. But what are these *means* to love yourself? How come we love to spend time with everyone but ourselves? Being alone doesn't translate to being lonely. I could not uncover and face my insecurities until I came up with a daily routine of spending time alone in prayer, quietness, and meditation. That was such a gift of love to *me*. I even noticed some scars in my body that I had never taken note of for thirty-five years of my life. I mourned and embraced them and forgave the people that played a role in causing them! See how much love was flowing from me to others. But first, I had to overcome the fear of being alone, so I could know this Phidia girl, love her and *then* share that very same love with others.

Jacob *took time* to understand and appreciate himself, his background, his mistakes, his journey and to forgive himself for his faults including swindling his brother. And when you forgive yourself, you can forgive any other person. That gave him an opportunity to appreciate his parents' faults so he could forgive them and take ownership of his contribution to the mess. No wonder, we never hear him blaming his mother for anything. At the time, people around him had dubbed him a corn man, but that did not stop him from giving himself another chance; *what do they call you and your tribe? Racists? Angry? Haters?* Don't let that stop you from forgiving yourself regardless of your mistakes that might have contributed to the name. Jacob just set the pace for us! But that gentleness with himself could not happen before he took time to know himself then embrace his journey—the successes, failures, and the participants.

You can't embrace part of your journey if at all you want to be secure. That is the process of settling one's identity and finding love for self and for others. Selfishness is a sign of people who have no love for themselves no wonder they are so care-less about themselves that they can trade their peace and integrity to temporarily satisfy a want. They hate themselves so much that they wouldn't embrace an opportunity to learn patience a virtue they would need through their lifetime. *Selfishness is a self-love deficiency overflow affecting the people around the victim.* Such people don't need to be criticized. Instead, we should arrange for them more lessons on self-love. They need more of it than less of it; that contradicts the traditional cure we have always prescribed for selfish people—that they need to love themselves less.

I suppose both the privileged white folks and the underprivileged black folks need to take this *emotional and psychological sojourn*. We need to invest time on ourselves to know and heal ourselves from the roots where it all began. We must embrace our backgrounds, our mistakes and those of our forefathers then proceed to forgive ourselves and them too. Like Jacob, we must accept our role in this mess and stop putting the entire blame on our forefathers. Let's admit that black or white we have failed in many ways with regards to racism so that we have no need to be angry when someone else points it out.

Once we make that admission, we shall begin to experience so much peace within which will lead us to be gentle with ourselves and others, and thereby giving ourselves another chance to make things right. This is the chance we shall run with to collaborate and deliver a shelter and create *real* value through the privilege. But we must set the foundation right; secure *self-loving* humans, reflecting that love on fellow humans. You don't have to stop fighting for what you deserve, just load your pistol with the bullets of love. C'mon, people, let us trust the *sufficiency* of the weapon of love and run with it to transform this privilege into a benefit for us all.

The 'Practicals' of Love

The scripture according to Mark 12:31 says, "… You shall love your neighbor as yourself…" You cannot love anyone else until you can love yourself. Loving others is like looking into a mirror. You get what you give to the mirror. If you don't like what you see, then improve your input. If you have a deficiency, then we can only expect a deficient love on this other end. You can't give what you don't have and the highest love you have for yourself is the highest measure you can reflect on others. Show us how much you love yourself and others by taking *action* to secure your identity. Hate is developed through envy, incorrect perceptions or bad experiences and manifested through anger and resentment. We must get to the root cause for real victory. We may never agree on everything, but we must agree to fight with bullets of love. We will not abandon accountability, but we will demand it with love. That must remain the rule of the game. Below is a step-by-step process for reloading your cartridge with the bullets of love.

1. Identify the Thorn: Trace a people, person, or relationship that you feel resentful or angry about. You could be having several, but you can only work on one at a time for effectiveness, so pick one. Putting a finger on it and calling out the person's name or the specific race of people resurfaces the issue from the subconscious mind and gives you a chance to experience the intensity of the pain and emotions you have been trying to suppress. It's like cleaning a wound that has been abandoned. It can be excruciating, but there's no shortcut for healing. I recommend that you journal your way through the process.

2. What and When? Find the root cause. When did you first begin feeling like this? What really happened and what was the situation before then? Following my divorce, I developed a hatred for men. I was being very irrational, but it was a coping mechanism to "get revenge" on my ex whom I felt that he had all the rights in the society while I seemed to have none. My hatred was based on anger for what he did to me and envy because he was the privileged one in my society. I had to get back to the root cause of my anger when I decided to cure myself. In this stage, you need to be specific with time if you can. In my case, I would write down that I started hating men in 2014 when Phil betrayed our love and used his privilege as a man to intimidate me.

3. Before and After: Hopefully, you have a better past to act as an anchor for comparison purposes, if not, don't worry. We will create one because we can do it through others' experiences or our own imaginations. In this stage, we look at both extremes; one with a delightful past and another with a nasty present. In my case, I would write, "I used to see men as an adorable representation of selfless love, power, and security. Now, I see men as cruel, arrogant, selfish favorites of an evil male-dominated society." Marrying the two extremes helps you realize the missing beauty of a changed perception.

Pick out the specific words you have been using against the person or the specific group of people. "Stupid" was the biggest word for me just because I couldn't find a better word of revenge for my offender, what about you? This is where we expose the stereotypes — for instance, men are users, women are gold-diggers, black people are violent, white people are racists or whatever the case might be. *The hatred will always manifest itself in words before actions.*

Recognize that your actions are based on your perceptions and words. Based on what you think and say about the person, the actions can only agree. You cannot act any different from the two. Your sentence would be something like, "I can't stand men, I have no respect for women, I don't believe in love, I don't trust black people, I hate white people," and so on.

4. The consequences: We are free to justify our decisions, but we can't avoid the consequences. The hatred and anger we manufacture for the "rival" will devour us first. But we won't know unless we get attentive to the details. Put your life on notice and see how your energy, emotions, health, productivity, relationships, and work have been affected by your new status. I did not realize how sick I was until I was admitted in hospital. My career was on a downward trend; I was put on a performance improvement plan three consecutive times. I was so emotionally absent that I had to relearn how to hug my children again! I had a blanket called, "I am stressed" to cover the real damage all the time until I couldn't cover it up anymore. Anger and bitterness take away your energy and everything else including your dreams. Some people die, literally, because of anger. See how much retrogression you have made since you became hateful. That is the *maintenance cost* of hatred. The reality of that loss can help you back to your senses.

5. Accept reality: If denial is more destructive than the offense itself then why hang on to this enemy that claims to be a friend? Lead yourself to embrace your reality. "I am divorced, he has moved on, white people are privileged, or the society favors men over women; I may not be able to change any of that, however angry and hateful I get."

6. What is the mutual benefit? Apart from recovering all the benefits lost in stage four, there's a common benefit that can act as an incentive to both of you. For me and my ex, our kids were the incentive. I had to recognize that I cannot show my kids another father because they already have a father regardless. I would do anything possible to give peace to my kids by reassuring them that mom and dad are not at war. They are only divorced, and that's it. For interracial relationships, we both want coexistence for the benefit that comes with it. If the white person uses his privilege to defend blacks or the underprivileged, he will be cleared of guilt, shame, and the hassle of protecting the privilege, which means that he will be able to enjoy its benefits. In addition, both sides will experience more peace and economic prosperity. What is the mutual benefit in your situation? That is the driver that can help you replace the bullet of hate with a bullet of love.

CHAPTER FIVE

Reverse Strategy: Trade Positions in the Battle of Privilege

A Sobering Moment

A few days after the unfortunate killing of George Floyd, I had a short conversation with Emily who was one of my customers. On a Monday morning, both of us were struggling with a rollercoaster of emotions. For the purposes of this discussion, I am happy to disclose that Emily is white, and I remain black; nothing has changed so far. I love colors, and I enjoy calling people by their ethnicity, because it is supposed to be magical and fascinating. Unfortunately, I am forced to be careful when I use color terms because it has also become a battlefield in our country and society. People have lost sight of the beauty in diversity which was God's objective in making us as different as we are. This explains why there's stigma in calling my friend white, which is supposed to be a proud part and parcel of her identity.

There was so much tension during this period and as was my practice, I started every conversation by acknowledging how difficult the situation was not just for black people but also the nation. There was so much hate circulating, especially through social media, I felt that this was a way to keep our sanity while we fight with love and compassion.

"Emily, this must have been a difficult week," I said. "Absolutely," she answered. She was trying hard to hide her emotions, but her compassionate nature almost betrayed her. It was a challenging moment for her as she tried to comprehend everything. "We may not have control over what others do but the two of us can join our candles of love and fight the darkness of hate in our own little way," I interrupted the silence. "Which side are you on?" she asked. "God's," I said. "I value what God values, which is love," I sounded like a preacher, huh? Fair enough for a loyal PK!

As for Emily, I expected her to quickly nod in agreement because the confidence in me had me convinced that I had "presented a very strong case," but no! She wasn't going to just take that. Something else was the matter. Looking at me with undeterred conviction she said, "At this point in time, I don't think we need to fight for everyone's right because then we lose sight of the real problem. It's like having a critically ill person and a healthy person coming for an ordinary checkup all being accorded the same level of attention. We need to fight for the rights of the oppressed. Why would someone who is privileged need help to fight for their rights? They possibly have more rights than they perhaps need!" Wow! Her remarks were very weighty. She opened my eyes to a new perspective on the entire issue. I hadn't seen it this way before. The next five hours or so I couldn't get over her words. It felt like I had received an urgent call to say something about the crisis. This was the call that initiated the transformation of the very manual I mentioned in my introduction (which was initially meant for my kids) into this book.

Do you think Emily had a point? Is there a possibility that this is what the battle of liberating the oppressed in this country lacks? Is it possible that the person fighting shouldn't be the one fighting, and that explains why they keep losing the battle? Can an oppressed person liberate themselves or another oppressed person? Maybe so, but how long would it take them if it ever happened at all? Isn't there a chance that one privileged person with a different attitude could make *the* difference that has costed the blood of thousands or millions of underprivileged people to achieve? Are there chances that the change that has taken the underprivileged decades to attain could be realized within days if the privileged *took over* the battle? If these are the kind of questions streaming in your head, then you just found a tried and tested answer.

Troubled by Privilege

During my high school years, I played on my school's basketball team. I wasn't the best, but I also wasn't the worst. Back then, where I come from, basketball wasn't a big deal as is in this country, otherwise I would have stood no chance. We used to have internal competitions for different grades or same grades, but different classes. I might have forgotten several details, but not Mr. Kenny, the referee of the 12th grade team and Risper, the captain of my team, for reasons you will soon get to know. Mr. Kenny was also my English teacher and I seemed to have found favor with him from the word go. I was the easy kid that followed instructions and strove to stay loyal to parents and teachers. I also did very well in my academics but not so in basketball, but that did not water down my favor with Mr. Kenny for some reason.

Back then, I had strong morals and values, which I suppose I still have to this day. I guess my strong Christian foundation from my cleric parents was a major contribution to this. I also believe those factors played a major role to my appointment as the school's deputy president during the 12th grade. (Back in my days, you were not elected by the students, but appointed by the school's administrative office). I still don't know what exactly won me favor with Mr. Kenny, but I liked it that way for some reason. I hope that doesn't sound creepy. We had two teams: -Simba and Chui; both are Swahili words that mean Lion and Leopard, respectively. I was on team Chui.

On my team, we had Colley, the daughter of the school's board Chairman Bill. Mr. Kenny and the board chairman both came from the same village, a factor that probably contributed to them being childhood friends. Clearly, the referee had some vested interest in our team, which kept manifesting itself with no effort on our part. It wasn't a good thing, but it was what it was. Unfortunate as it may sound, there were several occasions when we got away with so many mistakes and sadly the other team could clearly see the favoritism. They would raise their concerns, but they would just be swept down the drain. It was a battle of the weak against the strong, the underprivileged against the privileged. The underprivileged team fought hard to make things right, but they always fought a *losing* battle.

We were strong, since we had the power of the referee, the board chairman, and now the school's deputy president. On the other hand, the Simbas felt helpless and defeated. To make matters worse, Mr. Kenny would insensitively tell them, "You don't have to be in this team, you have a choice." Thinking about it now, I still cannot believe that he actually said that to them. I am not that old, but recounting this story makes me realize how much time has passed and how old I have eventually become. I don't think that the today's so-called alpha generation would tolerate this kind of treatment. For the Simbas, this was just salt added to an injury. They had no option but to stay and keep their mouths shut to avoid being in bad terms with a referee who was also their English teacher. This created *bad blood* among the teams, which were already graced with opinionated and strong personalities.

Change of Guard

Risper, my team's captain, was the oil inside this body of water. A very intelligent, gentle, humble, and open-minded young girl, she was the voice of reason. Each time, she watched this situation unfold with a troubled soul and kept asking me what we needed to do to end the hostility between the teams. But I was hesitant to get involved. I already had enough enemies, why add some more? As the "big office appointee," that automatically qualified me as a rival to most of the students who saw me as a watchdog. For that reason, I always took a low profile, more so if there was someone else in charge, Risper was. So, after several discussions with her, we agreed that she would call a meeting with Team Chui. During the meeting, she would tactfully lead the team to face the fact that our team was being favored at the *cost* of other participants in this sport. Not only was it at the cost of the other team but also at the cost of our *peace* and relationships in the 12th grade.

When you receive something unfairly it puts the most precious thing you have at stake — your peace. Who doesn't want to protect their peace? Is it worth spending your life running away from the shame and guilt of causing your *brother* pain for your pleasure? How hateful can you get toward yourself to be careless about their agony? When we are selfish, we deceive ourselves that we are gaining while in the real sense we are losing. We only *appear to be* benefitting. So, wasn't our self-love a reason enough to fight for the Simba's rights? These were the facts that Risper put before the team when she called an impromptu meeting ahead of a match. There was an uproar when she said that our team was enjoying a *dangerous* privilege. Can a privilege be dangerous? We struggled for a few minutes to get our team to settle down and internalize that perspective. Through her discreet and likeable personality, Risper brought sense to all the members except two. You will always have a few stray sheep that don't see the need for a shepherd! Those are the people that the law has to bulldoze into embracing the honorable thing.

With only two members in opposition, we were good to go. Risper and I booked an appointment with Mr. Kenny. We did not want the other team to know that we were addressing their pain just for the sake of our teacher's integrity; hopefully, he still had it. However, with almost twelve members on the team it was hard to keep it a secret, hence information about our meeting leaked out. Our discussion with Mr. Kenny went well and although he didn't admit to anything, things changed after that. It was interesting to note how much our relationship with the other team transformed just because we acted for their good. Even more so the fact that we did not blow our trumpet as we set out to fight for them. It was a strong gesture that our motives were driven purely by love and compassion and that shifted their perspective from seeing us as rivals to caring partners.

We with *one* bullet tamed a privilege that took the underprivileged Simbas about four months of a fruitless battle. They were fighting to kill the privilege, but we fought to tame it. We did not stop becoming Mr. Kenny's favorites, but we prevented this favor from devouring our friends' joy because at the end of the day, there was life after the game. We couldn't force Mr. Kenny to like the Simbas as he did us because that is a free-will decision. However, we could take *advantage* of our likeability to influence how he treated others with respect to us. Did we have some sort of magic?

If the privileged taking on a battle for the underprivileged is magic, then yes, we sure had it! *The battle of privilege was reversed.* The underprivileged soldiers (in this example, the Simbas) were sent on leave while the privileged soldiers (Team Chui) faced the in-house giant of their own privilege. They actually did not need to fight; they just tamed their own elephant from roaming and causing havoc to their friends. That is how powerful it is when the beneficiary of the privilege faces the bigger picture of the consequences and owns the fight for the benefit of all. Sometimes out of short-sightedness we only see the immediate gratification without considering the long-term impact. That's how this battle of privilege needs to be approached. Life is too short yet too precious to be lived in shame and guilt for using our power to destroy our brethren. What a joy when we choose to live it honorably and peacefully.

ME TOO MOMENT	Have you ever had to choose between your privilege and relationship?
	In one word, how did you feel about your choice?

Recruited by Love

Our situation in high school was way easier than is the situation between black and white folks in this country. For the longest time, the black person who represents the less privileged has been left on his own to fight the injustice perpetrated by the white "lords," at least as I see it. (I do not seek to dismiss the few privileged white heroes and heroines who are not part of this "black person's abandonment.") Notice that he is facing a battle too strong for him. His counterpart has the final say, courtesy of these unfair systems. The masters of injustice invested so much power on the white folk such that unless he *yields* willingly, there may never be enough force to subdue him. Well, that said, I never rule out the power of miracles because I have seen countless. But I wouldn't want to sit and wait for them as far as this issue is concerned. The damage is so intense because black folks also represent so many other oppressed races fighting against white privilege. After all, while I refer to blacks pretty much exclusively in this book, racism is also a problem for Jews, Hispanics and Asians, not to mention the fact that there are numerous underprivileged groups across the world who also have their challenges with privilege and who has it and who doesn't.

Recall the story of the Jewish family that I discussed in the previous chapter. The battle never ended until Jacob (who was the privileged son) *decided* to fight for Esau, the underprivileged brother. He was the *first* one to take action to heal the relationship because he understood the power that privilege vested on him, which made his fight more efficient than if Esau did it. Jacob *allowed* himself to feel some empathy for his brother's pain for losing his privilege despite this having been an agreement between them. This guy was a gentleman despite being a last born (not that I undermine the capacity of a last born), but he could have used that as an excuse to get away with this. Not Jacob! He chose to use privilege's power to catalyze the so much needed healing. He fought to keep his underprivileged brother from whom hate had separated for twenty years. He fought to heal him with kind words. He understood that his brother had a right to be angry just as does the black person. He did not dismiss Esau's anger.

Privilege gives you an edge over your counterpart. Whether we agree or not, the system has empowered the white person in such a way that any fight that the black person puts up is dismissed as anger or violence. Not that I deny the existence of both, but sometimes and perhaps for the most, it's just a perception. It will take the white person's willingness to *lay down* their privilege for others to become beneficiaries too. A change of attitude from both sides is inevitable.

This, therefore, is a call for the black and white folks in America to shift their positions. The goal is for the two to *trade* their positions in the battle of privilege. Trading here implies that white folks will stand in the battlefront for the black person, while the black folks safeguard the privilege from the front. Notice that this is a complete shift of roles from what has really been the case and that this strategy has no deficiency whatsoever. This calls for a calculated risk to dare trust; trust that your *brother* has got your back and will act in your best interest as you do the same. Calculated in the sense that these interracial soldiers must go through loyalty testing before they can be trusted. Just like military personnel when they are in a war zone, each must trust that their fellow soldier is acting in their best interest, but these soldiers go through a recruitment process. Their trust is not "blind" and that way they believe that the person at the back will keep their back side safe no matter what.

We have to find a way to create genuine interest for each other. This is only possible by realizing that as one American family, one person's trouble is trouble for all however much we try to imagine it otherwise. The fire we kindle for one another will end up consuming us all because we share one basket. We aren't independent of each other, are we? That is the driving force behind a *change of attitude* toward each other which is the *first step* of reconciliation and also self-recruitment into each other's defense forces.

The Sword in the Mouth

Once the attitudes are set right, we are ready for the second step — *speak* peaceably to one another. If I am suspicious of you, there is no way I will let you take my position in the battle line. This hatred and suspicion were created with *words;* it will also take words to break them. Before someone is dead, a word must have been said, which put the two parties on the edge with each other.

Recall the story of Jacob and Esau in the previous chapter. Esau *said,* "I am going to kill Jacob," and Jacob heard those words and then the hatred and suspicion began. Likewise, when Jacob was ready to end the hatred twenty years down the line, he sends a *word* to his brother saying, "This is a gift from your servant, Jacob." He did not stop there, he proceeded to the third and last step of reconciliation as well as self-recruitment (into each other's defense forces)—*action.*

For such a highly troubled relationship, you can't just show up for a hug out of nowhere and expect to get one. You would be taking a huge risk. Again, a peaceful word was not enough to break the wall; he needed to follow it with a confirming action. He gave him a gift, bowed down seven times, and then kissed his brother, Esau. Only then they were able to walk together.

We must acknowledge the *power of words* and use them to heal this broken world. Negative words, once they leave your mouth, become swords, slaying the target and unsuspecting passersby. There may never be any possible redemption for the damage. If you have nothing peaceable to say, please keep your word thoughts to the confines of your mouth. Everyone, both privileged and underprivileged, is hurting and we need to heal one another with kind words. Eighty percent of the hate will be cleaned with words of peace. Kind words are free of charge. Try saying something positive about the "other side." Find someone from the so-called "rival side" and having in mind that their pain is your pain, open your mouth and tell them something good. Intentionally become their medicine and see how you feel. Do you lose a tooth for doing this? I doubt it. If you can speak peaceably, then you can also act peaceably because the words prepare you for the action.

I think the expression that "doing something is harder than saying something" is not always true for all cases, for some the saying is harder, especially where breaking hate pertains because speaking acts as the *ground-breaking*. Not many people wait for the act anyway especially with the depth of the racial turmoil we have experienced. A kind word is way powerful to calm the storm. Besides, words seem to stick around longer than acts. Nevertheless, that does not undermine the power of the action which carries twenty percent of the healing as I see it. We sure need a complete package.

A Priceless Mistake

It was a Friday evening, and I had no intention to cook. Though cooking for people is my hobby, it is not the cooking that makes it a hobby but the people. I had just dropped my kids off at a friend's house for a sleepover. At the time, I was dealing with a lot of emotional issues following my divorce and all I needed was time to myself. Natty, one of my close girlfriends, had been pressing me to bring the kids to her house, so I could have some self-care. This was the day. With no people to cook for, I was ready to spoil myself with a different chef's menu. I dropped the kids off and headed to dinner in one of the neighborhood restaurants. Eve, my BFF, had, on the other hand, offered to spend some time with me that evening.

We had been in the restaurant for about an hour or so. The mood was great, and the place was full, typical for a Friday evening. I was facing the door a few seats away when five strange men walked through the door with their faces covered. I did not have enough time to comprehend the events because there was too much happening simultaneously. One man took charge of the entrance while pointing a gun at us. Another man headed to the cashier and I could hear a tussle as he forcefully asked for the money. By that time, we were all lying down with our faces to the ground. The other three were harassing the victims with kicks and blows as they ordered them to give up their cash, cards, and other valuables. They worked in a coordinated manner with one person to inflict fear, a second one to take the belongings and a third one to carry them. All these details I got from the edge of my eye as they terrorized my beautiful friend, Eve. I still can't believe how much time they had!

When my turn came, the ruthless fear agent kicked my shoulders and followed with the orders, "Bring everything," he said. In the process of handing over my wallet, but still scared for my head, I forgot that I wasn't supposed to look up, so I did. Their faces were covered except their eyes. When my eyes met with the terrorizer, he sort of stared for a second and then said to the rest of his posse in a loud whisper, "She is one of us! Leave her alone." That was it, they moved to the next victim. I was paralyzed with fear and confusion. I needed some explanation, but they were busy getting what they came for with no time to waste. Some mistakes can be priceless, both in a good and a bad way. This was one such mistake. Sometimes we want to explain a situation further, but we genuinely can't. I am sure you want some more details. Me too! To this day, I still don't know why and how I was considered one of them even though that apparently saved me.

Have you ever felt like you did not know yourself very well and that you need more details about you? That was me that moment and for many days after. I did not know whether to celebrate the victory or to worry that I was *forced to belong* to a nasty group of people. And that was not just it. The fact that I silently and helplessly accepted to be claimed by a terror group was extremely disturbing. I was left to explain to the rest of the people who heard what transpired, in what way I was one of them. You know how people like to compare notes after a common tragedy? I was just quiet because I had no one to compare my story with. Did I look like a thug and if I did what part of me did? *Damn it!*

Could it be that "his marijuana" had just started kicking in at the time he got to me, so that I looked familiar to him? But how come it didn't work on others after me? Or was it the big hairstyle that I was wearing for the day that looked like their signature style? No offense to those that like big hair, I do my hair that way sometimes just to compensate for my sort of little self. But that's beside the point. Did this dude see me somewhere in the neighborhood? Perhaps it was one of those bad boys that I passed by everyday as I went to the store? Or did God just send another angel, as He sometimes does? And was this just the best way for the angel to show up? Couldn't they have just left me alone without making an announcement that I was one of them? Some questions were just meant to stay unanswered.

Forced to Belong

Anyway, I wish to clarify that as a loyal pastor's kid (PK), I have been a good girl for the better part of my life. Never have I ever been involved with a gang or anything close or even far from it. I hope I cleared my name. But then, I still wonder, do such things happen in America or any other part of the world? Or is it just an African thing and particularly, a Phidia thing? Since then, I felt like these boys were spying on me whenever I walked the streets of Nairobi the capital city of Kenya or anywhere around my estate. I couldn't wear my favorite hairstyle for more than a year. I was forced to relocate to a different neighborhood. I am glad that my friend Eve knew me well, otherwise this blunder or whatever you may call it would have cost us our dear friendship. If that happens to have been an oversight from their end or a slip of tongue, then it was both costly and valuable.

But herein lies the real question — *why was I so scared to belong*? Isn't that supposed to be a good thing? Yes and no. Everyone wants to belong, but a forced belonging is not one at all more so when the claimed belonging is done by an undeserving party. There are some people who will try to recruit you into their circle of evil and they give you benefits so you find it hard to say no. I should have denounced this recruitment immediately. But I needed the *benefit* of keeping my belonging, so I kept quiet. I hope when the agents of hate say about you, "She is one of us," that you can do better than me; that you will be brave enough to denounce them *upfront* regardless of their offer. I say upfront because the more time you buy, the more likely you are to be trapped in the debris of hatred. Hate doesn't need to spend a day with you; a ten-second encounter is long enough to get you recruited and radicalized.

But remember, there are two sides to every coin. Forget about the identity of the person that said to me, "you are one of us." Let's focus on the actual words themselves. When someone says that, regardless of what disagreement had ensued before, something incredible happens. This statement steals the show, and the past gets washed away by the power of these words. Walls come tumbling, hearts melt with endearment and healing begins right there. More than ever before, we need to use every means of communication to tell each other that we are *one*, regardless of our skin color.

Whatever makes me *look like one of you*, however negligible it might be, that is what you should *fix* your eyes on and go after. Why focus on our differences if we have something in common? And if you were ready to shoot me with hate, just listen to the faithful commander of your heart saying like the goon, *leave her alone, she is one of us!* Hopefully, you will heed the orders as did the goon in my ordeal. It doesn't take the power of marijuana to notice that I am one of you, does it? Likewise, I shouldn't need to ask, "who are you?" We should begin to identify ourselves not by our skin color but by the *trademark of love* manifesting in our interactions right from the word go because we are in the *same defense force* fighting a common enemy known as hate. That trademark of love should make it easy to identify you. Make sure you have it.

ME TOO MOMENT	Have you ever found yourself unable to denounce evil because you were afraid of losing some important benefits?
	In one word, how did you feel afterwards?

You Belong ...The Evidence

My dentist is white. I believe I have the best one in the world. It would take a lot of effort to convince me otherwise because they meet one of my greatest needs, the need to belong. This clinic stands out in so many ways. They have a safe way of bringing you into their space. They make effort to know you as a person, not just as a client. They may not use words like that goon did to me. They just engage you in a way that tells you that you are one of them. They persuade you with actions to drop your guard and be a part of their family. What better way to do business in the 21st century?

They take a risk to make strangers part and parcel of their family. I am sure sometimes it bites them, but still, they don't stop doing it. They understand that some family members will always bring trouble, but also that the benefits of a family far outweigh its pain. That is the perspective that will help us in recruiting each other to our defense forces with the words, *you are one of us!* There is no better time to tell each other these words than now as we watch the world fall apart with hate and racism. We must use all avenues to pass this message around. During the robbery discussed above, you must notice that my thug guy spoke words, and actions followed harmoniously.

Don't just give me peaceable words, go ahead and show me then I will know exactly what you mean. We can miss your words but not your actions. We need both. If a heartless goon could keep their sharpened sword from devouring "one of their own," how much more can we drop our sword of hate for the sake of each other? Be my soldier and I promise to be your soldier. If we got this, the recruitment of officers is done, and we can start taking bullets for each other. I am a beneficiary of such relationships with privileged white friends.

If you are black and don't have such a relationship with a white person, I am sad on your behalf. You are missing out on the *fun* behind interracial relationships and likewise for the white person.

It could also be the evidence that you are a racist especially if these people are all around you. What a beautiful thing it is when a black person says to their white counterpart or vice versa, *you are one of us, step aside, I can do this better for you!*

Resignation Letter

Black folks need to accept that the current strategy has been time-consuming, emotionally draining, and non-effective. This admission must be followed with a resignation letter from a front-line officer. There is *no time* to serve notice; this is a destiny call which is both very important and urgent. I don't mean that black people should give up the fight. It is just time for black people to trust that there are a few (or hopefully many) privileged white heroes who have a *genuine* heart for the black people and the underprivileged. Individuals who are not only disgusted with the shame of the unjust, discriminatory systems but are also fiercely bold enough to utilize the power of privilege to defend and advance the victims. These are ordinary individuals who may not be in the political or legislative arena yet, but powerful in their own way. There is hopefully someone closer to home that can do a better job and then the only work left is to identify and collaborate with them. That doesn't leave the privileged at a loss for defending the underprivileged. It is a strategic way for the privileged to milk *real value* out of privilege by entrusting it with the underprivileged to secure it. Let privilege defend itself for its worth so that the privileged can sit back and enjoy it. *Oh, how I love this!*

Stepping back is not always a sign of quitting nor is it a waste of time. A step back from the front seat is a great chance to usher the underprivileged person to the place of awareness and to notice critical yet often overlooked details that are instrumental in this battle. Behind the scenes gives you an opportunity to identify these champions who don't define fairness on the basis of who the beneficiary of the privilege is. We still have such people, but the black person will often miss them as long as they stay in the front lines of the battle. The firing line is a risky place that keeps you very engaged and ready to attack the enemy not because you want to, but because that's the only way to stay alive. I am sure you have seen how people stay on edge on race matters, ready to attack anyone they deem to be a threat to their tribe and themselves. This means that you can't maintain the battlefront and still have the luxury to notice these champions.

Likewise, white folks have to be deliberate in identifying and connecting with the black folks who are no longer on the front lines. They are looking for faithful soldiers and willing to give the same faithfulness to *protect a privilege that also protects them*. You can't miss them because of their *deliberate open and warm attitude* toward the privilege and the privileged despite the circumstances. They may be disgruntled but they focus on what adds value to their lives and others. It will take a privileged white person who is at *rest* from the pressure of a battle frontline to notice them. The fear of losing and the insecurity that comes with this privilege must be dealt with if shifting of positions in the privilege's battle will happen.

The secret to more power is power sharing! But this won't happen until we are at peace with who we are. The white person must understand that their importance doesn't lie in the privilege but in who they are in relation to the privilege. Always remember that *you are not the privilege itself* and that any negative discussion about privilege can happen without affecting your emotional stability simply because you are your own self, period! And we know who you are by what you stand for. We have to take a mental shift so we can see things from the right perspective. Your identity doesn't need anything to hang onto, it should just be. I hope we realize that there is a shortcut to ending this privilege battle and that a change of position is inevitable for both sides for us to actualize the results faster.

The best part of this change is that it marshals a battalion of *better* soldiers to accomplish more than you would achieve on your own, which means finer results within a shorter period. These soldiers will find it easier to fight with love than you would because they are fighting an internal battle (as was my case with the story of our basketball team fighting for the Simbas), which is not directly aimed at them. That makes them more sober soldiers than you because emotions aren't getting in the way of the fight. They will call out the hater in their camps *but* with love as one of their own. They only shoot with one objective and that is to heal. They will do a selfless fight for the greater good of one family, the human family. You sure want to have at least one of such an interracial relationship!

Each side understands better the devils they are dealing with. Only a white person can tell the real fear surrounding this privilege and why it has to be so safely guarded. The black person may assume that they know but the truth is that they really don't know until they hear it from the person dealing with it and vice versa. This implies that white folks know the real problem or the root cause, hence they are better positioned to find the cure. It is possible that black folks have been dealing with the symptoms instead of the real cause. Likewise, the black person would do a better job of *protecting* this privilege that sweats the white person to preserve.

The reason the systems have been adamant about giving equity is the fear that the white person will *lose* their place in the new society. Oppression and killing of black people are a sign of that insecurity. How about if the white person lets the black person take guard? If he is the enemy to the privilege, the easiest yet most lasting solution is to make him the defender of that same privilege. I remember in my high school years that the teachers applied this rule to their benefit. You remember those hard-headed students who always broke school rules and influenced other students to do the same? One of the best strategies to tame them and their followers was to make them the gatekeepers of the very same school rules.

How can the underprivileged be made the gatekeepers of this privilege, the very privilege that has in the past hurt them? What will turn them from being a threat to the privilege to becoming defenders of the same? If you are scared for your life, you can either invest in ammunitions against the threat or in a relationship with the threat. I suppose that the first is more expensive and difficult to maintain than the latter especially if the threat is a family member.

I hope I have convinced you to hand over your resignation letter and let love recruit a *better* soldier than you for the battlefront of privilege, for your good.

One is Not Enough

There are times when the privileged have acted in good faith but the underprivileged couldn't receive it. I caution the privileged that this will not be a one-shot kind of a thing because of the extent of the existing damage. It will take consistency over time from the privileged to break past that barrier. You don't stop when you get rejected once because you know what you want at the end of the day. But again, wisdom lies in discerning when you have outgiven your capacity because some people won't receive love whichever way you "serve" it. Don't kill yourself trying to convert such people into your faithful soldiers because it may never happen. Spare that "close-range" love for the next prospect who is meant for your defense forces but leave some "safe-distance" love behind for them.

Whatever the case hate is not an option. Likewise, the underprivileged must be deliberate to let go their misgivings to receive the gift of love from the privileged so they can give back the same love to protect privilege. Love and trust must be given *enough* chances to produce the shelter. The question is, what do you gain by holding onto your suspicion? We must focus on the bigger picture in this issue. It will take a constant collaboration from both sides to transfer this battle to the ones who have the proper tools to fight.

I shared a story of my struggle in getting a house. What a relief when my privileged white girlfriend decided to step in to find out what had caused the delay! She had a better understanding of the systems and the people in charge of them than I did. She was willing to help, and I was ready to receive her help. At the beginning of our relationship, I wasn't as confident receiving her help, but her steadiness led me to the place of being at ease. We have many privileged white heroes who know how to spot the need and apply their privilege to satisfy the need. But they must be met by *open-minded* black heroes who don't shy away from a helping hand, heroes that keep their eyes on the things that matter most and whose identity is secure. Have you allowed your insecurities to hinder your ability to receive help or support others to be better?

One More Die-Hard for me

"How mean could you get? That was so insensitive of you!" This was my privileged white friend, Sally, calling out Julie, who is also privileged white. Both are my friends on social media. You would think that Sally was defending her space but no! She stepped right into *my* space to safeguard it because she felt that someone was taking it for granted. She sensed that *one of her own,* a fellow white girl was not treating me kindly. I did not ask her to defend me. She just opened her eyes, saw the need, and jumped in full swing without feeling the need to *ask* for permission. Wow! I dare say that you will find such heroes and heroines exist within the privileged white community. You just have to be attentive to see them and open your heart to receive them.

The above incident was the aftermath to a post I shared on one of my pages. As I said earlier, there is not so much to hide about myself.

So, anyway, I made a post about how I sexually shared a husband with my adopted daughter for three years. As you would expect, this prompted a series of reactions. Among them was Julie who asked, "Sharing your husband with your daughter? What the heck could have been wrong with the three of you?" I believe the question was very genuine, but it probably came off as insensitive to most readers. A public speaker's life is often subjected to public opinion and critique, which is just supposed to be part of the package. In any case, she had valid concerns. So, I responded by saying, "Julie, something was definitely wrong, which was exactly the reason why I shared this so that others can keep their sanity." Then, I moved on.

Unfortunately, Sally would take none of that. She fired the bullet, which then prompted a heated exchange with Julie and mind you, this was *all on my behalf!* She was out to make Julie see how insensitive she was to me, and Julie was just not going to have it. It was so intense that I had to come in and quell the fire by telling them both how much I trusted and appreciated their intentions. Phew! What a relief when I finally calmed down the storm but more so that I had a take-home for the day. How often do you have people fighting on your behalf especially without consulting you? The sweetest part is that Sally and I have never met in person. We are just friends on social media, yet she was sensitive to the pain of a black girl she has never met physically. Perhaps she would have done the same for a fellow white girl, but the fact that she so boldly transcended the messy racial divides to speak up for a black girl was the big deal takeaway.

Sally had the option of minding her business or just feeling bad about it and perhaps sharing with a friend. But she went beyond the feeling. She was not only thoughtful like most people were, but she was also bold enough to confront it. Not only did she feel the love, but she also acted it out. How beautiful was that! I believe our world is ailing as a reason of a "felt love," which never manifests itself in real life. A love we cannot touch is not love at all. All our frontline soldiers need to possess this kind of love, a love that moves. If I let you into my battle frontline, don't come for a joyride, I am looking for a soldier. There is so much *unrealized love* or other *potential love* out there. But whose life does it change? This lot of unrealized lovers does not cause any trouble, but they also don't condemn it. They maintain what I call a "grey" position because they fear for their safety and the color grey is the color *between* black and white. By so doing, by being grey, they indirectly support hate. Are you this person by any chance?

A Homecoming Ceremony for Your Soldier

Remember that the first step of identifying a probable frontline soldier is their *open and warm attitude* toward the "other" side. They don't dismiss the facts, but they also major on the *possibility*. So, how do we help our prospective soldiers to move from potential love to what my physics teacher would call *kinetic* love, which is the final and practical part of the recruitment process? This is a place where that very love goes through an experimenting process to confirm the worthiness of the soldier before they are brought on board to do what they do best. Again, this is a critical step at which the potential love is let loose to adopt and fight and as such the interracial parties begin to experience it within their relationships. Sally had just passed this test with flying colors and gotten a confirmation as a member of my defense forces! Wow!

But how could someone I have never met in person, boldly step into my world without fear? What *role* did I play in making Sally feel welcome into my space? First, I initiated the relationship by asking her for friendship on social media. An underprivileged black girl asking a privileged white girl for friendship! In this country, they are not expected to be on very good terms, so this was a great starting point. Then, she received the love with kindness and gave back the same and there lay the warmth in her attitude. Mark you, I asked several other white girls who, for some reason, either did not receive my love request or they received but never gave it back.

Asking was the first step to signal an invitation into my court. Then, I openly discussed racial issues while keeping a bipartisan stand, I was not out to defend my tribe. I gave equal measures of love to both whites and blacks and she noticed that. I maintained an open mind and a welcoming attitude. I had no grey areas as far as what I stood for. She sensed that she was an *equal* stakeholder in how I interacted with her. She felt *received* in my world. There was *safety* for her within my territory and that gave her the freedom to act in good faith without feeling the need to ask for permission. Wow! What a beautiful relationship right there!

Who is your team of diehards? Identify them and in a gentle yet clear way, send the message that they are *welcome home*. Yes, I call it *home* because this is where they were *meant to be* in the first place. Black and white folks were supposed to be united as a family of humankind, guarding each other's back, and taking each other's bullet because they share *a lot* in common including one economic basket. But the "fourth world war" caused by privilege, sent the soldiers into exile. Now it's time for them to come back home. You need to make them a beautiful homecoming celebration. Make them feel *needed* and *wanted* at the same time. Let it be known that they will not be treated as suspects but as family.

Strive to give these soldiers the assurance that they are free to activate their love with you and you will receive it with all genuineness and that you will also give it back, but in a better version. Sometimes, because of the existing misgivings about each other, we tend to see a threat even when it doesn't exist. Each side needs assurance that they are in a safe space for them to *activate* their love. We tend to think that white people don't have safety concerns since they are on the powerful side that invented this trouble. Not really. They are as human and as haunted as the underprivileged. They have to constantly figure out how to maintain their position and subdue the angry black person whom they don't feel safe with. They also need assurance that they are safe and free to extend the privilege into a shelter and that this good gesture will not come back to torment them at some point.

Love is a Force

We might know a scripture in John 3:16 which says, "For God so loved the world that He gave His only begotten Son, that whoever believes in Him should not perish but have everlasting life." This famous line in scripture has been given for us to emulate; the bar has already been set. What excuse do we have for claiming to love with no evidence? There's no love without giving. Is your love big enough to let go of something valuable? Is your love sufficient to produce an exhibit?

In my early twenties, I had a close friend from college. Benny always claimed to have a special kind of love for me, until we had it tested. One day, I had a bad fever and I needed someone to take me to the hospital. He was the first name that came to mind, so I called him. It was in the middle of the night. When he picked up the call, he could tell from my voice that I wasn't okay. "You don't sound well. Is anything the matter? he asked. When I told him that I needed to get to the hospital, he mumbled words that sounded like he was half asleep, and the call was disconnected. I called him again two times and the calls went unanswered. As a young adult, I knew what he meant, so I moved on to call another friend.

The following day, Benny called, apologizing, and claiming that he was half asleep and thought our conversation was sort of happening in a dream. Perhaps he was being genuine, but do you think I had time for this? You guessed right! I was so "done" with this "love thing" from that day forward. What kind of love doesn't give? I am well acquainted with the several "categories" of love, but I have no idea what class this kind fell into. I am not as mean as I might sound, and Benny and I are still friends. He actually won't mind reading this. I just happen to have experienced enough counterfeit friendships, that I can't miss the original kind. Anyway, he should have been grateful that I at least picked up his call after the ordeal. I think that was very gracious of me. I did not prove him wrong, love did. Sometimes you feel sorry for people, but other times you must let things be because that is how they were meant to be.

ME TOO MOMENT	Have you ever been let down by someone that claimed to love you when it was within their power to help you?
	In one word, how did that feel?

Love is kinetic energy. It moves, it has speed, and it is felt. Love is a force; you can't miss it. Let love call out the wrongs *without* exception even when the perpetrator is a member your family or race. Let love demand accountability. Why is the battle being left to the victim to fight on their own when there are so many kind and loving privileged Americans? How about having these amazing human beings spring into action? The impact is not the same as when the victim side does it. When someone whom you deem to have your best interests at heart calls out your action, there is more responsiveness than when it comes from someone you don't have as much trust in. This is for obvious reasons.

It would have been different if the white police officer who killed George Floyd was called out by a fellow white officer or by a white legislator. I bet it would have changed many others of like mind. Perhaps the demonstrations would have ended sooner if the white prosecutor did not dilly dally in prosecuting the white officer. But in the spirit of this book, let us also celebrate the white legislators and custodians of justice who took over the baton and ran with it relentlessly until justice for this case was established.

Lack of ownership on the perpetrator's side leads to escalation of the battle. What the victim side wants to see is acknowledgement and ownership. How beautiful it was to watch different ethnicities marching and declaring their solidarity for black lives! I watched that with tears of joy seeing the battle taking a different shift. While the public corporate manifestation of our love in action is critical, there's so much more that we could be achieving at a personal level. In our one-on-one interaction with the underprivileged, we can defend and protect, give hope in place of despair, courage in place of fear, value in the place of devaluation, life in place of death, and in so doing, rescue a destiny.

If the privileged take over this battle of privilege, a lot of precious time will be saved, and the results will be epic and that's not all. The underprivileged will in response, protect that privilege—of that I have no doubt whatsoever. Giving is like sowing, the gift comes back to you in a different and *better* form best described by the scripture as "pressed, shaken and overflowing." That is how selfless love can *reverse* the strategy in the battle of privilege by recruiting us into each other's firing line. There has never been a better time than now for both sides to partake in this historic moment as we turn the privilege into a shelter for the underprivileged and a *real* value for the privileged.

Caution: Avoid the temptation to rush the process of recruiting interracial soldiers. These are people that have access to the "bedroom" of your heart, they know your vulnerability and if they are not trustworthy, they can easily use the information to destroy you. Remember to be patient with the search and testing period until you find a worthwhile soldier. Never admit an interracial soldier into your defense forces until they have passed the recruitment process. They must earn your trust for you to allow them to fight your battles as you fight theirs; otherwise, it's okay to love them unconditionally from the periphery. You are also at liberty to keep a "wait list" until you are comfortable enough to graduate them into the security forces. Letting someone into the firing line to protect you is a serious business because a life is at risk. All the best!

The 'Practicals' of Love

1. Identify the struggle – Recognizing your pain and its root cause is the beginning of healing else, how can one be cured unless they first get diagnosed? Pinpoint an area of struggle in your life that has been a challenge to resolve and one that you believe someone else from the "other side" has got it all together. In my case, it has been handling racism and maneuvering the systems of privilege to get to my destiny and support my children to do the same. If you are not comfortable with conflict, then that is your thorn and all of us will likely have different struggles. Please beware that sometimes our blind spots hinder us from seeing our challenges. If necessary, this activity can be done with the help of a friend or a member of the Double MC club.

2. Admit the need for help - The underprivileged people need the privileged to fight for them and the privileged need the underprivileged to safeguard the privilege so they can enjoy the real value of it without fear, guilt, or shame. In this case, both the blacks and whites need each other in equal measures. Making this admission is a sign of humility and selfless love and a massive milestone toward racial collaboration.

3. Find Your Soldier - Identify an open-minded love-driven person from the "opposite" side, (I would call this person a hero or heroine of love) for the privileged, find an underprivileged person and vice versa. If you already have interracial relationships, you will have an easier time because all you need is to pick one that you are most comfortable with. This stage calls for patience, humility, and a daring appetite for risk. *Allowing* yourself to see the good in someone you would rather not (just because of an existing contention) is vital and worthwhile in making this step a success. There will be some trial and error involved. If your first choice doesn't turn out to be what you were looking for, then you have to find another candidate. It's just like job recruitment. You must interview several candidates and then pick the best. If you are lucky to get all the qualities met with the first interview, that doesn't mean you stop. We need as many soldiers as we possibly can because the goal is to form a battalion of soldiers. Please note that we are *not* looking for perfect people in this step. The key qualifier is the *attitude* of the person and what drives them. They must think *equality* and bear the trademark of unconditional love with the bigger picture in mind.

Remember, the interview doesn't take one day; it takes as long as a relationship can take. That means you don't have to do one at a time, you can have multiple interviews going on at the same time. If the interviewee happens to have read this book, they are also at liberty to conduct a parallel interview on their interviewer. No one needs to disclose their agenda. This is the only interview that happens without a posted job advert.

Show a genuine interest in their lives, celebrate them for breaking racial barriers and *expect* the same from them. If the celebration is one way, that is a red flag of a troubled relationship, and walking away might be the best option unless you feel bold enough to find out why they don't which, in my opinion is a little risky for interracial relationships.

As the relationship grows, you should be able to discuss racial issues without fear because you consider each other family. Share your strengths, weaknesses and struggles and seek to understand theirs. If they don't reciprocate, then you can have them in the outer circle and perhaps someday they can join the defense line. Don't, however, bring anyone to your battlefront unless they are genuinely interested in you.

4. Give them the Power - Once you have chosen a candidate, empower them to act on your behalf. Let them know that they don't need to consult you whenever they have to fire a bullet to secure your space. Knowing that they are trusted both with words and actions gives them the needed autonomy to act on your behalf.

5. Give Back - Other than trust, there is no better reward and motivation for these soldiers than reciprocity. Don't lose your diehard soldiers because of your own selfishness or uptightness.

CHAPTER SIX

Keep God in Perspective: A Shortcut to Loving Imperfection

The 'unlovable' Type

A few years ago, I had a friend who had a very special child. Nikita was the kind of a child that you would want to flee from at the slightest opportunity. If you are a parent, you probably understand what I'm talking about. My children were always torn between play and avoiding the drama of this energetic, naughty, and stubborn little friend who often visited us. At four years old, she was more than qualified to win a medal for being a Drama Queen. On top of that, she was a spoiled little brat whose mother wouldn't correct at all. As the only child of her mother, and the only granddaughter maybe that was the expectation within her family. She was extremely entitled. These circumstances were a major influence in developing Nikita's character. Her mother, Katie, was one of the sweetest people I have ever met. A very gentle, warm, and kind personality indeed and she highly resembled her daughter.

Having gone through a nasty divorce, Katie was still engrossed in court battles over the custody of little Nikita. She really wanted to convince her daughter that she was the best mom ever, whatever that meant. Because of these factors, she was under so many forces that she wasn't sure which one to submit to as far as parenting this little girl was concerned. Being close friends, she was fond of dropping her off at my house over the weekend so she could enjoy some good company with my kids as she ran some errands.

Immediately Nikita arrived on the doorstep of my house, my life would be forced to a standstill. All there was to do was to repeatedly use the words *stop* and *no*, as I ran after her, collecting not just the toys but everything else she scattered all over the place. She spared nothing she came across. She seemed to believe that the floor was the best place for everything and that scattered was just another word for beautiful. Unfortunately, my *nos* and *stops* fell on deaf ears. She had a complicated blend of adorable energy, a big attitude and stubbornness. By golly, she came for a playdate and she made the best of it at my expense! Hopefully, I don't sound mean to this little angel, as I genuinely aspire to give you a true picture of her character. I'm sure by now you have an idea of what I had to deal with at least two weekends every month.

My Child ... A No-Go Zone

I suppose it would be very normal to expect that I couldn't stand Nikita, not because she wasn't my child but because her behavior did not impress me at all. I recognize that parental love is supposed to be unconditional, but I am also the kind of parent who believes in rewards being given both ways. If you get rewarded for something good, then fairness requires that you also get rewarded for what is not so good.

My kids love to say how unfair things are when fairness favors their court. When the fair part lands on mommy's end, then they would like to wish that discussion away. But I am always faithful in reminding them that the sword cuts both ways. With that at the back of your mind, you know what fairness for Nikita would mean according to my parenting dictionary. I should have taken her by the horns, but I spared her. On a typical day, she was supposed to get several time outs before she *earns* a hug but I ended up skipping the first part of that plan.

At the beginning of the relationship, I tried to cope with her without saying a word to the mother. After two months of it, I was suffocating. So, I made an executive decision to deal with her the same way I handle my children. Under the "new management," Nikita was supposed to collect all the toys that she dispersed all over the place with no help else, she would have to be grounded with no more toys. That doesn't sound mean, does it? She cried, threw tantrums, resisted, tried to manipulate me by telling me how she just discovered that I didn't love her but eventually she budged. That Saturday, she only received one time out instead of four! I thought I was being very gracious until an hour after the pickup when I got a call from Katie.

"Phidia, I wish to be very clear with you. Though I appreciate your support, nobody, and I mean nobody, gives my child a time-out without my permission." This gentle girl was really fuming. I had never experienced this side of her. For a moment, I was almost sure it was a friendship prank, but I was in for a rude shock. I waited for that *I was just kidding* but it never came through. I wanted to reason with her, but she wasn't in the receiving zone. So, I just apologized even though it didn't make any friendship or discipline sense to me.

Since I had no intention of asking for permission for every time-out, I needed to find a different coping strategy. Katie was the kind of person who believed in me and all my dreams without censoring them. Such people I call "destiny incubators." People who believe in everything you are and in everything you want to be. They feed your dream with the necessary words to keep it alive. I don't let myself lose any of them unless it is a matter of life and death, and this situation did not qualify for this description. Henceforth, I wasn't going to allow something this minor to affect our relationship. In any case, Katie was dealing with a lot, and I needed to be there for her whatever that meant. Moreover, her sweet personality won her favor with my kids, who in turn loved her very much. I wish I could just choose her and leave out the troublesome Nikita, but that would mean shooting her in the heart, which I wasn't ready to. She came as a complex package, and I decided to accept it as is.

Inside the Laboratory of Unmerited Love

The only weapon left for me to make this relationship work was my usual trademark ... *unconditional love*. And it was *my* business to make it work. As for Nikita, she was having a good time whatever that was. She had long moved on after reporting me to her mother with no clue of what I was dealing with courtesy of her energy, stubbornness and now her mouth. So, here I was, struggling with such a bad attitude toward a four-year-old! I just could not envision how I was going to give this love in the first place especially after the reporting ordeal. And as if not bad enough, next time we met she had the audacity to tell me innocently yet sassily, "My mother will call the police on you because you don't like children." And shortly after as if she had already forgotten that "I don't like children", she had a "humble" request, "Ms. Phidia, do you have a water gun?" It was play time and suddenly, I had transformed into her "favorite" auntie. If you wore my shoe for the day, what would you do? I guess that is a story for another day.

Imagine the tug of war between my heart and mind at that moment, with the former pulling toward love and the latter toward hate. Isn't it fascinating that the mind believes in *earned* love while the heart desires *unmerited* love? And perhaps you may be wondering, "What the heck was wrong with this Phidia woman? She *should* have just understood that this was only a kid." Sure, she was, though it didn't feel like I was dealing with one. Maybe I just needed someone to help me understand how a four-year-old kid knew how to make an "appropriate" face to get what she wanted? Isn't that supposed to be PR? You mean kids at this age also have one? Never mind. I guess *understanding* my thought process helps you connect with my predicament at the time.

Under the prevailing circumstances, my brain had established huge signage with the words "DO NOT ENTER" written in red, right at the gates of unconditional love for little Nikita. But being a Type A personality, the word defeat also does not exist in my dictionary. Not when my relationship with a special person like Katie was at stake. I was going to do it *just* for the love I had for Katie if at all that made her happy. Journaling is a big strategy of victory for me. So, the following weekend I purchased a little diary and named it "A Thousand Ways to Love Nikita." I chose a thousand because it gave me the impression of an abundance of possibilities to make this work. But honestly, I wasn't even looking for a thousand, if only I could just find one! So, with my mind screaming "IMPOSSIBLE," I was hoping that the diary's title would silence this impossibility. Within me, there was such a commitment to love her anyhow!

ME TOO MOMENT	Have you ever been forced by circumstances to relate with an unlikeable person just because they belonged to a close friend?
	In one word, how did you get through it?

My Poisonous Secret

Even so, I had concerns, in case someone bumped into the little book. It had all my emotions toward Nikita expressed without editing. I wanted my *struggle* to remain a *secret* since it was not obvious in the first place. Or, perhaps, I was ashamed of the struggle itself. I thought of giving Nikita another name just to conceal her identity, but I was adamant. That wouldn't feel authentic, I wanted to deal with real stuff. In the process of thinking whether to change her name or not, what I feared befell me.

One Friday evening, I was going through my little journal in preparation for the playdate of my kids with Nikita the following day. Then, I had to rush out to pick something up from the store leaving the "top secret" on my bed. My daughter can be nosey, so she stumbled upon it. This led to a long conversation when I came back. Inside the little book, I had highlighted all the annoying things about Nikita's behavior, exactly as I perceived them. Nothing was sugar-coated at all. Alongside each behavior were my feelings towards her that were evoked by that behavior. Now as fate would have it, this was no longer my secret but our "secret." I wanted to bury my head until this was over but there was no one to hand over my cross to. I just had to carry it to the end.

So, I opened to her about my *struggle* with loving Nikita. Surprisingly, she was so intrigued to discover that the woman she considered a super woman had her own challenges too. All she ever heard me say throughout her short life was, "Love, love, love," which gave her the impression that I did it effortlessly. Discovering this new side of me was freedom to admit her reality. That created a haven for her to share her difficulties as she was also troubled by this relationship with Nikita whom they had frequently yelled and screamed at each other. With two of us sharing the same boat, why not row together? We decided to find a way to support each other to overcome our struggle. We both loved Katie; there was no question about it. She was the auntie that my daughter could tell anything to and trust that she would be understood. Henceforth, we both had a common point of reference that would become our anchor toward loving Nikita or just coping with her, whichever worked.

Just a Struggle; Not Surrender

Part of the strategy to win this battle was to be each other's keeper. We agreed to always be aware of one another around Nikita. Then, we came up with a hashtag whenever either of us was being driven by negative emotions following Nikita's actions. Either party was supposed to shout, "for LK," which meant "for the love of Katie" and the other party would pick up the message and act accordingly. It was a fun moment for my daughter who felt so special for getting a privilege to "sort of" give her mother orders. The deal worked. It wasn't easy at the start but within a few weeks, the little angel gave in to unconditional love and our relationship with her turned around for the better. It was as though our anger had been a motivation to her attitude and now, she no longer had the drive!

First, it should surprise you that the same people we keep away from our secret struggles are the same ones that can help us. Why do we feel embarrassed about our *battle* with challenges? Because we think we are the only ones going through it? Or has society taught us that struggling is a sign of weakness and so we would rather conceal it? And how safe are we with that secret? Could we be feeding the monster that would devour us at the end? How come we feel "safe" provided we can hide our little secrets and suppress our attitudes about this or that color of people? Maybe we need to realize that sharing our pain is a demonstration of courage and our "freedom pass," which could be the exact motivation that another person needs to admit that there is a thorn in their flesh too. Furthermore, it's just but a *struggle* and not a surrender. Provided you haven't thrown in the towel, you shouldn't be ashamed. That's why it is called a struggle because you are putting in a fight. Opening about it invites others into your boat, which means the chances of surviving are higher. Two are better than one because when one falls, the other will raise them up.

So it was that any time my daughter Hadasa used the hashtag "for LK" that the image of Katie and the beauty of her personality would be so vivid before me. The wonderful memories of our relationship would flood my mind, and my eyes would see Katie in this cute, little, stubborn, naughty girl. That would melt my heart with love, and kindness would prevail. Provided it was done *for* Katie, it was worth it. It was magical to see how my attitude and consequently relationship with Nikita changed. I developed so much tolerance and gentleness for this little girl, so much that my kids felt threatened and often complained that I loved her more than them.

Give It Until You Make It

So how did I move from enduring Nikita to genuinely loving her? Any time I wanted to snap because Nikita was acting crazy or driving me nuts, I "pulled out" the picture of her mother from the gallery of my mind and her seemingly flawless personality. Instead of seeing Nikita, I would be face to face with Katie and that was just cool with me. I saw beyond the stubborn, little rebellious girl. I went outside the box.

I saw more than my naked eyes could see. I looked with my heart. I would end up embracing the little angel at the most awkward of times. Then, she would just look at me and a few times she wiped her teary eyes feeling torn. I guess she was torn between the guilt of the undeserved gift of love she just received, when she had expected an angry, hateful ranting, and the beckoning of her personality to try it again! Within me these words were loud and resounding, "This is not just Nikita, but the daughter *of* my sweet friend, Katie. There's definitely some of that sweetness in her too!"

I changed from calling her Nikita to calling her KatNiki just to incorporate her mother's name into her name. At first, she shook her head vigorously and feistily said, "That's not my name, I am Nikita." I should have seen that coming long before, huh? But then we negotiated, and she accepted the nickname. I had to make sure that I did not lose sight of Katie to love Nikita otherwise, I had no other motivation. If the mind is convinced, then the game is over!

That just drove me to the place of seeking to *understand* the little girl even more, which translated to more love and compassion. It was unbelievable to see how much I could love the seemingly undeserving Nikita simply based on her mother's personality and the *relationship* that existed between the two of us. I turned every annoying instance with Nikita into a light, fun moment. I convinced my mind that it wasn't a big deal. I had an explanation to my kids and to myself for everything she did just because my love for her mother *covered* her faults. I highly doubt that without Katie being in the picture, there would have existed any relationship between me and little Nikita. She gave me no motivation at all for one. It was *all* about her mother Katie and the special love I held for her.

Love at Your Own Risk!

I like being genuine most of the time, whenever I can safely do so that is. I suppose that I am in a safe space right now. All humans can be pissy in one way or the other, it's just the degree that differs. You will never find a perfect one. There are people that you cannot relate with on their own capacity just because annoying is who they are. With such people you need a go-between for a relationship to exist. I see them everywhere, even in church, and I could be one of them for someone else. For some, they sort of rehearse how to be annoying while for others, they just find themselves doing it naturally. As far as I'm concerned, the former gets on my nerves rather than the latter, I don't know about you. If I discover that you have been practicing how to drive people nuts, that really vexes me. And, you know that such people exist with no apology. For this lot, their day is not complete until they stir up someone's nerves.

On the reverse, I have a different attitude toward the second group of humans. For them annoying is a natural part of their personality, and I try to understand them for the most part. But that said, as things stand today, there is not a reason convincing enough to bring black and white folks together. With every new day comes another reason as to why the two can't co-exist. The hope of ever getting the two sides to engage in a meaningful relationship dwindles day in and day out. Frankly, there seems to be more reasons to tear each other apart than to build up one another. Having said that, however, is there any hope in this hot mess?

Certainly, yes. Hope does exist. But it calls for a change of perspective from both sides. The game cannot be won from the mouth. The win has to be registered in the mind before the mouth can manifest it. How can a black person break through the shambles of pain, loss, anger, and vengeance to love a white person? Similarly, what "magic" does the white person need to change his attitude toward a black person? How can he begin to see him as an equal being that is deserving of honor contrary to what his forefathers taught him to believe? No promise that black or white folks will make any adjustments to their behavior, if at all, for you to expect that to become a motivating factor. And even though we form strong interracial relationships, do you presume that the parties will be perfect? Absolutely not! You must find something *independent* of any of the parties for any sustainable change. What control do you have over others' actions? If people choose not to change, then what hope remains? Do we just continue the hate *as if two wrongs make a right?*

We are faced with the same dilemma that I was with Nikita who gave me no promise, neither did she make any effort to help change my perception of her. She wasn't even interested. The entire process was in my hands to hate or love. She was not aware of my resolutions.

I just did not like how our fight was affecting my relationship with someone I *loved*. I did not consult Nikita. I just made up my mind to put forth an effort to change things. Have you gotten to the place where you can be genuine with yourself? How long can people live a lie about their racial perceptions? The fact that a black or white person's struggle with negative racial perceptions is not obvious doesn't cleanse them and that applies to all races. Hopefully, they have not surrendered. No wonder my assumption that it is just a *struggle*. The next step is to face the real monster.

Imperfection Loved Via Perfection

At this point, I consider it paramount to make this disclosure; that being a Christian woman all the principles and concepts of this book are borrowed from the Bible. Now, if you happen to identify with them so far, chances are that you possibly don't mind hearing a little bit of the Bible, as long as I keep it *brief* and *relevant* to the objective of this book. Having thus said, it would be baseless to bring this chapter without making some references to the scriptures and Jesus who is the *icon* of selfless love and giving for the Christian faith, having given His life to pay for the sin of humanity. Perhaps we will understand later in this chapter why He couldn't use a different way to save humankind. I am hopeful that by going through this book your attitude has changed and you feel secure enough to read this last chapter without losing your temper or feeling any pressure to do or say anything especially if you hold a different opinion. I promise that all you will find in here just like the other chapters is just, but love and your opinion is highly respected regardless. Again, as is with the other chapters this is a testimony of my life and an invitation to try my best practices. This feels like a greenlight to proceed together through this chapter. Thank you!

The call for interracial love and collaboration is beckoning us to a place of *security* and *maturity*. Giving hate just because it was given to you is immaturity resulting from insecurity whose intention is to *prove* a point to the offender. It's time to make up your mind like a hero or heroine, independent of what other black or white folks do and all other races and decide that you are going to play your part in creating a shelter and transforming privilege into *real* value. This means that you find a reason *bigger* than yourself and the other party. For me, that reason was Katie. What reason can hold you up for a lifetime to keep your love for whites or blacks and all races undeterred everyday as annoying as they may be? What is that constant factor that does not change with your mood, age, circumstances, people's behavior, actions, or whatever else you may think of? I bet, just as in Nikita's case, that factor has to do with *who they belong to* and the existing *relationship* you have with that person they belong to.

First, acknowledging that these vexing humans don't belong to you is very sobering. It keeps you from assuming autonomy in the way you deal with them at the face of disharmony. It also saves you the wrath of whom they belong to unless you really want some. I wish I knew what wrath awaited me for just a simple time-out on Nikita and that what looked good to me *wasn't* acceptable for Katie. Someone's kid is the center of their heart. Katie did not mince her words and neither do I wish to mince mine on behalf of our Creator. I believe that we were all created by God. Now, I respect them that do not recognize the existence of God. With that in mind, based on the journey of security that we have walked together through this book, I wonder if it's okay to conclude this— *That the act of humans acknowledging the existence of a greater supernatural authority over their lives could possibly be the highest level of victory a secure human can attain.* Insecurity drives us to a desire to control everything because we think surrendering is a sign of *weakness,* and we are *afraid* to trust anyone else to do it because we assume that we are the *only* ones who can keep things "perfect." If this contradicts your beliefs, please don't mind it.

The point is that there is something supernatural about our existence that we have no control over, and that is what I refer to as God the creator. So, is the one who made us supposed to just dump some living bodies on earth without an objective? Does any manufacturer make a product without a purpose? If that doesn't resonate well, don't we have plans for our children? And where did we learn all these habits of good parenting from? Isn't it the image and likeness of the creator in us that makes us behave like Him?

Don't we see ourselves in our children? It's all good until they reflect the dirty part of us, and we are like, *who do you belong to*? Either way, it is our image and sometimes likeness in them, whether for good or bad, just as His image and hopefully His likeness is in us. I use the word "hopefully" because though we look like Him from outside, we may not act like Him. And although His likeness in us may be tampered by our corrupted and fallen sinful, selfish nature, we cannot completely get rid of His person in us. Isn't it more serious then that we are *His* image and likeness as opposed to mere products from just another manufacturer? Whichever one you bear, whether His image or likeness or both, you qualify to be honored and treated with dignity *just* for it if nothing else.

Someone asked me a very genuine question, "Why does the creator have to be a male?" "I don't know," I said, "But it doesn't bother me. He can choose to be anything provided it doesn't affect His personality, His power and my relationship with Him. I don't feel insecure in any way," I said. What matters for me is not the creator's gender *but* who they really are. And yes, power for me is key because I have no business with a powerless god. As a descendant of a Kamba and a Kitondo girl, for that matter, I like overseeing my life only to a certain extent beyond which someone more powerful than I must take responsibility. I love to have some fun with life without being careless, and that means at some point, I must relinquish the steering wheel of life to one who can do what I and my kind cannot do. That is the beauty of "*belong-ing.*" Trying to be in control all the time is too stressful anyway. As a single mom, I know that better now. Or maybe it's just me. But that's beside the point.

So, if these people like Nikita belong to someone, how can we then expect that the very creator whose image they are doesn't care about blacks, whites, or any other race while imperfect as we are do care for our own children? Do you realize that even when a son turns into a thug, a true parent will still look at him chained up and cry, *Oh, my son!* Do you think God the creator is different? Absolutely not. He is the hallmark of parenthood. Do you suppose that you can get away with oppressing others or just hating them because they are annoying to you? Don't you realize how frustrating Nikita was to me, yet I needed to *ask* for permission to correct her behavior? And even though I did not like that approach and I was too prideful to take it, that did not change Katie's stand. Much as I did not think it meant sense, I had no option as far as making decisions over Nikita was concerned and if this Nikita issue would sever our beautiful relationship, it wasn't worth it. I had to choose my battles.

Do you suppose that you can go on oppressing or killing someone's creation and get away with it? Aren't you scared that you are overstepping your mandate with someone more powerful than you? I don't mean to inflict fear, but I don't think you can continue being casual about how you treat blacks, whites, and all the human races just on account of *who they belong to.* If that doesn't change a thing in you, maybe the issue could be the *relationship* you have with Him.

Knowing who they belong to is less effective if there isn't a good relationship to hang onto especially in the heat of the moment. If I had no relationship with Katie, I would have no business with Nikita. Again, staying away from the little girl would have been an avoidance strategy, which, at the end, would have left me judgmental toward her, angry with assumptions and ultimately deny me the chance to show love and compassion to Nikita. I eventually, through the love for Katie, gave myself an opportunity to realize that it was not the child's mistake to be what she was, but her circumstances and the people around her made her that way. We ended up creating a beautiful relationship with her and even a *better* one with Katie, and I was able to finally love her as a person.

'Cheat' the Process

How do we pledge so much loyalty to perishable things like our skin color, money, social class, fame, and what have you, things that abandon us when our time for demise comes, yet we valued them to the point of killing each other? Do you think our priorities could be upside down? Are these things worthy of the attention we give them? Do they really deserve our obeisance? If we focus on seeing things with an *eternal perspective,* we can overcome our selfish nature that is temporal. This very nature leads us to committing shameful atrocities because we considered ourselves better than others then we resort to blaming racism while the root cause is ignored. The battle against racism and hate may not be as effective unless we *introduce* God into the picture, which humbles us to see things for what they are and set priorities right. *How can we discuss the creation without involving the creator anyway?* Could that be considered as meddling? I bet any legally acquainted manufacturer would sue for that!

    Our aim is not only to refrain from hurting each other, but also to establish a *relationship* that can produce a shelter and a *real* value out of privilege. That means staying away from each other is not an option. So how can we have a fruitful relationship between two imperfect parties unless the glue of *unconditional love* is brought into the picture? Love is complete, perfect, and safe. Its description, width, length, depth, and height cannot fit in this book, let alone this line. Love is a wholistic package. The scripture in Matthew 22:37-40 says, "Jesus replied: 'Love the Lord your God with all your heart and with all your soul and with all your mind.' This is the first and the greatest commandment. And the second is like it: 'Love your neighbor as yourself.'" So, based on this scripture love is the greatest commandment which is *first* directed to God and then to humanity.

Loving God makes it easy to love these "crazy" humans because the love is not aimed at the *imperfect, undeserving* human but to *a perfect and deserving* God whose image they are. Then, as you keep giving love to the *perfect image of God* in them, they will, of course, think that the love is meant for them but that is your secret. This love strategy I call it a "via love" which is directed to something which the giver considers special and deserving within an undeserving target. The outcomes are worth the pain. It disarms the target, persuading them to drop down their guards and they begin showing you their vulnerability and kindness. Then you realize that no one is too strong for love, not even the angry or the radicalized terrorist. Kindness is the best weapon to avert wrath. The essence of wrath is to make a point and subdue the so perceived as an opponent. Kindness, for that matter, leaves the angry prover with nothing to prove and no audience to prove it to. That is the disarming process in action.

Do you know how many famous, tyrannical, and seemingly heartless leaders have fallen in the name of love? You realize with shock that inside that "terrorist" is a sweet, humane, and vulnerable boy or girl. That begins the connecting process with them as you strive to understand what led them to their ugly acts and the judgmental attitude is then replaced with empathy. That should drive you to love them the more.

> **ME TOO MOMENT**
>
> Have you ever done a "crazy" sacrifice in the name of love?
>
> In one word, how did that make you feel?

We will fight a losing battle unless we find a *tenable* cause for interracial love. Our love must break past common logic, facts, and conditions for us to realize the shelter and *real* value out of the privilege. It did not matter to me what Nikita did because my love was driven from within my heart and not outside. There has been a lot of paybacks manifesting in the relationships between black and white people. Revenge is a *cheap* strategy for insecure people who base their love solely on visible temporal things, the very things we hate, discriminate, and kill each other for. This speaks into our lack of eternal perspective on matters of life. We end up giving value to what doesn't deserve value and seeing things for what they aren't.

Interracial love can be very difficult if you don't like the person. Having a relationship with God is a *shortcut* to the process. This is really the only "acceptable" form of cheating. Have you ever loved someone's kids even before you met them just because you loved their parents? I call it love by extension which is a very powerful strategy. This is where you *create the image of the person you love in the person you are struggling to love and then direct all your love to that image in the person.* Then, as a result, the undeserving person finds themselves soaked in overwhelming unmerited love *for nothing of their own!* The vice versa is also true. If you have experienced an unpleasant black or white person, any sight of anyone close to that could translate to "hatred by extension," which is the idea behind stereotypes. That's the power of the human mind and we can make use of it to paint the world with love. Now, does that mean that if you hate the Creator then you could possibly unintentionally hate the creation? This is worth our thoughts.

From personal experience, relating to God has been way easier than relating to humankind. While humans are complicated and seemingly consumed with rules, God operates with only one rule, the rule of *love*. He doesn't focus on the do's and don'ts, He is attentive to one thing that fixes everything else — love, which is perfect. My kids are fond of saying to me, "I love you, mom," and most of the time, I don't give the generic "love you too" response. I just say to them, "If you love me, you will obey me." You should see the weariness on their faces because they expected that they could miraculously claim love with no responsibility on their end. If God commands us to love others and we choose to hate instead (because it is a choice), the problem may not be anything else but a deficiency of love for Him. How many crazy things have we done for people we love? Even things that don't make any sense logically speaking but they do from a "love point of view!" It shouldn't be very different in this case.

Whenever I am faced with an unlikeable or hateful person, the thought of whom they belong to and the love I hold for Him makes it way easier to still love them, and that helps to understand their struggle and be gentle with them instead of being judgmental. But just one second of focusing on them is overwhelming and I will suddenly slip into the pit of judgement! So, I must purposefully keep my eyes on the image of God in them. Every time you mention God, you get my full attention because of what He means to me. You may wonder why I love Him so much. Being a divorced woman and the stigma that comes with it especially in my community, friends and relatives keep shifting their positions on how they view and relate to me. That is not the case with Him, His love for me has remained constant and consistent, in fact I have experienced so much mercy, kindness and favor after divorce than before! I don't mean to suggest that you should get divorced so you can experience a better version of His love though. He just has a way of spoiling the so-called "unlovable" based on societal standards in order to prove a point to those that consider themselves "deserving." *Doncha love Him?*

When you are in love with someone, you find it easy to love their family and friends. You could easily miss many of their faults until the day that love "goes south," and then you would be like ... *what the heck did I love in this person*? It is not any different with God. His people become your people and they get executive treatment for *nothing* they have done or are. But first things first, a love relationship with God must exist. And if you wonder where to begin, you already have an express ticket just because of His image and likeness in you. You don't need a go-between to introduce you to Him. All you need is to talk to Him in your own words to give into this relationship. Yes, give in ... because He already loves you (creating you in His image and likeness is the very first evidence of that love) and has long been waiting for you to receive it.

God is *secure* enough to wait. Sometimes people struggle with waiting not because they have a busy schedule, but because they feel by waiting, they are stooping *too* low. They see waiting as a negator of their worth and that stems from not having a *solid* identity. Well, I expected a powerful God to break doors to show off His power and might, not so! He can stand at the door of your heart for as long as you live, gently knocking. Secure is who He is. How could a God who is also love be insecure anyway, when we know from experience and scripture, that love drives out fear, the same fear which is the magnet for insecurity? Now, racism and hate are signs of insecurity. So, am I right to deduce that finding His love translates to finding security which consequently leads to triumphing over hate and racism? Let us for a moment think about this…

Being in love with God is the beginning of all love. The scripture in 1 John 4:8 says, "He who does not love does not know God, for God is love." So, if He is love, being in love with Him translates to being in love with love itself! Picture that for a moment… We know that in a love relationship the two parties give, and no one can outdo love when it comes to giving. So, in this case love (God) gives first otherwise we have no love to give back because God is the origin of love. Anything else considered as love that doesn't come from Him is likely a "manufactured" counterfeit which can be poisonous. Therefore, imagine that we receive an overwhelming ocean of love from love itself (which is God) and we are satisfied and overflowing, then we give the surplus of the same love back to God the giver, and the rest to the people around us, wow! So, our love giving in this case happens from the place of *cheerfulness, ease,* and *abundance*. Now, the proportion of the love that we give back to Him in comparison to His "love bank" is like a drop in the ocean, yet He values it. Please note that we don't give back love to Him because He is in need; it's the same way as a parent you give your child a piece of candy and ask them to share with you to teach them to give! All God wants is to train us to love our neighbors because if we can love Him, then we can love anyone else because they are an *extension of Himself through His image.*

It's no wonder a heart filled with a Godly love is a satisfied heart which produces more love *than* it needs or a fountain of love because it is *connected* to the source. This excess love spills out back to God the giver, and then touching anyone in the surrounding irrespective of their color or race. And since this love is *unconditional* right from the author, it will in the same manner spill out unconditionally, adopting everyone regardless of whether they are racists, haters, prideful or angry. That is how receiving His love makes it easy to love Him back and share unconditional love with others. So, which version of love do you have? The original or manufactured? We just need to watch *how* you give it out and we will know.

So how much hate and racism do you think this fountain of love can withstand? Massive. I suppose as long as it takes to establish love in both the hater and the racist (not that I am an advocate of any of the two). That kind of a heart is unstoppable by any kind of hatred.

It doesn't look for any justification for love because there is so much love force from within and the springs are unstoppable. You can pay anything to get this gift of love from Him, yet it's *free!* He makes it easy to love anyone unconditionally because each one of us is a recipient of the same kind of love otherwise we are all guilty and undeserving of another bright day to live. How can such a gracious God be deniable of any request or command? Are you really looking for a way to make this world a *better* place? You just found it— obey His command to love your neighbor; neighbor because you can't pick and choose. In short, He requires us to love anyone around us regardless of their color or race because that qualifies them to be neighbors. But we must first be willing to receive the *original version* of love from Him, so we can find it *easy* to obey Him because we are satisfied with His love and have a surplus to share, first with Him and then to others, as an act of honoring Him.

Are you wondering what His name is? Just call Him God the Creator, because He is the only one, and if anyone claims to have a love relationship with Him, but they have no evidence of unconditional love, then we must hold them accountable for misrepresenting Him! Do I sound judgmental? I sure have no intention to, but before you cast any stone on me, the scripture above clearly says that such people don't even *know Him*, where knowing here is meant to represent a relationship. If this sounds too harsh in our current world where we are supposed to be "sensitive" to people, then I suppose the scripture is to blame, and hopefully I deserve to walk free from condemnation for this statement.

Is the Hater Doomed?

Putting the hater on the spot is *not* the objective but to show them the mercy available to them for a change. No hater or racist is beyond God's mercy, no one is doomed for eternal damnation except the devil who is the only one whose heart is not dichotomous in nature. He is so rebellious that even the principle of two sides to a coin doesn't apply to him. His heart only harbors hate. In fact, he himself is hatred, and so no possibility of love existing in him therefore, he has no chance to be recovered as we do. It's no surprise that he is the only one prohibited from reading this book because it won't change a thing in him. **We all have another chance to make it right** even if you have killed someone, God forbid. Ah! This concept of God's mercy is strange to the systems of humankind which are apt to condemn and once confirmed guilty your fate is supposed to be *quickly* sealed.

Humans will use all means to tell you that, "I can forgive but not forget." Not so with God. Being the love He is, this love is not only experienced in good times but also in adversity. He gives us countless chances to make it right and once He forgives, He will never take you through a guilty trip for the forgiveness as if you must pay for it. His forgiveness is from a *right* motive as opposed to some whose "forgiveness" is meant to inflict fear, shame, and guilt. Concerning His mercy, the scripture says in Psalms 136:1, "Oh give thanks to the Lord, for *He is* good! For His mercy *endures* forever." What can you do with a *forever mercy*? The word forever is nondepletable and inexhaustible. This is mercy with no beginning nor end, which the hater and the racist can take full advantage of at an amicable price called *give thanks*.

God will never ask you for anything else in return to this boundless, limitless, and overwhelming mercy except a grateful heart. And gratitude is not just in words but in a *consistent* practice of love for Him and for your neighbor. Returning to hate is undoing to the very attitude of gratitude and the more you have been forgiven the more you should love. Are you ready to ask for mercy for your role in advancing hate because we all are guilty in one way or the other? Are you humble enough to admit that you have fallen short as far as unconditional love pertains and receive His mercy? Do you have the commitment to walk the narrow path of unmerited love as the evidence of your gratitude?

If all external factors are held constant, what really is your fallback position? Is there an *intrinsic* drive? Are you willing to labor until the shelter is born? And while the willingness might be there is the force sufficient to carry you through a lifetime practice of selfless love? Do you have a motivation that can stand the test of time? Will your investment be adequate to push through until the privilege has transformed into a real value? If you have any doubt, then this is a loving invitation to you. Why not try my strategy? You have nothing to lose at the end of the day. And if you have a different opinion, I promise to hold you with utmost respect. This book is about love and this same love is what drives me to share my life with you perhaps it could make a difference. This very love triumphs over fear. Love is solid, kind and has no *pressure* associated with it whatsoever. You reserve the liberty to receive or reject it and still be held with regard for your decision. If you are reading this, I am grateful that you are still here and hope that this makes you feel safer to continue reading this last chapter.

ME TOO MOMENT	Have you ever done something that you felt was unforgivable?
	In one word, how did you get through it?

Swindled by God?

Is there anything for us in return for giving this unmerited love? Or is the God of unconditional love swindling us? Even though doing things for a person we love is satisfying, it is even more fulfilling to know that they notice and will *reciprocate* someday. Imagine trying to please someone who doesn't acknowledge you. You will wear out with time and move on to find a new love that gives back. A just and loving God understands this principle of giving and receiving, He, being the author of it, no surprise He gives us something to keep us going.

When George Floyd was killed, my love for my white brethren was tested to the highest level. I experienced all kinds of emotions from anger, hate, fear, shame, and anxiety just as much as I can conjure. I was caught in the middle of it when my eleven-year-old daughter asked me, "Mom, what are we going to do?" and then she broke down in tears. First, I had hoped that she hadn't even seen the video. As a mother, the last thing you want to discover is that your child is facing the same monster haunting you. That aroused the fighter within me who had surrendered to victimhood for four days in a row.

If you realize that you are the best among the worst, that should hype you up to act different. I needed to give an answer to this little soul. But not just an answer, it had to be the right one and be backed up with action. That's what I call "the practicals of love." So, I said, "Baby, I understand how you feel, it is difficult for me, too." For a minute or two we were quiet, as if to allow ourselves to feel and share our collective pain. "But we know that hate for hate does not produce love, and blood for blood doesn't bring life," I continued. She looked at me, staring blankly with desperation as though she expected something else, but I was done! These words had become the mantra of our family for more than two years. So, why was she looking at me as though I had said nothing? Then, she burst into tears again. "Mom, I never knew fear before, but this country has taught me how to be afraid." Those words stung my heart. Did we do all this loving business for two years just for nothing only to end up with fear?

The Promise and the Promisor

How did my little queen and heroine, a girl that had always been bold, taking on leadership roles from her first day of school end up in this state? Then I noticed how *empty* I felt, even after quoting our favorite love mantra's words to her. We both needed something more assuring than just words. For more than two years, we had relentlessly given love in the place of hate with the hope that things would get better. Unfortunately, they only seemed to get worse with the raw image of Floyd's killing on our minds. We were worn out, and we felt helpless.

We needed a *promise* to hold onto as we continued with the fight of love. A promise that the love we give shall one day be rewarded with something better than fear. An assurance that every racial discrimination-related pain shall be positively vindicated— positive because the vindication was not just about making the perpetrator "pay for it dearly," but more about the *restoration* of the loss and an *end* to injustice.

You and I have lived long enough to know that the weight of this promise cannot be delivered by a mere human. Long enough to know that not another election, or president or judge can deliver this commitment. At the end of the day, I still needed to say something else to this little girl. Something that held an *unfailing* promise in it. When I was growing up in the Eastern part of Africa, America was idolized. If anyone talked about the United States of America, it had to be on a perfect or powerful note. Some of us never knew that America could make mistakes. How naïve we were! We had this idea of a perfect country with perfect people, leaders, and systems. Well, that has since changed as we have gotten face to face with the reality. *So, if the superpower cannot give an unfailing promise, then who will?*

This excludes the scope of humankind because his nature is one that fails often. So, who has got this promise? Immediately I had an answer for her. "Child, I can't guarantee that I can do anything to prevent this from happening again, neither am I powerful enough to apprehend the culprits or even restore the lost lives. But remember the scripture tells us that vengeance belongs to God. If we choose hatred and revenge, we deny ourselves His *perfect* vindication and trade our peace therefore that is not an option. The black person is not here by flukes and so is everybody. He belongs to someone more powerful than all of us, God. One day, He will take vengeance, bring justice, restoration and establish righteousness." "Why can't He do it now?" she desperately asked. I thought on my toes and said, "Because He is loving and merciful by nature, so He gives people *time* and many chances to turn away from hatred. He doesn't take pleasure in releasing judgement on His own image and likeness. But He certainly rewards both good and evil so our love will be rewarded too. *For the love of God,* we must forgive and keep loving. We have to pass this test, baby."

 Her countenance drastically changed. I knew that being a fierce and competitive girl, the words test, and fail would provoke the fighter and the winner in her. And, if the words fighting and winning were in this case associated with love, why not! I was basically using all the available tactics to get through this as you would expect of a mother. "Do you love God?" I asked. "Definitely," she answered with her usual confidence. Then cautiously I said, "I am sure you can do anything for Him, right?" "Yes, Mother" she said." Phew! A splash of hope swept through my heart. Being an independent mind, this girl is the kind that has to be convinced within themselves to do something; I could have easily gotten a capital "NO." Thank goodness for the milestone. Then with more confidence I said, "Look, I am calling my *white* customers and friends to check on them. Do you want to call your *white* friends, Abby and Toni, so you can hang out?" I was very deliberate to use the words "your" and "white" to make her realize that the white was a part and parcel of *us*. She jumped on her feet with some enthusiasm just enough to conquer hate one more time. If I was doing it, then she was going to do it too.

Now, whether the hope I gave her was true or false may not be the issue here. Believing these words was worth every part of it if the results of the day were anything to go by. In any case she had *nothing* to lose but everything to gain by putting faith in these words. And she wasn't going to be the only beneficiary of this attitude; the white people around her and by extension all other races would be part of it. But her seeing my actions was more convincing than my words. Leading from the front is sometimes the only way to get the message home. The very same girl who fifteen minutes ago was scared of life, and sat in her bedroom crippled with fear, anxiety, anger, hate, shame and rejection had found her hope again. Not only did she find hope, but she also translated that hope into action. She went out to meet one more white person to break the barrier before it was fortified! *The longer you leave the racial barrier unattended, the stronger it gets.* I could barely contain my joy as I watched her pick up the pieces which despair had scattered all over the place.

Love and Justice Married

Whew! It was done! My girl was back, stronger, and better for another fight of love. Nonetheless, I must acknowledge that this was one of the biggest race-related nightmares I had ever dealt with for the two years we had been in this country. Big enough to affect my appetite for four days and to challenge our very foundation of love. I am grateful that we got to the end of the tunnel with so many important lessons. But where exactly did her hope come from? That day we dug deep to find it. Later in the day, I asked her what really made her optimistic, and this is what she said. "Because I believe that God is powerful and trustworthy. You also spoke with so much confidence." *Me? Confident?* She should know how I struggled to pronounce the word "white" that day. But never mind. I am just so glad my struggle was not obvious.

But the fact that she got a promise from someone greater than her, one that does not fail like her imperfect mother was a reason enough to find her hope again. Knowing that her love will *also* accomplish justice and restoration one day gave her a reason to give some more. Again, whether the person would deliver the promise or not, living in that hope was worth every investment toward defeating hate. And since the promise was not timebound, this meant that she was mentally prepared to love for as long as eternity takes with less temptation of giving up. I wouldn't be looking for anything more than this! That day, we revisited the issue of Nikita and created another hashtag to get us through the fire without compromising our commitment to unconditional love. Our new hashtag became "For LG" which meant "For the love of God." We posted several notes around the house to keep us reminded that if we had nothing else to love in a white person and any other race, then the image of God in them was worth our every bit of love.

Coming from a Christian background, I grew up with a perception that asking for justice makes us *mean* and *evil*. We are only called to love, period! Apparently, the same bible that asks us to love and forgive also promises us justice. *The existence of love invokes the existence of justice.* They are like alpha and omega. Both work in harmony like musical notes to produce a *rhythm of completeness.* No wonder they both appear within the same context in the scripture countless times, confirming their relatedness. **Please note:** Justice here means rewarding the giver of love and the intended receiver with what they deserve according to their actions. No one is left out!

So, why is the justice part overlooked by some people when God Himself doesn't? He says in Deuteronomy 32:35a "Vengeance is mine, and recompense." If the God of love is also the God of vengeance, then what makes you think that you can embrace one and not the other? Apparently, His vengeance is still driven by love, not so when we do it because then it will be our hateful emotions on the steering wheel. Notice that the person who executes the vengeance matters a lot. Remember that Katie warned me that no one does anything to her daughter without her permission? This is the same case with God. The haters and racists are His stray children and only He can deal with them, don't dare touch them *unless the touching is done by the hands of love itself through you, period!*

Be keen on the separation of duties and adhere to your job description lest you find yourself in trouble! So, when you go about loving, He will be doing the retribution on your behalf. Wow! I love this game! That God is always willing to do the "dirty part," on your behalf, so you can always look like the good guy. You sure are (a good guy) because unconditional love makes you one. Once you are done with your part, God lovingly yet fiercely like a lioness defending a cub pushes you to His back and says, "Have nothing to do with this, I got it!" Picture that for a moment, how does it feel? He doesn't mind taking the blame as He defends you and me, as long as you do your part. *How cool is that?*

But why can't He just defend us without asking us to do anything? Because that would again *compromise* His very nature of justice. I am the kind of girl who is very inquisitive and likes to make sense of everything as much as possible. So, if you ascribe to the traditional view that matters of faith and religion should not be questioned, I might unintentionally come off as annoying. I like the fact that I can make sense of most of the things in the Bible. Even though matters of religion are matters of faith, I prefer to reason with my faith than blindly follow. I guess that is a make or break for any believer whatever the object of faith is. This examination of our faith is necessary because it either invalidates our belief or helps us build more faith if at all the object of faith is valid. I appreciate that the Bible encourages its followers to ask questions, as seen in the scripture in Acts 17:11, so they can substantiate their belief.

Whatever faith you ascribe to, I sure hope that it allows you to question it because that is a sign of a secure faith and a *critical* part and parcel of fairness or justice. As an advocate of fairness, I believe that no one should be forced to be a follower of something they don't understand. I guess this explains why Jesus in Revelation 3:20 says "Behold, I stand at the door and knock. If anyone hears My voice and opens the door, I will come into him and dine with him, and he with Me." Nothing is at gun point as far as this sentence pertains, it is a relationship involving a willing giver to a wiling receiver. That's *justice* served. God, being as *secure* as He is doesn't get offended with our questions if we ask with an intention to understand the truth concerning His existence or His word, again the word "secure" won't let us alone! Do you know that *secure* people don't mind reading this chapter to the end without losing their cool whether they believe it or not? Seems like this word "secure" will "haunt" us until we put our houses in order.

ME TOO MOMENT	Have you ever felt guilty for demanding justice?
	In one word, why do you think you felt that way?

Who Is Your Icon of Love?

The bottom line is that you must do the loving first before vindication takes place. It is your love (giving) that opens the doors of justice. Talking about giving, who can outgive God? He doesn't preach water and take wine, no! From the scripture point of view, He gave the best that He could ever give as we see in John 3:16, which says, "For God so loved the world that He gave His only begotten Son, that whoever believes in Him should not perish but have everlasting life." If you are a parent, you know how much of a deal that is. But did God have to give His son? And are you also wondering where He got the son from? That should be a very genuine question whose answer I may not have. Perhaps we need to reserve that for a different forum so we can stick to my promise of keeping it brief and relevant. But maybe, reminding ourselves that He established the heavens and the earth, and we still don't know where He was standing at the time should remind us how omnipotent He is, but never mind. So, why couldn't He find some other means to forgive and reunite with His own image in a rebellious humankind? He had the power to just let go the offense, didn't He?

Again, the answer lies in His love *for* justice. God established justice before He established humanity. This very justice required that someone had to pay for the sin of humanity and who on earth could offer a *perfect* ransom to the God of all creation and still have a *right* to judge humankind? This person had to be both God and human at the same time— God so as to offer a *perfect* sacrifice to a perfect God, and human to identify with the pain and predicament of humanity and henceforth *qualify* to execute justice on behalf of God and humankind. That is why the God of love and justice could not "cut corners" to get the job done otherwise, because that would compromise justice. He had to let His son who is also God take a lowly form of humankind for love and justice to be established. His love to save humanity from judgement went first, and now He waits for an appointed time to execute justice in relation to *how* humankind handled the love. Do you notice that order within His justice system, that no judgement is passed unless love has been given? Wow! Furthermore, how can He ask us to do it right when He Himself can't? Whatever the cost, He was going to do it the right way, and sure He did by giving His only son! How passionate about love and justice could He get! If this is too much to comprehend, I understand, just remember the message here is how *important* and *related* love and justice are to God and that He can do anything necessary to submit Himself to both.

So, only God could come up with a perfect sacrifice and so He did painfully give out His only son Jesus. His giving was phenomenal. And who gives *without* receiving? Wouldn't that bring some sort of imbalance into the giver's life? We might know of a scripture in Luke 6:38a that says, "Give and it shall be given to you: good measure, pressed down, shaken together, and running over…" It's just a fundamental rule of life —if something leaves, something will come to fill the vacuum. The best part is that you get a better version of what you give because giving is like sowing. Even though it costs us our pride and selfishness to give love, especially to someone who seemingly doesn't deserve it, the outcomes are priceless.

Why do you think the scripture in Acts 20:35 Jesus is quoted saying that it is more blessed to give than to receive? He knows that this worked out for Him big time. He wasn't bullied into dying for our sins, His Father gave Him to the world upon which Jesus gave out His life for us, so two "givings" happened here and the receiving is what perfects the cycle. But important to note is that *whether the intended receiver receives your gift or not,* it doesn't affect your reward. Their actions only affect the giving and receiving cycle. Your gift of love will *still* be rewarded whether the person to whom it's given receives the love or not. That should encourage you to love and love and love!

At the end of Jesus' giving though a painful one, we are told in Philippians 2:9-11, "Therefore God also has highly exalted Him and given Him a name which is above every name, that at the name of Jesus every knee should bow, of those in heaven, and of those on earth, and *that* every tongue should confess that Jesus Christ *is* Lord, to the glory of God the Father.". Well, this is not a theology book and I acknowledge with respect that if you ascribe to a different faith this might not be very comfortable for you to read, but since the concepts of the entire book are borrowed from the Bible, then this example of Jesus feels closer home and therefore ask for your permission to use it. And if I missed *your* icon of love and selfless giving, please include them here with a red pen and feel the inspiration that comes with it. Now, whether you believe this scripture or not may not be the issue as far as this book is concerned, but the *outcome* of His giving is what really matters.

A Gift that Disrupts for Good

With reference to this scripture above, Jesus got some "superpowers" that no one else seems to have, powers to forgive sin (and give eternal life) and to *oversee* the justice system of Heaven and Earth. Two important things here— One, His giving of love produced unlimited life for humanity, because that's what unconditional love does; It brings life. Two, His giving of love *qualified* Him to administer justice on behalf of Himself and the recipients of that very love. These two words (love and justice) seem to be inseparable. His love both forgives sin and condemns it, how just! But do you think He deserves this kind of a reward?

Perhaps you have seen how some of His followers in the time past and even in the present faced with a difficult choice to either deny Him or die prefer Him to their lives. I have read, heard, and seen many incidences of how these followers of Jesus remain unmoved, even when faced with a death sentence from insecure people who would rather kill them because their insecurity cannot embrace anything different from what they know. How desperate insecurity can get! You must hate it and be compassionate to its captives. And I am not sure if these atrocities amount to some kind of "racism" on their own, but whatever you may want to call it, I wonder if these "superpowers" that Jesus got out of His selfless giving have anything to do with the passion and adoration that His followers exhibit toward Him or is it just radicalization? That is a story for another day.

Whatever the case, the take home here is that the *magnitude* of your giving determines the magnitude of what you receive in return. And here magnitude doesn't necessarily mean the quantity but especially the *quality* (the sacrifice involved and the motive). Have you seen people who help the underprivileged in society as a showoff, yet their hearts are far from their gift? Well, this kind of giving does not "do a thing" to the giver nor the receiver (because looking at this example, *a real giving is supposed to transform the giver and the receiver too).* If your giving is not genuine, at some point, the gift is bound to turn into a poison to you and your target, so it's safer not to give in the first place. It is very hard to hide the attitude accompanying your giving if at all you can.

Please Note: The outcome or reward of Jesus' giving had *no* correlation with our receiving. The Bible is full of stories of how people rejected Him while others received Him, yet none of that rejection could stop His reward. Immediately Jesus was done with giving out His life, God the Father *took over* the process. He raised Him from the grave as written in Romans 8:11, back to life with a promotion of a name above all names and that was it! But why did God the Father take over the process after Jesus finished His giving, yet most of us rejected His gift? Because when you give love to undeserving person on account of *who they belong to,* you are giving to the image of God in the person. Therefore, God Himself "stands up" in honor of your selfless act and receives your gift! Yes, I dare say *stand up* because God honors those that honor Him according to the scripture in 1 Samuel 2:30, and selfless love given on *His behalf* amounts to honoring Him. So, where on earth or heaven did you see anyone honoring another while seated? I guess I have presented a good case so, let's for a moment picture that standing ovation from God Himself… *Don't ya love this?*

ME TOO MOMENT	Have you ever mishandled a stranger only to be haunted by guilt after discovering who they really were?
	In one word, why do you think you felt that way??

More than a Standing Ovation…

You have no *excuse* to let hate wear you out, your love giving should prevail over the response of the intended receiver because your eyes should be on the image of God in the person, and you now know very well *how* He receives your gift. Once your selfless love is given, sit back and watch, because God takes over the process. You must have seen how loving people attract so much favor in their daily living despite their challenges. I am a living proof of this from the time I chose in my heart to forgive and unconditionally love my ex-husband and our adopted daughter. I can only describe the experience as "living under open heavens!" That should motivate you to stay at it, keeping your *inner* eyes not only on the beautiful sight of a *standing ovation* from the God of all creation as He honors a hero of interracial love, but also the reward that awaits your giving in this life and the unlimited life to come. Always remember that your gift of love is *complete* regardless of what your *physical* target does with it.

This gives us a better understanding as to why Jesus, in the scriptures mentioned above would ask His followers to consider giving *more blessed* than receiving for two reasons: First, giving creates an opportunity for you to automatically receive. So, you don't have to worry about receiving if you can focus on the giving; it *effortlessly* comes as part of the deal! Second, your giving gives you a *better* gift in return than would be the case if you decided to solicit for the gift. I mean, if you sit and ask people to give you, you get a short deal because you miss a step in the *giving and receiving cycle* known as *addition and multiplication*. This step is only triggered by your gift which is the platform for the so called "pressed, shaken and overflowing" magic described by the scripture in Luke 6:38. This magic is what I refer to as addition and multiplication of your gift before it is handed over back to you. No wonder giving is better than receiving because it perfects the receiving.

Caution: This principle doesn't do what I would call "selective fulfillment." It doesn't first sort out the seed to separate the bad and the good. The principle is ONLY responsible for the *addition and multiplication and not the nature of product, the quantity and not the quality*. Your type of input will determine the quality of the product. If the seed is hatred, it will, in the same manner as with love, proceed to add and multiply, so you will at the end of the season receive a good measure of hatred pressed down, shaken together, and running over! I don't want to be around you when that package is delivered because that parcel of doom is more fatal than the deadly Hurricane Katrina of the year 2005; my heart goes out to the victims.

Who is your icon of selfless love and giving? As for me, I just shared mine. The bar has been set, there is no way we can play below it. I sure hope and pray that you will abundantly sow unconditional love especially into this racial turmoil, and that the overflowing gift of unmerited love will in return sweep you off your feet with *exceeding joy, blessings and unspeakable favor* for this life and the life to come! And not just for you, but all your loved ones. Always remember that God is your *invisible* target and recipient of your unconditional love through an imperfect human and once He receives it, He does the pressing, shaking and gives it back with an *overflow* and this very overflow of blessings and favor is *not* for you. You have no business with the spillover, do you? You already have your cup full. It is for the people around you starting with your loved ones. Wow! This business of giving unmerited love is just worth it!

But then, the love that rewards the lover with kindness is the same love that rewards the hater with judgement and if humankind deserve justice, *then God too does*. That should be a fair statement for anyone that understands how justice works. I guess this explains why the very God of love will *against His desire* judge his own image, because He doesn't compromise justice to favor Himself.

Please Note: If God never gave His son Jesus, and the son never gave His life, then they both would have no basis for executing judgement on the world. It is the gift of love that opens the doors of justice. Likewise, if you don't love your neighbor regardless of their color, race or actions, then you also have *no* right to justice.

I hope I have given you enough motivation to admit the deficiency of your "kind of love" in order to receive from God (the source of all love) the original copy that stands the test of time. I sure believe that by submitting yourself to this reality, your interracial love will prevail over every circumstance. I pray that you will be able to resist the temptation to revenge hatred for hatred, as you enjoy a love relationship with God *now,* at the same time *looking forward* with excitement to your bountiful reward.

Forgive, But Not Like an Idiot

Refuse to suffer inferiority and don't get into a deal without understanding what is in it for you. From experience, religious teachings tend to favor the perception that asking for our fair share is evil. Yet,

God doesn't give commands without a promise because He knows that some things just don't work. He is the essence of fairness. He doesn't extort people. It is an honorable thing to be the *receiving giver* and not the *giving giver,* with one hand giving and the other receiving. That has no relationship with evil at all, it feels so right in every way because it's just fair, and God is a God of fairness, otherwise where did we learn it from? Have you by any chance seen how much of this word (fairness) and its "relatives" we have all over the scripture? What do you make of that? And perhaps you wonder why I sound so passionate about this subject. I was once brutally held hostage by this mentality of one-way giving.

Having been a church girl all my life, I thought I was meant to give all of me until there was nothing else to give. I read the Bible one way. I had a bad relationship with receiving. As a marketer, I made good use of my mouth and sure enough, I acquired good clients. What a quality job I gave to them! I had no doubt whatsoever but asking for the same quality into my pocket was a tall order. I either felt embarrassed or undeserving. At times, I felt as though I was a bother to the giver, even when excellent service had been rendered. How awkward! It took a lot of reading, prayer, and journaling to change that. That's how stubborn this mentality can get. So, if you are still struggling to be the receiving giver, I completely understand. If claiming your fair share, not just with business but also in relationships feels like digging on a rock, I can relate. Yet, this is a critical part of dealing with racial issues especially for black and white folks whose racial wrangle is a big mammoth in this country.

Having God in the perspective doesn't mean being an idiot. God is a rewarder of obedience. The call to love our *imperfect* neighbors is *not* a pleasant one for the mere fact that we have no choice over who becomes that neighbor. That means that most of us will have to deal with people we don't like and love them the *same way* we love ourselves. *How difficult!* No way this would be doable without a promise from God. Jesus talking to His disciples according to John 15:14 said "You are My friends if you do whatever I command you." That is a promise within a condition.

I wonder if anyone would reject an offer to be a friend to the God of all heaven and earth? Only someone who does not know who He really is, which is understandable. I would do anything possible to be a friend to the president of the most powerful country in the world, yet they are just mere humans like me. What about being a friend to an Omnipresent, Omnipotent and Omniscient God? Imagine how you graciously deal with your BFFs despite your imperfections; what do you expect a perfect God to do with His BFFs? I don't think there is any promise greater than this and that is what I would call a *real privilege*. But incase being His friend is too overwhelming, then here is a more direct one: The scripture in Psalms 103:6 says, "The Lord executes righteousness and justice for all who are oppressed." But then the big question is: Can you trust a promise from a random stranger?

One time, we were strolling around at a trade fair with my children when a random person who seemed to be child-friendly approached us holding a stick and said to my little boy, "If you break this stick, I will give you free ice cream." He wasn't holding any ice cream but nearby, there was an ice cream truck. It was summertime and the sun madly "revenging" on us for something we couldn't tell. I expected my son to get excited and quickly reach out for the stick. Instead, he looked at the gentleman and asked, "Who are you?" Well, I never saw that coming. The guy never answered, he moved on to ask the same question to another little boy around us. I watched the kid break the stick and sure enough he got the ice cream. I was shocked and frustrated at the same time. It didn't make sense to me that a seven-year-old ignored a promise for ice cream on a hot summer day. That was not all! What did who this person was have to do with this ice cream? Unfortunately, it was too late to ask these questions. We missed the ice cream but didn't miss the lesson. My little boy was not going to jump into promises regardless of his need for the day, unless he knew the promisor. *It is the relationship that makes the promise reliable and binding.* I guess this deserves more thought.

God wants you to love and forgive with *hope* and *expectation*. He wants you to have some *fun* in exercising your interracial love. No wonder He gives a promise, something to look forward to in the place of your sacrifice. Of course, it's a sacrifice when you choose to love someone who does not deserve it. How about withholding your vengeance to manifest love and compassion?

God doesn't want us to forgive like losers. He wants us to forgive from the winning side. *Hope* must accompany our love and forgiveness, otherwise we have been defrauded. The relationship is the basis of our hope and obedience on the account that we are well acquainted with the person handling our issue, His intentions and competence. He will not just execute justice, but when He does, it will be the perfect thing we have been waiting for. Yet, our greatest motivation is not the justice *but* the *love* we hold for Him. Don't just tell me to let go, give me a promise that you got it. I won't let go if I know I will fall to the ground. That's the essence of a promise within a relationship. In this case, it *transfers* the responsibility for justice to someone else who can do a *better* job than you and leaves you with one responsibility— to love, which makes your life way easier than if you were to do both the love and the justice part. So, when you see me smile while I should be knocking down people's heads, be wary. That doesn't mean I am a fool. I forgive through love but holding on to a promise for *perfect* justice.

God's Exam Paper

I recently was served in a coffee shop and I realized they offered an opportunity to tip the staff. I also witnessed the client ahead of me giving a tip. So, from the kindness of my heart, I decided to tip the staff who was very gracious to me, but I was in for a shock. There were two of them, a lady and a gentleman standing next to each other, and both took part in serving me. So, when I gave them the tip, they looked at me as if a bit surprised or disappointed or both then the lady asked me, "Are you looking for change?" "No, I mean, it's a tip for your kindness," I explained for a second time. I have a little bit of an accent, so I hoped that they perhaps did not understand me at first. The lady looked at the gentleman standing beside her, as if to get his opinion. Then the gentleman thought for a few seconds and said to me, "Are you sure?" Immediately, I experienced their insecurity attempting to choke me, I felt little for a moment then I thought to myself, perhaps they had never seen a black person or girl for that matter tipping or something?

I guess I should apologize that the issue of race had to be part of my contemplation, maybe it was uncalled for. I was just trying to be generous with understanding and giving them a benefit of doubt. After all it was an ordinary tip, so I don't think it was the size of it that bothered them. So, what made them think that this adult woman wasn't sure? I was almost ready to judge them. Then I realized how much *compassion* they needed, so, with gentleness and firmness I answered, "I am sure, just take it, thank you." Then I walked out with "sort of" a gracious swag, shaking off that littleness imposed on me, to recover my authentic self. But what the heck do you think that was or perhaps there was no heck in the first place?

How do you see a black person? As a slave who is unworthy of honor just because historical injustices gave you that perception? Or, as an angry troublemaker? What is your perception of a white person? Do you see him as the evil supremacist who has killed your innocent loved ones and has everything going for him? Or is he the assassin of your willpower to live through disenfranchisement? Are you a white person who believes that a black person is economically and socially limited from sharing the same neighborhood with you? How about a black person thinking that no successful privileged white person has deservedly earned their success? You may be justified in your own way to hold on to your perceptions but whichever way you see the other race, it will affect how you relate to them immensely. And may I humbly suggest that the attitude described above is a bigger monster *than* systemic racism itself. The most important thing to remember, however, is that regardless of how annoying and unlovable they may be, or how many stereotypes and evidence of cruelty that exist around them, someone made them for a purpose, and it may not be right for us to pretend that we know that purpose better than Him.

The scripture in Proverbs 14:31 says, "Whoever oppresses the poor shows contempt for their Maker, but whoever is kind to the needy honors God." Taking matters into your own hands is taking the wrath of God upon yourself. None of these people had a say into their existence. God created them for His own purpose and has placed all of them in different situations to *test* their hearts and those around them as an opportunity to earn rewards. God is not having an "OMG moment" concerning the social status of black folks; neither is He for white folks nor any other race.

All our actions including our mistakes are factored into God's agenda for our lives. He knew how things would go in this country before it's establishment. He *allowed* some to be better than others yet allowing does not equal condoning, and If I am free to choose, it doesn't also mean that I am free from consequences. He had the power to keep this from happening. But rewarding is His "hobby" and a component of *justice but* testing which is also part of the justice process is the only way to qualify for the rewards. If we, as humans, love to give tests before rewarding, then God the ultimate author knows that even better. So, based on how the privileged and underprivileged have been conducting themselves around each other, *is there a possibility that this country has failed the test of the God of love and justice?*

Referring to the scripture above, that person you hate is more than what meets the eye. When you see them next, remember they are a representation of *God's exam paper* right before you. Do anything possible to pass it like my daughter did in the aftermath of George Floyd's death. If that person is God's workmanship, then it would be a fair conclusion to say, hating on them especially on racial lines is indirectly hating on God the "manufacturer" because the person had no business in what color they came in. Disregarding a black person equals disregarding God. Hate for a white person is hate on God! And this applies to all humankind. It doesn't matter what justifications we can produce for our actions. The fact of the matter remains that all these atrocities are being committed against God. Do we want to be that brave?

ME TOO MOMENT	Has anyone ever treated you in a way that made you see yourself lower than the original you?
	In one word, how did that feel?

A Manufacturer Under Siege!

When the scripture talks about honoring the needy, it implies that we are not going to deal with perfect beings. Yet, whatever their state may be, God shall not excuse us for treating them with contempt. If that were the case, then whatever issues you have with the "product" should be addressed with the "manufacturer" whose competence is in question.

We are the same "product" from the same manufacturer but packaged in containers of different colors unto the pleasure of the manufacturer. There is no point in bickering over this. We know the truth, and COVID-19 just gave us more facts to work with. Let's be bold enough to face this truth, that we are as human as the next person. Once that point gets home, then let's ask ourselves the important question, who am I really? Yes, I am a human being but what exactly is my identity? The other questions like Why am I black or white or Why am I privileged or underprivileged can come afterwards. If the first question is answered well, the rest will fix themselves.

When we miss the manufacturer's *point of view* then we cannot get anything else right. No manufacturer would make a product for the sake of just making it and so the same is with God. Remember, we are not products but rather His image, and that's more serious. Every one of us has a unique purpose. There is no need to compete or destroy one another. We all have our space that no one else can take and even if they try, they can never do it exactly like us. The problem is not the *skin* but the *sin* (missing the author's perspective). Oh, how I pray that we begin to see each other through the eyes of the Creator then we will realize the beauty that lies in our differences including our skin colors (and all other physical attributes) and cultures!

The Priceless Sin

While the word sin triggers a feeling of judgement and a sense of being under attack, the real meaning of it is *missing God's mark or His point of view.* If we get His perspective on who we are, we also know who the other people are, which has nothing to do with their physical attributes. That resolves the big question of identity—who am I? In a typical situation, the name that your parents called you and your father's name come first in answering this question. Then you can proceed to tell us more about yourself. So, do you know what name God the Father of creation called you?

Is your real identity black or white or is it the image of God your Heavenly Father? If you get this right, then you can ask the question of race and privilege without anger, bitterness, or shame. As I said in one of the previous chapters, **racism and hate is a sign of insecurity**. Failing to answer the first question (who am I?) is the genesis of so many other unanswered questions. And the only evidence we have that the questions are not being resolved are the countless incidences of human degradation in our society.

We are not here to devour one another but to nourish and bring relief to each other in our current world whose weight is extremely overbearing. Inside each of us is a beautiful therapeutic fragrance to get one another through each day. Let's not lose our focus. We are here for something bigger than ourselves. We are making footprints as we pass by because yes, we are bound to *pass by* whether we are black, white, brown, or yellow.

We won't be here forever; who wants to live in such an imperfect world for eternity anyway? A flawed lifetime is more than enough, no surprise the scripture encourages us to look forward to the revealing of a perfect world by the God of love, justice, and righteousness. Whether it happens or not this is worth everything. I bet anyone who ascribes to optimism would want to give this a thought. It helps us set our priorities right, accord value to what deserves value and gives us the hope we need to love unconditionally, enjoy this life and be more productive. If you are a believer of positive thinking, then this should be music to your ears. But that is beside the point, the most important thing to remember is that the footprints we make will follow us forever. Let us not overstep our mandate, the actual colors are His business, but the fragrance is our business. The color of the candle is His business, the light of the candle mine.

Stick to the boundaries, don't ask me to respond to anything that touches His space because I will mislead you. I invite you to *hold me accountable for my character but not my color.* If my color bothers you, then be bold and address it with the "manufacturer." I was just made, and I don't have more details than that unfortunately. As for now, don't be a distraction to me because I am busy making my footprints count, preoccupied with earning my points and committed to making my rewards. Yet, I don't have so much time at my disposal because every minute and everyday counts. For that reason, you can have all the love, whether you deserve it or not because I have my perspective and priorities set right. You are invited to join me in this kind of attitude so we can defeat racism and hate.

ME TOO MOMENT	What is your real identity?
	Why do you identify yourself as such?

This is the Glue

I have so far shared five strategies that help me stay on course against hate this chapter excluded. But I would miss a truthful moment if I didn't admit that the five sometimes hold very little meaning for me, especially in the heat of the moment because of my selfish sinful nature. But this last one of keeping God in perspective seems to be the *anchor* upon which the rest are sustained. Don't lose sight of His image and likeness in me, though sometimes it's been marred by my flawed nature and external influences. And when I don't *deserve* the love, please remember that *God's image, however little of Him there may exist in me, surely does.*

When your point of reference is yourself or society, then you can only go as far as morality can take you. Believe it or not, even morality has its own limitations. It can only last as long as your will power, and that will-power can also fail depending on the nature of your motivation. So, when it fails, what is next? I bet you revert to your default selfish, imperfect self.

Removing the creator from the creation is like having the only available pilot sucked out of a plane in the middle of the flight. You know that such things happen, right? And that His cockpit crew has neither an alternative pilot nor a first officer, huh? That amounts to a *massive disaster* in the middle of nowhere! Does it feel like we as a country and the world are making a free fall from the sky, looking at the current level of racism and hate? Have we lost the ONLY Captain in the flight? Are we crashing, with billions on board? *God forbid!* We MUST make emergency decisions before it's too late!

Man, without a higher authority over him, becomes a god to himself and works everything in favor of himself. He can do anything, provided it benefits him, except for the fear of punishment, if there exists any at all. Like a mirror, he gives back what he receives. If we allow people to influence our actions, then we will likely give out more evil than good. *Man referencing himself on fellow humankind is the epitome of a failed society.* If we intend to extend this privilege into a shelter and transform it into a *real* value, then we must shift the center of focus. I suggest we need to begin seeing each other not for who we are, but most importantly, for *whose* we are.

Selfishness is already wired into our human system, and no amount of legislation can or will change our hearts. This is evident with evil being the hallmark of the modern world in recent times despite tightened legislation. Lawlessness has become a global pandemic in our society today. A change of behavior may be short lived, but a change of heart prompted by a changed attitude is more reliable. Honoring God is the beginning of honoring our fellow humanity. His unfailing supply of unlimited love makes it hard enough for our hearts to give into hate. The average human loves back when love is given. That's not a big deal. Going above the average human ability to give love in the place of hate calls for finding a bigger reason. Do you love Him enough to "violently" rebel against the beckoning voice of hatred just to love His perfect image in me?

The world will continue to add more and more vexing humans. You know the kind of people who look like they are on payroll to develop your peacekeeping skills? You can't adequately deal with them unless you have the words "hold your peace" written on your fist in underlined bold red! With the failure to do this, they can lose their head any moment. Not because you hate them, but for the simple reason that you have given them so many opportunities that nothing else is available but the fist. They keep pushing you and you keep stepping back not for cowardice but for the sake of peace. Yet, the more you step back, the more they push and now your back is leaning against the wall because all your precious space has been intruded upon! They are "experts" in this business and so they always succeed in driving the heck out of you regardless of how much effort you put to keep your cool. What really can hold you from giving them heck right back? What restraint do you think it takes if such people happen to be your next-door neighbor? Perhaps you are thinking… *I will just avoid them, what is the big deal?* Maybe not!

Consider my experience with this neighbor who would so often be furiously knocking on my door to tell me what another neighbor told her about my son. "I was told by one of the neighbors that I don't want to mention their name that your son said my son is bothersome," she said one time. Then another time, there was also something else, not once and not twice. "Tell your son to stop playing with my son," she repeatedly told me. I was so close to invoking a "restraint order" on her, not because doing it was fun, but I needed some peace to enjoy my house without unnecessary doorbell rings. A few things bothered me about this whole saga: One, why was she acting on hearsay? Two, all my neighbors seemed amazing people, who was this neighbor that told her about my son if at all there was any, perhaps it was a cooked story. But in case she was honest, then was there a *secret* agent of hate in the neighborhood who at face value looked like a friend to me and backbiting me at the same time? Three, why was she sending me to tell my son to stop playing with her son, while she could instead tell her son to stop playing with mine? Was she secretly *recruiting* me as an agent of hate?

Though I refused to take her nagging orders to spread hate and allowed the kids to continue playing together, this example serves as evidence of my claims on how desperate good humans can be vexing at the same time. You have to be alert, to identify them and their secret mission of giving you an *assignment of hate*. But how do we overcome the temptation to accept their "recruitment offer"? Or better still, how do we tame our fists from acting upon such humans who labor so hard to make their hatred *your* "screen saver"?

Did you presume that the law would provide a "perfect" guide on how to handle such people? I certainly have high regard for the law, but I also think that its capacity is extremely overrated. Sometimes things on the ground may be different and all you have is the law of love towards a perfect God to guide your decisions as you think on your feet. How can we keep God whose image we are out of the picture of our struggle with racism and hate?

The Beauty of Surrender

You have the power to choose what to see and what you focus on to magnify things before you come into a screaming reality. I was able to see beauty inside that little but annoying and strong-willed Nikita because I focused on Katie's image in her. What is your point of reference when you look at black or white folks? Yes, with the realities of racial killings by white cops on black people, and black people expressing their anger in overbearing ways, and with all the emotional, psychological, and socio-economic damage on black people, with some innocent privileged white civilians forced to bear the sin of their fathers or their fellow whites, so much water has gone under the bridge. No words can adequately cleanse the past. There will always be anger and finger pointing, and it seems to be getting worse with everyday realities aggravating the situation. How can we stay afloat in expressing unmerited love?

If we *allow* ourselves to be permeated and driven by our love for God and consequently others, even the *wait* for justice will not *drain* us. We will not only *enjoy* the process but also the justice when it comes because it will just be a *top up* to an already satisfied heart. Did I say satisfied? Yes, you can be calm and contended in this messed up world when you allow love to germinate peace, hope and joy within your heart. But priorities must be set right. Love is a cycle that begins with the Author of it who is God because He Himself is love. Anything else could be a counterfeit and may not endure the test of time.

I hope and pray that we can establish a trusting relationship with Him. Only then can we relinquish the justice business to Him as we instead give our undivided attention to creating a shelter and *real* value out of the privilege by collaborating through the medium of unmerited love. That is precisely where freedom begins—when we take a *calculated risk* to release our pursuit of justice to someone else better than ourselves other than compromising our peace by taking the law into our hands. Please note that my statement does not mean to suggest that we should abandon the pursuit of justice through the available justice systems. Instead, my point is that we should *refrain* from hate as a means of vindicating ourselves so we can commit ourselves to unmerited love as we allow God to handle our ultimate justice because we trust Him. *Oh, how amazing is the beauty of surrender; it is the highest position of power only reserved for bold people who seek real victory.* What peace, what a joy to know and understand this concept!

High-Risk Pregnancy

Remember, we do not seek to kill the white privilege. After all, "she" is an expecting mother whose death would cost us a beautiful bouncing "baby" called the Shelter. We are on a mission to summon all certified "midwives" and relevant "surgeons" to bring their expertise to the delivery room because this is a complicated pregnancy. Hopefully, no surgery is required, but, if need be, then I am afraid we have no choice. We are dealing with a high-risk pregnancy in which the baby requires close monitoring before, during, and after birth to ensure that he or she is in good health.

Historical injustices and racial struggles make the birthing process a difficult task. They pose a threat at each of the three stages above. That means that the work doesn't stop at the baby's birth because there are many adversaries seeking every opportunity to get rid of the baby. We are not out to share the privilege, the white person can keep it, but we need to create a benefit for all racial divides out of the privilege. We must focus on the *baby* and not the *labor pains*. Keeping our attention on the labor pains results in a blame game and fuels more hate. We should translate all our privilege-related experiences into opportunities to bring forth the shelter and reload privilege with real value.

I don't mean to shatter your hopes, but the truth is that our legislators don't make the best "midwives" or "surgeons" for this delivery process, but we, the civilians, do. It all starts with us down here. We are the very people who hurt each other; we are the same people that can heal one another. The kind of relationships we create with the next-door neighbor, that fellow parent at school, or that person you frequently sit next to at the place of worship matters a lot if our baby will not only be delivered safely but also grow to maturity. Whatever the case may be, we need quality relationships based on mutual feelings and experiences. Relationships that respect, trust, hold up, defend, advocate, and persevere at the very least. Yes, *perseverance* is part of the package because there is nothing quite like a rushed pregnancy. One week takes seven days and there is no strategy to shorten it. This is one of the many things that require utmost patience. It takes two imperfect human beings to tangle, and we must not leave patience out of the equation.

Pointing fingers must stop. We need each other to safely deliver a shelter to protect the oppressed and ultimately our economy too. Only then can privileged white folks walk with their shoulders high with no fear or shame for being the custodians of this privilege. The benefit will eventually be felt by both sides. The faster we admit this, the sooner we can begin the project. But we should also be warned that prolonging the labor pains could lead to the loss of our baby. While the travailing of privilege is a good sign, it could turn deadly in no time.

Speed is of the essence, and if you have been reading this book until now, you hopefully have the qualities of the highly sought-after midwives and surgeons. It's nothing out of reach, it only calls for a different attitude and mindset toward the white privilege and consequently each other. We *all* have a chance to mine value out of white privilege, no excuse! Begin to create interracial relationships *now*; do not procrastinate and let us set a pace for the world of privileges on how to handle privileges once and for all! C'mon, let us do it like Pros! May all roads lead to the delivery room and may each one of us take part in this *historic* moment. *Don't miss!*

I Dream...

I dream of a world where my personality, color, or race will not determine how much love I get. I breathe the fresh air of hope of a world painted with the fingerprints of love. A world where the words of this book will be the fabric of school curriculums. I see little kids carrying a copy of this book in their backpacks, I perceive a generation rising, one that will grow with countless possibilities of unlimited love, a generation that will find racism a strange word. I see millions of the Double MC clubs in every nation, state, county, city and neighborhood embracing diversity with fun and privilege with power; I behold imperfection loved with the eyes of perfection, insecurity washed away by the ocean of true love and self-understanding. I sense an unstoppable tide and a shifting of mindset ushering in a world that is not scared of surrender. And yes, I perceive a new secure world where the strong bow themselves to the weak and the privileged to the underprivileged. I hear the sound of victory, with the fear of yielding conquered by unconditional love under the supervision of unlimited, timeless, boundless in-exhaustible mercy. Yes, I see a people relented to the incredible peace of surrender, and a world submitted not only to God but also to one another in love regardless of color, race, ethnicity or even personality.

The 'Practicals' of Love

This chapter is very personal. It consists of my best practices that have given me victory repeatedly in the area of unmerited selfless love. I have had so many reasons to hate, just like most of us have. And still, I don't think I am done as of yet. And all through, this last strategy has consistently given meaning to my sacrifice of undeserved forgiveness and love. If you hold a different opinion, I totally respect that. The intention is to help us connect with a reason bigger than ourselves—one that can stand against time and circumstance. That way our attention will shift to the things that matter most, which are so often ignored in our pursuit for perishable things which are the reason we hate and kill each other.

Below are questions that, if answered genuinely, should help you take a mental shift, change your priorities, and find a sustainable reason to love a flawed human species, yes, a cause bigger than yourself or a fellow human. Some questions could take a long time to answer, so don't get frustrated when you can't get the answer in a day's time. All answers are within you, but you must spend consistent quiet prayer (talking and listening to the Creator through your inner voice) and meditation times to get the answers. This is a very personal journey, but you can walk with a genuine accountability partner of a like mind who is committed to finding authentic answers to these questions. You will know their honesty by their attitude toward the questions. Take your pen and journal, relax, focus, and let the inner you find the answers. Here we go....

1. Who am I?
2. Where did I come from?
3. What am I here for?
4. How long am I here?
5. Where am I headed to?
6. How am I going?
7. How do I feel about my departure?
8. What shall I be remembered for?
9. What is exciting about where I am going?
10. What matters most to me in this life and why?

You are free to add as many questions as can help you connect with your eternal value. These are very sobering questions that we may not feel very comfortable to face. But they open us to "the real stuff" about our own lives. We spend our precious few days in this world chasing money, cars, houses, and fame—things that don't pledge any loyalty when our time to depart is at hand. Racism and hate always has something to do with these. This practice of *evolving* is supposed to change our priorities, because it helps us see things for what they *really* are and not what we think they are. **Caution:** Do not ask these questions if you have a preconceived answer, you are not genuine or ready for the truth.

If you still feel void or restless after answering a question, you need to revisit it until you feel restful and peaceful. It is okay to ask someone you trust to help you find the answers as long they have answered these questions for themselves. Please know that no one can answer these questions for you, they can only ask you more questions to help you find more clarity in answering the question.

Whatever the answers be, please share them with someone and see how you feel. If you don't feel brave enough to share them, that could be a sign that you haven't found a truthful answer yet. You may need to revisit. I recommend revisiting these questions *daily* to help us keep the right perspective toward ourselves and others.

I pray for us as we seek the answers that we will indeed find them. My hope is that finding the answers will change how we see ourselves, our race, other races, and all of humankind. May this journey humble us to a place of surrender, rest, peace, and joy— first with ourselves and then with others so together we can experience and share unmerited love.

Give Me Hope...

As I watch the ruthless killing of innocent men and women, little children crippled with fear for the "sin" of their skin color and others forced to pay for a sin of racial discrimination committed by their ancestors, destinies brutally snatched away by hate, and a world troubled with anger, hatred, revenge and pointing of fingers, I keep thinking, "What court could vindicate this?" For all single mothers that have to raise their children single-handedly, the homeless and lonely kids whose fathers racism and hate robbed, for devastated mothers who have lost their sons to racial killings and innocent faithful police officers battling PTSD for someone else's cross, I wonder, "What court could avenge this?"

Yet, it's not just the revenge. I want justice *with* restoration. But who can deliver this? I keep expecting a day that someone more powerful than the strongest of humankind will overthrow the human courts, chambers corrupted with the selfishness of humankind. I can only hope that what is lost shall be restored someday, yes, by the author of life. I lose nothing for hoping, so let me be. After all, everything I lean on seems to fall apart. Give me hope beyond my eyes, one far above the highly flawed humankind justice systems. Lead me to a hope greater than the overwhelmed United Nations watchdogs, one that I can't feel, touch, or see not because it doesn't exist, but because it is too high for my little fingers to reach and my limited eyes to behold. An expectation that a short, troubled lifetime cannot steal from me. Give me a hope that mankind in his cleverest and most cunning endeavors cannot interfere with. Tell me about the perfect powerful God of Love and Justice.

Acknowledgements

Bringing this book into reality has been such a journey of devotion and commitment that can only be described as a "labor of love," which several people took a part of either directly or indirectly. Therefore, I extend my most profound appreciation to the following:

My beloved children Queen Hadasa and Prince Joses for laboring with me, praying, advising, and taking care of me until this book was completed. "Hada," your words, "Mom, you need to be bold in your writing; you should say, I believe not I think," held my confidence into accountability through the entire book. Thank you for keeping me on check with my writing timelines, cleaning the dishes and fixing for me a cup of tea so I could stay focused on the job. You told me in many ways, *Mom, I love and believe in you.* "Princo", your advice every evening, "Mom, remember to wear your light protective glasses," not only protected my eyes but also reminded me that there was so much love at home that we could afford to share some through this book. Thank you for cleaning the floors and clearing the trash so that mommy could write one more line. When you requested to read the first chapter of my book, that sealed my confidence that someone else couldn't wait to do the same. What a privilege to have you as my accountability (and prayer) partners and best friends. You mean more than the world to me!

My godly and loving parents, Pastor Cosmas Maingi and Joyce Katile, for giving me the childhood foundation of unconditional love and compassion, which is the blood that flows through every single vein of this book. The "crazy" faith and boldness you engraved in me as a little girl indeed came to my rescue in accomplishing this daring task. Oh! You are everything I would have asked for in a parent!

Pastor Shadrack Mwonga and Jennifer Mwau, my spiritual parents for watering the seeds of love, forgiveness, and compassion. Thank you for faithfully walking with me through my own "practicals" of love when my unconditional love and forgiveness were tested to the core inside the "laboratory" of trials and temptations. I almost got trapped in the debris of misjudgments after a messy divorce if you never told me who I indeed was. I am forever grateful for your constant reminder throughout my insane moments, that vengeance belongs to God. What more shall I say? I am truly favored to have you!

My amazing and instrumental siblings, Faith, Samson, Dorcas, John, Calvin, Michael, Mercy, Samuel, and my beloved late sister Judy, for offering me free experiments to exercise unmerited love and giving me a new perspective on the word *family*, which is a key concept of this book. I owe you for who I am and look forward to our next experiment! I love you.

Eva (Mama Comfort), little Comfort, Emmanuel (Emma), Faith (Fey), Brenda and Pastor Geoffrey my extended family, and mentees, for always making sure that I knew what I meant to you even in my worst. Thank you, Pastor G, for reminding me what an amazing big sister I am to you. Eva, how could I give up my real self with the resounding words from you, "You are my super mama and my heroine!" Aren't these the vibes I needed to fly to this side of destiny? And FYI, little Comfort believes that I am the only one that can "wrestle with a monster," *don't you believe her?*

Pastor Obed Musumbi and Joyce Mwashigadi my "second family" for the gift of a timeless love that believes and upholds. Knowing that I can safely fall on you without asking has sharpened by selfless love skills which is what this book is all about. I guess this is what they call "learning from the best!"

Jackie and Sarah, my "adopted" family, I wonder where you got the guts to invite a terrified foreigner and a single mother with two kids and no job from a hotel to live with you! Sarah, you will always be the sweet, caring big sister to my kids. Jackie, you earned yourself a new title, "Mom Jackie," which my kids still refer to you by. You preserved three destinies through a "risky love," no wonder your name will be mentioned wherever this book is read.

Christie and Francesca, my die-hard sisters, for believing in me and all my dreams even when I had no evidence for it, and taking care of my children as though they were your own. You and your husbands ensured that we did not sleep on the streets when things were hard for us. Francesca, my kids believe that you are a better chef than me, and do you by any chance think that this makes me feel insecure? Never! And how can I forget the sacrifice you made those days to make sure you gave me a ride to my cleaning appointments! Christie, your husband must be delighted to hear that the camera stand he gave me to launch myself on social media is still intact. Far be it that I should forget how his truck was always available to move us from one house to another, five times within five months! Not even one of them did you miss. You never abandoned us until we found a permanent home! You knew my need even before I said it, and you boldly, like a lioness, showed up to it. And what more should I say? If this is not the true definition of sisterhood, then someone should help me understand it.

To my special sisters and prayer partners, Alexis, Jackie and Latoria for believing in me and praying relentlessly that this book will be read and applied by millions until love wins. What a gift you are!

Ian and Toni, our privileged little special white friends who make such amazing play buddies and mutual friends for my kids, oh, how we love you! Thank you, Kathleen, and Nicole for letting your kids hang out with my kids; I doubt you knew which country I come from or what car I drive because that didn't seem to bother you as a prerequisite. What heroines of love you are!

To Joshua Kiio and Lilian Katuma, my former colleagues, fellow countryman/woman, and Kamba kinsman/woman who, five years ago, prophesied this moment and promised to be the first buyers of my first book, I hope that was not one of those "Just kidding" moments! Whenever I talk about authentic friendship, undeterred faith, hope, and inspiration, I will always think about you! Joshua, constantly reminding me in your "sort of" Nairobian Swahili that *"Phidia, unaenda mbali,"* always does the magic in arousing the warrior in me! Lilian, thank you for living the legacy of a true Kitondo girl by doing less love talk and more love walk during my lowest moments. If selfless love and a friend indeed were a person's name, then that should be your new name henceforth!

Ms. Lulu Massawe the finance guru, for making an invaluable call at the right time and choosing the right words to make me angry enough to deal with my insecurity. And to Dennis Massawe the business pro, your faith in me was everything I needed as I began the journey to discover myself. You challenged me to write a book, and this looks like it! Thank you!

To Coach Holley Mignosi and the Soulful Speaker Sisterhood, I never knew how much love I had until I met you and you said, "Phidia, you are just but love." Then I realized that my real name is Love and that there was something unique about my love, so special that the world would appreciate even a small portion of it. Isn't this very love the life of this book because you spoke, and I believed you? And what else does coaching entail?

To Coach Jessa Grace, you have such prowess in transforming the Author into an Entrepreneur. She sure must be bought! Or how else do we saturate the world with unconditional love?

Coach Gilbert Ang'ana my former boss, resilience has found a new meaning since I met you. You may never know how much of it went into actualizing this book!

Amy Gray, the photographer, that photo session did not feel like business at all. It was a glorious manifestation of a privilege in the powerful hands of a loving-kindness, security, and prowess! What a beautiful blend!

Bridgette, thank you for opening your house to my two kids and me. It was in your home that on a warm June summer Wednesday morning, at 5 am, the first few sentences of this book were scribbled. Had I been on the streets, I doubt I would have answered this call!

To my friends and former colleagues Alice, Amos, Bilha, Carol, Fred, Jackie, Joshua, Lilian, Makena, Margaret, James and all my friends and cheerleaders, what can compare to a friend who believes in you? That is who you are! Jackie, always my number one fan! Eunice Makena, you never give me a chance to forget how far I have come from! Amos Okoth, my former boss, it has been six years and your precious words at my lowest moment in life, "Phidia, you have a massive potential; I doubt you know," don't seem to leave me alone. Could this book be a sign? Please tell me… Fred Okello, your "hashtag" statement, "Phidia, I see greatness in you, if you can't see it, I will lend you my eyes to see it," has been my zip line to get me across this scary assignment. Isn't this what friends are for?

Dr Jason Reesor and the amazing Town Center Dentistry team for a service that flawlessly manifests the true meaning of the word "family" and "belonging," which is the heartbeat of this book. I consider myself lucky to have experienced both in their authenticity!

To all my customers, especially (but not limited to) the privileged white ones for "trespassing" the racial limitations to entrust a black immigrant woman with your home and much more. Special mentions must go to:

Alyssa -- Only God knows how many times you have said to me, "Phidia, look at how pretty you are!" So, how could the privilege make you my sister, prayer partner, confidant, destiny incubator and cheerleader? Thank you for your prayers, follow-through, humility, advice, kindness, and grace. Your faith in me was an accelerator in making this book a reality. What an example of faithfulness and a well-managed privilege!

Bobbie -- What an easy sweet personality you have! I have never felt the need to try and be anything else other than my real self in your presence because of the genuine love atmosphere everywhere you are. How is this still privilege?

Cathy -- I was not just a cleaner, but a part of your dining table guests every other Wednesday. In so many ways you said to me, you are a member of this family!

Elizabeth -- Your precious gift from Italy? I still have it. It hangs on the wall as a reminder that the privileged and the underprivileged can exchange love through the hands of meekness.

Emilia -- Your privilege wasn't obvious because your humility and kindness took the stage rendering it irrelevant. Oh, wow! Your cinnamon toast is the best! And, what a sweet baby you have. She has taught me to love more, be free spirited, and have fun with life. She certainly got it from you and your husband.

Emily -- Your love and compassion flowing through your adorable boys will always be my invincible evidence of the possibility of taming hate through the transfer of kindness within privilege. I am still mesmerized that they always thanked me for cleaning their bedroom as if I wasn't paid for it and asked if they could walk on the just cleaned floor of their *own* house just because they cared adding some more work to me. Wow! Tell me if that was still privilege.

Frank -- You taught me how to eat *real* crabs and just for your information, that menu has been expensive to keep up with! Talk about the laughter we shared with my kids swimming in your exotic pool on a hot summer day and Uncle Frank being the big baby that you are. These are priceless memories of how human and friendly privilege can get. And yes, the privileged and the underprivileged shared the same table etiquette with no itches.

Geeta -- Yours was not a white privilege, but your wallet was privileged through hard work that bore results. How come you never looked like it? How did you and your husband transcend the social class gap all the way to my level to share my world? Thank you for the Christmas gift that blew my kids and I away! Clearly, privilege is just another word as far as you are concerned.

Jagu -- A different kind of privilege that makes your home very warm and serene. For you, nothing matters more than laughter, kindness, tenderness, and caring for people. Imagine how beautiful when all this is crowned with the meekness of your husband!

Jen --Until I met you and your husband then I realized how easy it is for the words privilege and peace to fit in the same sentence. Your home is just but a haven, and what an adorable son you have!

Julie -- To you a privilege is nothing but creating a haven of peace to you and the people around you and your sons did not disappoint in manifesting it! I sure needed that tenderness and fully enjoyed working in your peaceful home.

Karen -- What an authentic girl you are and a family you have! No wonder you have the most gracious teenage kids I have met who generously appreciated my cleaning as though I did it for free. They sure picked it up from your sweet, real self. You have proven that there is no excuse for using privilege as a scapegoat for misdemeanor, and yet still, that privilege doesn't have to deny us being honest with ourselves and others.

Kathleen -- Thank you for caring if we had a Christmas tree. Though the one you gave us died, (I guess we didn't do a good job of keeping it) the act of your caring nature is forever embedded into our hearts. Who could imagine that the privilege does care when the media doesn't do enough to show us this side?

Kelly -- The African artwork in your house tell it all. How could it be that easy for privilege and diversity to shake hands? No wonder our relationship feels more of friendship than business!

Kelsey -- "Phidia, how are you doing financially with this pandemic? My husband and I are thinking of increasing your schedule frequency to help you get through this season," that was your text to me, Kelsey. I would fill this book if I had to write how you walked with me in sickness and in health. You and your husband are so privileged especially with the blessing of a loving kindness and contentment. I need no other evidence that a secure privilege regardless of its name has the power to empower!

Laura -- Even with so many trials, you were so privileged with a contagious sweet attitude and even found time to check on me and my kids. I wish I could get some of that which seems to naturally flow through you. I looked forward to every sandwich you made to ensure I did not work on an empty stomach as if that was your responsibility. How could your privilege come so close to serving the underprivileged?

Lesley -- I did not know you long enough, but those months felt like eternity because both you and your husband together with your adorable children demonstrated what it is to be loving, kind and accommodating. They never missed a moment of charming me with their smiles and thoughtfulness. Was that still privilege?

Linda -- Thousands of miles away from home, I found a mother inside the privilege. So gentle, grateful, caring, jovial, kind, and warm, your personality cannot fit in this one sentence. My kids looked forward to the special gifts you sent them every other Tuesday. What a beautiful encounter we had with your privilege!

Paul -- You did not say much but your actions told me everything I needed to know. When I talk about advocacy, your name always comes to my mind. You seized every opportunity to advertise my business. I was sold by your privilege and the privileged bought me.

Pri -- Your privilege was a little different. A beautiful blend of tough love and compassion; you wore the right shoe for the occasion. We fought and reconciled enough times to make us sisters. How adorable!

Robert -- How you cared about my workload as if you were not already paying me for it! The music and the ginger ale made it more like a party than a stressful work environment. Privilege well represented.

Sandra -- My kids now call you "Auntie Sandra" and I promise I had nothing to do with it, but your actions did. It was more than business for sure. When one takes their time to make some masks for their housekeeper's family and to remind her to wear them to stay safe from COVID-19, is that business or love? For me, that is a sister and I found one right within your privilege.

Stephanie -- Your privilege was so present and accommodating that you and your husband learnt some Swahili words to use every time on my paycheck as a way of connecting with me. If that was nothing to you it meant the world to me!

Susan -- I did not know how open and engaging the privilege can get until I met you. Thank you for telling me in many ways that privileged or underprivileged we are all human and sometimes share the same life challenges.

Tammy -- I wondered how did the privilege trust a black immigrant woman that much on the first day? Now I have the answer … because love trusts. Your gifts to my children were special. And what an adorable lot of kind and respectful teenage girls you have. Oh, how approachable privilege can get!

Tara -- You were more of a girlfriend than a client, teaching me how to stay positive and sharing tips on how to be a boss lady made me realize that the privileged and the underprivileged could share the same business strategies. How about your husband sharing his favorite cooking recipe! Humility and warmth suffer deficiency when it comes to defining both of you. I don't mind if this is what privilege is all about!

Terri -- You did not let your pain get in the way of kindness. Pre-COVID-19, I got a deliberate hug every single day I cleaned your home as a testimony that black and white is just a mere dress, covering the same content known as *human*. And, what a gracious lot of young adults you have in your three kids. Do you know how many times they came by to ask me if I was ok? If this is what privilege is about, then we need to create some more!

And to all the heroes of interracial love including Amelia, Ashley, Gwen, Mickie, Sally, and many others, and to all the men and women who have been instrumental in shaping my life and this book, people who perhaps did not move the world but did one little thing that meant the world to me, thank you! May this book be the reward for your contribution to my life and ultimately to the world.

About the Author

Inspirational Speaker, Author, Love, Forgiveness, and Passion Coach, Phidia Maingi is the CEO and Founder of Rescue the Passion Global, which seeks to empower people to transform their lives from disaster into dynasty and mess into merry through the magic of building their careers inside their Absolute passion. She comes from the school of thought that your Absolute (highest) passion is a package of completeness and overflow. Having been divorced at 32 years of age by her first love and husband of eight years who then married their adopted daughter, she embarks on demystifying the concepts of love and forgiveness as the main pillars to unwrapping the treasure inside an individual's deepest passion. She refers to this process as "The Money Plus" of Passion.

Ms. Maingi has helped many people through her life experiences to find their wholeness and abundance through maximizing on their Absolute passion to attain fulfillment in health, relationships, career, and wealth creation. Having reconnected with her utmost passion after more than fifteen years, she inspires and helps others to do the same. Her unique way of teaching and coaching makes the transition process fun. Phidia enjoys cooking, cleaning, interacting with nature, hiking, and travelling.

To find out more about Phidia Maingi and
have a life-changing experience, contact her at:

Rescue the Passion Global
P.O. Box 26909
San Diego, CA 92126
phidia@rescuethepassionglobal.com
www.rescuethepassionglobal.com

CPSIA information can be obtained
at www.ICGtesting.com
Printed in the USA
BVHW041344210921
617185BV00016B/407